Media and Communication Technologies

A Critical Introduction

Stephen Lax
University of Leeds

palgrave
macmillan

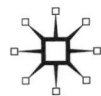

First published 2009 by
PALGRAVE MACMILLAN

Palgrave Macmillan in the UK is an imprint of Macmillan Publishers Limited, registered in England, company number 785998, of Houndmills, Basingstoke, Hampshire RG21 6XS.

Palgrave Macmillan in the US is a division of St Martin's Press LLC, 175 Fifth Avenue, New York, NY 10010.

Palgrave Macmillan is the global academic imprint of the above companies and has companies and representatives throughout the world.

Palgrave® and Macmillan® are registered trademarks in the United States, the United Kingdom, Europe and other countries.

ISBN-13: 978–1–4039–9889–7 hardback
ISBN-10: 1–4039–9889–2 hardback
ISBN-13: 978–1–4039–9890–3 paperback
ISBN-10: 1–4039–9890–6 paperback

This book is printed on paper suitable for recycling and made from fully managed and sustained forest sources. Logging, pulping and manufacturing processes are expected to conform to the environmental regulations of the country of origin.

A catalogue record for this book is available from the British Library.

A catalog record for this book is available from the Library of Congress.

10   9   8   7   6   5   4   3   2   1
18   17   16   15   14   13   12   11   10   09

Printed and bound in China

3 8002 01720 925 7

Media an⟨

and Communication Technologies

Also by Stephen Lax

Beyond the Horizon: Communications Technologies Past, Present and Future
Access Denied in the Information Age

Contents

List of Boxes

List of Tables

List of Figures

Introduction

Technology is central to communications and the media. That much is obvious. We are frequently reminded that in the first years of the 21st century, many people carry around with them each day a collection of technologies that a generation ago would have been unachievable, unaffordable and in some cases unimaginable. A modest mp3 player can hold a library-full of songs, a simple mobile phone can call more-or-less anywhere from anywhere else, while a slightly more advanced version can provide high speed access on the move to the whole of the internet. These simple statements cannot reasonably be disputed, and in discussions of the role of communications in everyday life, the role of technology is often described in this straightforward manner. It is seen as a fixed entity – it just does a particular job. However, this approach understates its importance in understanding media and communications. Just as any study of these fields would naturally include the economic and political aspects of communications – for example corporate structures or the regulations imposed by governments – the social factors in the development of communications technologies must also be considered. The particular job a technology does is a consequence of economic and political decisions, as well as technological capabilities.

Equally, of course, certain features of the media and our modes of communication are dependent on the ways in which technological systems operate. For example, as we shall see, mobile phone systems have been in operation for more than 50 years, but it was only when a cellular transmission system was developed in the last two or three decades that they became adopted to the extent with which we are now familiar. This is a technical reason for the growth in numbers of mobile phones, and without asking about the details of novel technological developments (why was a cellular system critical?) there can be only limited understanding of some of the more hyperbolic, bald statements about new technologies such as those hinted at above. There are also economic and political aspects to that technological development. In other words, to continue with the example, to understand fully the growth in mobile phone use (and its possible consequences), we need to consider both the technological and social factors together, and the same applies to all technological systems.

Studies of media and communications typically adopt one of two approaches to technology. A recurrent tendency places technology clearly in the foreground in any analysis. Typically, 'boosterist' explanations of the role of technology in society talk principally of the 'effects' and 'consequences' of technological developments, proclaiming inevitable social upheaval (both beneficent and detrimental in varying degrees) or even 'revolution'. While such hyperbolic accounts feature throughout history (for a discussion of this tendency, see Carey 1992), in recent decades the emergence of information technologies and, later, information and communications technologies (ICTs) encouraged a flurry. Alvin Toffler (1970, 1980), amongst others, predicted a host of social changes resulting from the widespread deployment of interconnected personal computers, including the decline of industrial work and its replacement with the 'electronic cottage', in which new 'artisan' workers would connect to the workplace from home. The titles of two edited collections, *The Microelectronics Revolution* (Forester 1980) and *The Information Technology Revolution* (Forester 1985), betray a similar overwhelming outlook. Such boosterist accounts of technology's ability to effect change do not hold back: Negroponte suggested that the incursion of new communications technologies into every aspect of our lives would ultimately render us 'digital beings', while Gross suggested that television brought about the end of communism in the 1990s (Negroponte 1995; Gross 2003). In these approaches, the role of technology is paramount in bringing about social change and, moreover, the assumption is clearly one of linear causation: the technology may not be considered merely as a fixed entity, but any changes that do occur in the technology are often claimed to bring with them far-reaching consequences for society and individuals. Attempts to explain the social consequences of technological development in this way have been subjected to much critical analysis in which simplistic linear models are dismissed as crudely deterministic, and during the 1980s and 1990s a number of more considered accounts emerged in a novel discipline of the sociology of technology. Nevertheless, as Cavanagh notes, as the internet attracted increased scrutiny from the 1990s onwards, such criticisms tended to be forgotten (2007: 138). For example, amongst many other authors similarly inclined, in 1998 Cairncross listed 30 ways in which 'the communications revolution would change our lives' (Cairncross 1998; by the time of the second edition in 2001, the list had reduced in number to 25 life-changing effects).

A second approach to technology is offered in what might be termed critical social accounts of the development of communications and media, often based on political economy. These tend to analyse, justifiably, the interplay between issues of corporate ownership, regulation and economics. So, for example, in a discussion about the emergence of satellite and cable television in the UK the emphasis is on government economic policy (encouraging private companies to provide services) and regulation (relaxing content rules in comparison with public service broadcasting) as explanations of developments (for example, Negrine 1994; Curran and Seaton 2003). However, technology, though not neglected in such analyses, usually fulfils a secondary role, whereas technical aspects such as the capacity of different cable systems and the bandwidth demands of television transmission are also deserving of investigation in this context. In more recent accounts of 'new media', the enabling effects of the technologies' attributes *are* recognised as important, for individuals (for example, in enabling greater participation, economic and political, in society) and for social relationships (state versus individual; local versus global), but again further treatment of technology is limited (for example Lister et al. 2003; Flew 2005). In these examples, the importance of social forces is quite reasonably subjected to critical analysis in explaining the development of media, both old and new, but the technologies in question are largely taken at face value, as mere enabling agents, in what is sometimes referred to as the 'black box' approach to technology – that is, while other factors are regarded as social processes deserving of exploration and analysis, the technology is simply an object that allows something to happen.

So while the first approach can be criticised as neglecting the wealth of historical and sociological evidence which demonstrates that technology cannot be regarded as an autonomous, singularly determining factor in social change and ignores a host of social forces at its peril, the second, critical approach, though more credible in linking technology with social processes, tends to neglect or at least relegate the changing nature of the technology itself, seeing it instead as the fixed, black box, entirely the consequence of a historical sequence of social forces. Certainly, technology *is* conditioned and constrained by the various social influences upon its development, but it also does have effects which depend significantly upon its technical capabilities (and limitations). If the booster approach outlined here overstates technology's 'effects', often dramatically, then the critical approach can be claimed to underplay them.

The approach taken in this book, therefore, is one which sees technologies as social products, that is, as the results of social processes such as investment decisions, political intervention and consumer response and equally as social products which have technological features that constrain or otherwise help explain the consequences of their use and their subsequent development. While readily rejecting the crude, boosterist explanation of the place of technology in media and communications in favour of one which recognises the importance of social factors, the following chapters attempt to augment this critical analysis by also examining the technological basis upon which they operate. Just as the social factors are continually changing, as economic and political priorities shift, for example, or consumption patterns alter, the continual and rapid pace of change in technology means that it is necessary to examine some of the underlying technological principles that govern communication rather than describe a particular fixed point in technological development (for example the latest music compression format). To fully grasp the implications of newly emerging digital techniques, for instance, it is important to explore factors such as the economic motivation behind such developments, as well as the technological basis upon which they occur. An appreciation of the fundamental differences between digital and analogue systems is helpful in understanding why one particular digital coding technique might be seen as superior to another. Equally, exploring the basic technological principles of communication helps to establish the process of technological change as a historical one, since many of these principles are common to all communications systems and were established at the outset of the exploitation of electrical technologies for communication.

Indeed, one of the deepest influences on technological development *is* history. It is impossible to come up with a completely new idea, either in technology itself or in its usage. Clearly much technological change is a development or enhancement of what has gone before, and even 'breakthrough' technologies depend on the use of previous technologies. The development of one technology, such as the computer, makes possible new experimental techniques (for example, based on computer modelling) that aid further development of another. Thus 'new' technology depends critically on its history. As MacKenzie and Wajcman put it, 'Even what we might with some justification want to call revolutions in technology turn out to have been long in the making' (1999: 9). In terms of usage it is even more likely that new technologies will very obviously be enhancements of previous technological systems, so that usage patterns are already established into which any new technology may readily fit, whereas a truly novel usage would have no immediate, obvious application. Webster suggests that in fact many new developments in ICTs embody the familiar and economically successful principles of television: 'Why offer anything different when television has shown itself the public's favourite leisure technology?' (Webster 2006: 136). If the history of a particular technology is an important part of explaining how things are done today, it is also a useful check on the frequent proclamations that all the technological systems we see before us today are completely unprecedented and herald a new era. For example, as noted above, the mobile phone was being used from the 1950s, but the idea goes back much further: in fact in the 1860s, in the earliest days of electrical communication, it was conjectured that such facility would become possible and a call would open with the now familiar exchange, 'Where are you?', followed by an appropriate response (see p. 32). Equally, while many argue that the internet is changing our world in ways never seen before, is it reasonable to argue that the first telegraphic communications, particularly the overseas links of 150 years ago, were any less remarkable?

Because of this historical influence on technological development, this book follows a more-or-less chronological sequence of technological innovations. It opens with the beginnings of electrical communications in the 19th century, although of course mechanical technologies had assisted communication before then. However, with the expansion of industrialisation in full swing, the speeding up of physical transport with the coming of railways brought with it the need for more rapid communications, and the application of electrical technology was a decisive factor as it allowed communication to take place faster than a train could travel and to overcome the limitations of the previous mechanical and optical devices (for example, electrical communication would continue to work in conditions of poor visibility). The congruence between physical transportation and electrical communication is demonstrated by the observation that in the initial phases of the electric telegraph, its cables were carried alongside railway lines – wherever the railway went, logically so did the telegraph (there was also the more prosaic reasoning that the railways had already established rights of way needed by telegraph cables). The expansion of the railways also increased the need for the standardisation of timekeeping (until the mid-19th century, different cities operated to local time – for example, midday in London preceded midday in Plymouth, around 300 km to the west, by some 20 minutes). From 1852, the telegraph was employed to assist by communicating a common, national Greenwich time signal from London to major cities connected to the rail network (Morus 2000).

It was with the telegraph, then, that some of the foundations for modern technological communications were laid. It was also where a number of trends were established, recurring periodically as new communications technologies emerged in later decades. In summary, in Chapter 1, we note that the electric telegraph emerged at a particular moment in history that encouraged its development for predominantly economic reasons. Its first users were business organisations, but initial interest was limited, and certainly public interest in using it was very low. Marketing and public relations were important then as now, and a number of publicity stunts and public demonstrations were mounted to show the device in operation, securing much admiration in the press but, again, proving less successful in promoting its widespread adoption. However, as is often the case with communications systems and especially with networks, the device became more attractive the more it was used, a kind of virtuous circle, and in time companies which did not use telegraphic communication began to be (or, at least, began to feel) left behind. Once established, it also prompted research into technical improvements, culminating in the telephone which would replace it. The telephone grew, albeit rather more slowly than is often imagined, into a far more extensive network than the telegraph had ever been, principally because it was a utility that could be operated by the non-expert and so was planned as a network that extended beyond public tele-graph offices and into all businesses and homes. Though incorporating many of the features of the telegraph's operation, the expansion of the telephone network demanded the establishment of a number of electrical techniques and standards, such as automatic exchanges and subscriber dialling that persist today. This rather simplified summary serves merely to suggest that we can observe similarities between the emergence of different technologies, though of course each also has its own peculiarities.

Once again, as Chapter 2 demonstrates, the emergence of radio communi-cations at the end of the 19th century and its subsequent development serve as exemplars of the ways in which technological progress is shaped by social forces. Though knowledge of the technical requirement for radio was steadily growing, it was not until Guglielmo Marconi identified a clear market, namely the British Admiralty, for whom communication without wires was a neces-sity, and the Post Office, who could imagine the financial advantages of no longer needing overhead telegraph and telephone lines, that financial moti-vation spurred developments on more rapidly. Yet less than three decades later, 'radio' meant something completely different, something entirely famil-iar to us still: the continuous, one-way transmission of sound, be it music or speech, from one place to a multitude of listeners. Broadcasting took advantage of, indeed depended upon, the technical characteristics of a system originally intended to do no more than merely replace a wired form of communication, the telegraph, with a wireless version of the same. The technical possibilities were not enough on their own, and we see that broadcast radio came about as a consequence of particular changes in the social make up of society.

In contrast, with radio having established the idea of broadcasting, television could be seen as almost an inevitable development. Chapter 3 shows that the idea of transmitting images rather than simply sounds down wires (and later, naturally, without wires) had in fact been imagined and, to some extent, inves-tigated before radio became established. Of course, television now dominates broadcasting in most people's imaginations (and in more concrete ways: of the BBC's spending on programming, around 90 per cent is on television and 10 per cent on radio). Thus most technical developments in recent decades have taken place in television, and these demonstrate the complexity of the mix of social and technical factors at work. For example, the introduction of digital television currently taking place in countries across the world has been constrained by the technical limitations of digital signal processing and the eco-nomic difficulty of offering new equipment cheap enough to persuade viewers to replace otherwise perfectly functional analogue receivers. The emergence of new television platforms such as cable and satellite is discussed in Chapter 4 and demonstrates the importance of political decisions by governments, as, particularly in the 1980s and 1990s, broadcasting policy came to regard television (and, to some extent, radio) more as a commercial rather than a public resource, paving the way for both subscription services and the use of potential two-way networks like cable systems as mere alternative, one-way broadcasting platforms. The identification of digital broadcasting as a replacement for its analogue counterpart illustrates this tension further, as the importance of government support for public service broadcasters in driving digital television adoption becomes clear. This is considered in Chapter 5, and the technical background to digital broadcasting is discussed as implying the beginnings of a slow, but long anticipated, convergence (at the technical level at least) between broadcasting, computing and, later, telecommunications services. Indeed, as Chapter 6 shows, for decades computing remained aloof from any form of electronic communications technology, indeed aloof from electronics (such as the transistor and integrated circuitry) altogether for a while, emerging instead into a post-War culture of 'big science' (including *inter alia* atomic energy and space exploration). Only when enthusiasts and amateur 'hobbyists' began to show that there was no *technical* reason why computing could not be small scale and personal like other forms of electronic equipment did the idea of the computer as a communications device begin to take hold and, like the radio during the first quarter of the 20th century, 50 years later we see the discovery of alternative uses for a technological system ultimately overshadowing its initial conception.

If it can be accepted that the telegraph began the new era of electrical and electronic communication, making an unprecedented and decisive distinction between communication and transportation, it is less easy to judge where we now find ourselves almost two centuries later. Novel developments there most certainly have been: broadcasting was a social form which had not existed, or even been considered, before amateur enthusiasts began playing around with radio. The digital techniques of computing were intended for processing numbers, and only after several decades had passed was it considered possible or desirable to apply the techniques to communication. With the use of wireless systems to provide mobility, described in Chapter 7, there is one sense in which we come full circle: the desire, expressed 140 years ago, to be freed from cables and wires is finally realized, and there now exist almost three times as many mobile phones than fixed telephone lines, with the equivalent of almost 50 per cent of the world's population owning one. As the chapters in this book demonstrate, as we move through the ages, each new technological 'breakthrough' has been accompanied by proclamations about the consequences for society, invariably ignoring the wider complexity of the technology-society relationship. Today, the same tendency remains in evidence. With unprecedented levels of access to technology, many continue to speculate on what this will mean for society, and this continuing tendency is considered in the concluding chapter: for some it implies the end of the old material, industrial world and the beginning of a new, more hopeful information age, while for others the concentration of these technologies in a relatively small number of privileged hands confirms that technology, so often acclaimed as securing a route to a more prosperous, egalitarian future, actually offers no simple solution, no 'technical fix'. Whichever view is expressed, however, it is all too often argued in terms which follow one of the two trends outlined earlier, that is, an argument that overlooks the importance of the technology itself. In our inevitable and necessary speculation about the future of an ever more interconnected world and its inhabitants, a deeper appreciation of information and communication technologies as both technical and social entities is vital – and in this respect it is hoped that this book might contribute a little to understanding that world.

The Early History of Technology and Communications: The Telegraph and the Telephone

Technology has always been used to assist communications. In one sense this includes the printing press and other means of recording text and images, but other techniques have also been applied to allow rapid communication over great distances. The lighting of a succession of bonfires built on the tops of hillsides across southern England signalled the sighting of the Spanish Armada in 1588 for example (and numerous hills across the south coast still retain the word 'beacon' as part of their name, such as Ditchling Beacon near Brighton). Two centuries later, optical telegraphs contained an array of moveable boards or rods, different arrangements of which representing different meanings: mounted on hilltops alongside an operator equipped with a telescope, coded messages could be relayed over long distances from device to device (and again, 'Telegraph Hill' is a landmark which can be found on many maps). Semaphore signalling was thus relayed across France during the Napoleonic wars in the early 19th century, and such 'pre-electric' telegraph systems were also installed in other countries, including once more southern England. These had the advantage that the message could travel more quickly than by sending it on horseback, but also the great disadvantage that they relied on the visibility of the apparatus. Poor weather or, in the case of the semaphore, darkness would render them useless. An emerging alternative, which was less affected by these adverse conditions, was to use electricity as the signalling medium.

The early 1800s saw a great deal of experimentation with electricity and its possible application as a motive force. This was a period of great industrial expansion, and this inspired much scientific and technical activity to support it. The looms in the great cotton mills were powered by steam which required the transport of huge quantities of coal. Electrical power, while some way off, was a superior prospect. It was well established that electricity could be carried through wires, and work by Hans Christian Ørsted in Denmark and later by British physicist Michael Faraday showed that in the presence of a magnetic field, a current-carrying wire created a force between magnet and wire. This was later to become the basis of an electric motor but equally had potential as a signalling or communication device. An electric current travelling down a long wire could cause an indicator device to be moved at some distance from the source of that current. While numerous attempts were made to realise such a device, the first commercial electric telegraph was patented in 1837 by William Cooke and Charles Wheatstone, who successfully developed a device that could be used by the rapidly expanding railway companies which needed some means of signalling messages up their tracks faster than their trains could travel.

Around the same time in the US, the development by Samuel Morse of an alternative signalling method based on a coding system in which a sequence of dots and dashes represented the letters of the alphabet – for example a dot followed by a dash to represent the letter A, or three dots for the letter S – made for a more reliable telegraph which rapidly became widely adopted. Developed with Morse's assistant Alfred Vail, the Morse Telegraph needed just one electric cable, unlike the multi-wire Cooke and Wheatstone device, and electrical pulses sent down the wire caused a hammer to make an impression on a piece of tape passing through the device. A later development caused a sounding device at the receiver to emit either a short or a longer note. In each case, the telegraph operator decoded the message either by reading the dots and dashes off the paper tape or by listening to the sequence of dots, dashes and gaps on the sounder. While demanding greater skill of the operator, the latter technique speeded up the reception of messages still further.

Once again, Morse and Vail sought to identify a likely market for their device and like Cooke and Wheatstone teamed up with the railway companies to demonstrate and further develop their telegraph. The first installation linked Washington and Baltimore, a distance of some 60 km, and in 1844 Morse famously transmitted his first public message, 'What hath God wrought!' to the assembled dignitaries. Thus, just as the railways had begun to connect, or open up, vast areas of the North American continent, the telegraph accelerated the process by means of electrical communication. Given the ease with which telegraph lines could be installed in comparison with railway lines, the telegraph arrived in many towns and cities before the railway; the Western Union Telegraph company installed the transcontinental telegraph line from the West Coast to East in 1861, while the Union Pacific Railroad only finally connected the ends of the continent some eight years later.

Already, in this briefest of accounts of the origins of the electric telegraph, we see a number of features common to many technological innovations. From the outset there were a number of different technical approaches to the problem of distant signalling – the two systems described here, those of Cooke and Wheatstone and of Morse, were by no means the only systems in operation, though these were the two that developed most successfully into working, commercial systems. Working largely in isolation from each other, and often in ignorance of each other's progress, these groups of people were each in their own ways tackling the same perceived problem of how to speed up communication. The eventual triumph of Morse's telegraph over its competitors (including Cooke and Wheatstone's) was down to its simplicity (one cable rather than five) which made it more reliable and cheaper. The need to identify a market and secure business partners at an early stage is again a recurring aspect of technological innovation – without such interest, naturally, it becomes more difficult to develop a new device or system.

Celebrating Technology: The Telegraph's Reception

While the railway companies were an obvious initial market for the telegraph, given that before it they themselves possessed the quickest means of getting a message from A to B, Cooke and Wheatstone in the UK and Morse in the US anticipated that other businesses and also members of the public would be interested in its use. Both sought to impress political and business leaders of the wonders of the new devices but found that, more often than not, the new electric telegraph was seen as a technological curiosity rather than a useful new communication device. The telegraph was greeted similarly by the press (ironically, in time to become avid users themselves of this new technology). Here was a device which demonstrated the wonders of modern electrical technology, but at public exhibitions where it could be seen in action it was being used for no more than a chess game played between Washington and Baltimore. An early poster displayed by the Great Western Railway in London invited members of the public to come and see 'this interesting and most extraordinary Apparatus' in operation, again drawing attention to its novelty as much as its utility. Tom Standage recalls a number of events that over the next few years slowly began to demonstrate the worth of the telegraph as a useful communications tool rather than an object of curiosity: in 1844 *The Times* newspaper was able to report the birth of Queen Victoria's son within 40 minutes of its announcement; in the same year, a pick-pocket, Fiddler Dick, was caught when he alighted from a train on which he had been hoping to escape; and John Tawell was apprehended on 3 January 1845 after his description was telegraphed to London when he had boarded the Slough to London train following the murder of his wife (Standage 1998: 50–51). In the press reporting of these events, the role of the electric telegraph was recognised as instrumental: *The Times*, reporting 'the accouchement of Her Majesty' on 7 August 1844, added 'We are indebted to the extraordinary power of the Electro-Magnetic Telegraph for the rapid communication of this important announcement.'

So while it took some years for the telegraph to become appreciated for its potential to open up the country to long distance communication, once awareness had begun to grow so did the excitement both in the press and wider commentary. The laying of cables under the sea, linking up different countries in the 1850s, and in particular the successful connection after a number of attempts between Europe and America in 1858, heralded a new future allowing people to communicate in manners never before known. This excitement was understandable, for it made possible instantaneous communication between distant places previously separated by days – for example, to be able to send a message across the 60 km between Washington and Baltimore and expect to receive a reply within minutes rather than waiting until, perhaps, the next day would significantly change the way people interacted with one another, and in time also alter their expectations of interaction. More dramatically still, to be able to communicate across oceans within minutes rather than the weeks necessary beforehand provoked some to anticipate a future world of peace and understanding. Writing in the year of the completion of the Atlantic Telegraph cable, Charles Brigg and Augustus Maverick argued that the telegraph 'binds together by a vital cord all the nations of the earth. It is impossible the old prejudices and hostilities should longer exist, while such an instrument has been created for the exchange of thought between all the nations of the earth' (cited in Carey 1992: 208). Twenty years earlier, Samuel Morse, who of course might be expected to see the positive side of his new invention, had already suggested that as the telegraph spread across the US, 'the whole surface of this country would be channelled for those nerves which are to diffuse with the speed of thought, a knowledge of all that is occurring throughout the land; making in fact one neighborhood of the whole country' (cited in Czitrom 1982: 11–12). Brigg and Maverick (who were not alone in their thoughts) simply extended Morse's logic to the international dimension. Sadly, they were thwarted by the failure of the connection to work satisfactorily. Although signals *could* be sent between the end points in Ireland and Canada, they were of poor quality and interpretation of the codes was very slow. The system got worse and worse and eventually failed completely on 1 September 1858, three weeks after connection was first established.

The response to this new communication system is reminiscent of much of the comment that was made a century and a half later, in the early days of the internet and World Wide Web. For example, the rhetoric about the new device fostering a more peaceful society, where differences between peoples would be overcome and understood, compares well with comments by Howard Rheingold, one of the earliest protagonists of the internet; he described the internet as 'a tool that could bring conviviality and understanding into our lives and might help revitalize the public sphere' and offered a 'vision of a citizen-designed, citizen controlled worldwide communications network' (Rheingold 1994: 14–15). The sense of greater understanding between distant people and cultures, a feeling that the world could be imagined more as a community, was most famously expressed in Marshall McLuhan's notion of the 'global village', first put forward in 1962. It is a recurring theme – each advance in the power to communicate over ever greater distances and in shorter times has been accompanied by claims of the benefits to follow. Armand Matellart quotes from one such claim:

> Someone made a remark about the telegraph which seems to me infinitely correct, and which brings out its full importance, namely that, at bottom, this invention might suffice to make possible the establishment of democracy among a large population. Many respectable men, including Jean-Jacques Rousseau, thought that the establishment of democracy was impossible among large populations. How could such a people deliberate? Among the Ancients, all the citizens were assembled in a single place; they communicated their will.... The invention of the telegraph is a new factor that Rousseau did not include in his calculations. It can be used to speak at great distances as fluently and as distinctly as in a room. There is no reason why it would not be possible for all the citizens of France to communicate their will, within a rather short time, in such a way that this communication might be considered instantaneous.

This statement was made by 'man of science', Alexander Vandermonde (Mattelart 2003: 22). It was made in 1795, and the 'telegraph' to which he referred was a mechanical semaphore device, the first optical telegraph line in France, operating between Paris and Lille.

We will see that almost all technological advances in communications have generated similar excitement and idealism (and some, though not all, have even inspired poets to celebrate them in verse). Although the expectations of the impact of the first Atlantic Telegraph cable seem, in hindsight, wildly over-optimistic, dashed as they were by the failure of the technology, it would be equally misplaced to dismiss the anticipation as simply naïve and romantic. Newspaper reports at the time gave a real sense of the achievement and subsequent tragedy at the cable's failure in September 1858. For example, following the completion of the connection, *The Times* reported on 11 August:

> In the face of difficulties and dangers, the magnitude of which cannot be properly appreciated by those not engaged in the work, the engineers engaged in this undertaking have, with almost untiring energy,

adhered to their all but hopeless task with that perseverance which is sure, sooner or later, to lead to success.... Many serious difficulties had to be encountered during the six days and a half that the operations lasted, any one of which, had chance not favoured us, might have ruined the expedition and delayed the advance of ocean telegraphs perhaps more than half a century.

That this was a challenge testing the limits of technological capability was acknowledged in an article in the same newspaper some two weeks later, on 26 August. Headed, 'Will the Atlantic Telegraph cable last?' this extract concluded that the water in which the cable was laid was 'so still and so low in temperature as to retain it in security for a long time to come'. This was not to be – the eventual failure of the cable came five days later, a further *Times* article recording, on 17 September 1858, that

The sound of rejoicing for the completion of the telegraphic communication between England and America had hardly ceased on both sides of the ocean which has been so wonderfully intersected by the wire...when a gloom was cast upon all by the sudden and unexpected announcement that intelligible signals had ceased to come through the cable.

While these extracts, and the other daily newspaper reports from the expedition, give an idea of the momentous nature of the Atlantic Cable project for humanity at large, it is instructive to consider what else it represented. The electric telegraph may well have been something for newspaper reporters to celebrate and marvel at, but it had also become a vital element of business life, and it was this rather than any notion of a technological challenge or a more peaceful world that drove the attempts (and provided £350,000 of funding) to establish transatlantic connections. By 1858, the domestic telegraph services across the world were handling millions of messages per day; that year, one company alone, the UK's Electric Telegraph Company, transmitted almost a million messages over its 50,000 km of wires, the number increasing by an average of 28 per cent each year (Kieve 1973: 68). Typically half of these were generated by the stock exchanges in the main trading capitals of the world, with another third for other business uses; telegraphic messages for family or personal purposes remained a small part of its usage. Carey describes the importance of the telegraph for business transactions: it was the first device to completely separate communication from transportation. Before the electric telegraph linked up cities, the prices of commodities varied from city to city: 'the cost of wheat, corn, or whatever would be radically different in, say, Pittsburgh, Cincinnati, and St. Louis' so that each market was local and independent (Carey 1992: 216). This allowed trading under a process of arbitrage: buying goods where they were cheap and moving them to where they could be sold more expensively. These differences in prices between cities had already started to fall as railways, canals and roads were built, making transportation of goods easier, but the telegraph meant that all buyers and sellers were aware of prices right across the markets making the opportunities for arbitrage scarcer. In Carey's words, 'the railroad and canal regionalized markets; the telegraph nationalized them' (1992: 217). The development of international markets was an obvious next step.

By 1858 many countries had already been successfully connected by submarine cables, principally between Britain and the countries of its empire and, despite the disappointment of the failure of the first transatlantic cable, the further expansion of business required the effort to be repeated. A second cable failure, this time operating between Britain and India in 1859, prompted more intensive research and investigation, and replacement cables were finally successfully laid between Britain and India in 1864 and between Britain and America in 1866. This time the cable worked and international telegraphy expanded just as domestic telegraphy had done in the previous decades, enabling the further growth of trade between distant countries and, for imperial powers like the UK, the more efficient administration and control of its colonies (Headrick 1991). Numerous technological improvements enhanced the telegraph's capacity and reliability, and the electric telegraph remained an important communications device, particularly for international communication, well into the 20th century, despite the emergence of newer communications technologies. One of the key reasons for this longevity was the inherent simplicity of the Morse telegraph's coded message – a simple dot-dash signal is relatively easy to produce and to distinguish even in the presence of background noise, an advantage that is comparable with the on-off signals in today's digital systems – and this helped Morse's design succeed over competitors which relied on more complex cabling and signalling arrangements. One of the intended enhancements to the telegraph's operation, however, led to the development of a device that was to replace much of the telegraph's usage in the following decades.

The Telephone's Genesis

The telegraph's capacity to carry messages was limited by a number of factors: one of these was simply the speed at which an operator could translate the written word into Morse's dots and dashes, and operators became known for their skill and speed in doing so. Nevertheless, with demand on its use growing, at busy times a backlog of messages would build up to the point where some telegraph companies actually found it quicker to send messenger boys with bundles of written messages between nearby telegraph stations (Standage 1998: 89). Another limitation on the telegraph's capacity was the number of wires connecting telegraph offices. While a line was carrying one message, it couldn't carry another. The immediate solution was to string up another wire, and by 1866, when the Western Union Telegraph Company was incorporated, there were 827,000 miles of wire strung between telegraph poles across the US alone (Cowan 1997: 152). Pictures of street scenes in the second half of the 19th century show ever-expanding spider's webs of telegraph wires, and this physical expansion could clearly not go on forever. An alternative means of increasing the capacity, without the cost and complexity of adding yet more wires to the system, was explored. By the 1870s, a number of investigators were trying to send several telegraph signals simultaneously down a single wire by using different, separated electrical frequencies for each. If a message from one telegraph, with its own sequence of dots and dashes, were connected to a wire on a high frequency electrical signal, and another, completely different message was sent on a lower frequency, the two messages would occupy different frequency 'spaces' within the wire's capacity. At the receiving office, one telegraphic receiver could be designed to respond only to higher frequencies, while another could pick up just the lower frequencies. The device was known as a harmonic telegraph, because of its dependency on varying frequencies, or harmonics, and the process of sending more than one message simultaneously down a single wire is known as multiplexing. While this afforded a useful way of making more economical use of the telegraph cables, for some of the experimenters sending varying electrical signals, or 'vibrations', down wires also raised the possibility of transmitting electrical representations of sound via electric cable. Sound is carried to the ear by minute vibrations of air molecules, themselves produced by some mechanical vibration (vocal chords, for example, or the strings of a violin). If a mechanical vibration can instead be induced by electricity, then sound can be created from vibrating electrical signals (Box 1.1).

Box 1.1   Sound Conversion: the microphone, motion and electricity

For the telephone to carry speech signals down wires, some means must exist of converting sound into electricity. This is the role performed by a microphone, and it relies on the relationship between electricity and magnetism. Scientific investigations in the early 19th century had established how this relationship worked: if a magnet and a metal wire are moving in relation to each other, an electric current will flow in the wire. The size and direction of current flow depend on how fast and in what direction the relative motion travels. In other words, the state of the electric current is a reflection of the motion.

Air molecule vibrations carry sound from source to our ears or to a microphone. Though tiny, these vibrations can impart movement on our eardrums or, equally, on a diaphragm in a microphone, and if the diaphragm is attached to a coil of wire surrounding a magnet, an electric current is induced in the wire, and this current responds continuously to the air molecule vibrations. Hence, the changing current is a reflection of the nature of the sound that is producing it (Figure 1.1).

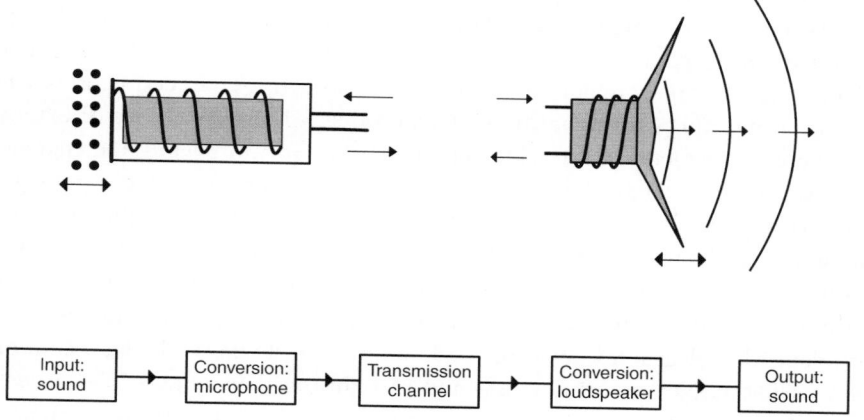

Figure 1.1 Microphone and loudspeaker: inputs and outputs

Those electric currents form the signal that is carried in the wire. At the receiving end some means of converting that electrical signal information into sound is needed. The electromagnetic effect that is used to produce an electrical signal in a microphone is reversible: if a wire carrying an electric current is positioned near a magnet, it will produce a force between them which can cause it to move, and the size of the force and any consequent movement depend on the size and direction of that electric current. A loudspeaker or telephone earpiece therefore consists of the inverse of a microphone. A wire coil surrounds a magnet, which is attached to a loudspeaker diaphragm, or cone. As current passes through the coil it causes the magnet to move, vibrating the loudspeaker diaphragm, thus producing sound. The way in which the diaphragm moves reflects the changing electric current and, since that current is produced by the air molecule vibrations at

Box 1.1   (Continued)

the microphone, the sound coming out of the loudspeaker should sound the same as that recorded by the microphone. The function of the microphone and loudspeaker then is simply to convert mechanical molecular vibrations to and from an electrical signal which is suitable for transmission through the chosen medium, be it an electrical cable or a radio wave.

Since the 1860s, people had toyed with the idea that it might be possible to use electricity in this way: Philippe Reis in Germany and Charles Bourseul in France had made simple sounds, humming sounds for instance, by tuning an electric circuit to create vibrating electrical signals which were carried down a wire and produced a mechanical vibration, and thus a sound, at the other end. While this was far from actually transmitting speech, two experimenters who had been working on the harmonic telegraph saw the possibilities of extending these experiments to carrying speech. Elisha Gray, a telegraphic engineer, and Alexander Graham Bell, who came at the problem from a different perspective as a teacher of deaf people, both filed a patent for a telephone on the same day, 14 February 1876, in Washington. Following litigation, controversially won by Bell, Gray went on to concentrate his efforts on multiplexing telegraph signals, while Bell pursued the idea of the telephone. Aware of the problems the telegraph's inventors had had in its early days – being seen more as a curiosity than useful device – and recognising that many of the speech-by-wire investigators were also motivated mostly by curiosity, Bell intended to promote the utility value of his invention. Like the telegraph before it, the telephone was demonstrated at shows and fairs, once more attracting admiration from the public and press but less from business interests. The technology, wondrous as it may have appeared in demonstrations, would not sell itself. Potential business users were lobbied, but businesses had by this time incorporated the electric telegraph fully into their regular operations, an increasingly vital business tool the more widespread its adoption became, and it was not immediately obvious what benefit the telephone would offer in that environment. As with the telegraph, efforts were made to market the new device, and Queen Victoria again presented a public relations opportunity when Bell presented her with a pair of telephones on a visit to London in 1876 (two is the minimum number of telephones needed, after all, if one is seeking to demonstrate its use).

Bell sought, initially unsuccessfully, to appeal to the big telegraph companies to back him in developing the telephone. In the US, the Western Union declined his request for funding. Bell then offered a vision of how the telephone would be used. In 1878 he appealed to the 'capitalists of the Electric Telephone Company' to fund this vision (Pool et al. 1977: 156):

> At the present time we have a perfect network of gas pipes and water pipes throughout our large cities. We have main pipes laid under the streets communicating by side pipes with the various dwellings, enabling the members to draw their supplies of gas and water from a common source.
>
> In a similar manner it is conceivable that cables of telephone wires would be laid under ground, or suspended overhead, communicating by branch wires with private dwellings, counting houses, manufactories, etc., uniting them through the main cable with a central office where the wire could be connected as desired, establishing direct communication between any two places in the city. Such a plan as this, though impracticable at the moment, will, I firmly believe, be the outcome of the introduction of the telephone to the public. Not only so, but I believe in the future wires will unite the head offices of telephone companies in different cities, and a man in one part of the country may communicate by word of mouth with another in a distant place.

He distinguished the telephone from its predecessor, the telegraph:

> The great advantage it possesses over every other form of electrical apparatus consists in the fact that it requires no skill to operate the instrument. All other telegraphic machines produce signals which require to be translated by experts, and such instruments are therefore extremely limited in their application, but the telephone actually speaks, and for this reason it can be utilized for nearly every purpose for which speech is employed.

This prescient scenario suggested that the telephone would go much further than the telegraph, that while it would certainly serve the needs of businesses, it would find further use among the general public rather than needing the services of 'experts' to operate it. Further, just as Queen Victoria had needed two telephones for it to work at all, the new telephone system would become more valuable to its users the more people connected to it; or, equally, people would be more likely to take up the telephone if the network was substantial enough – a self-reinforcing expansion of a true network, where anyone on the network can contact anyone else anywhere on the network. This clearly envisaged the telephone as a two-way communication device, but other ideas soon became apparent.

As later chapters will show, many novel technological developments have been anticipated by those developing them as fulfilling a particular function but have rapidly become adopted by others for quite different purposes. While Bell and his business colleagues saw the telephone as a communications network in the way that we know it now, in its early days it fulfilled a number of roles. Some of the earliest installations were private lines, for example connecting a factory and its owner's home. Other early adopters were doctors who could be contacted both at home and at their surgeries, hospitals and pharmacies. However, while these might be seen simply as precursors of the more public network that was to follow in time, demonstrations at public fairs and festivals presented a different side of the telephone. To demonstrate the telephone's sound-carrying capabilities to someone who had never seen one before, a telephone would be placed in a concert hall some way across the city and a festival visitor could listen live to the concert on a second telephone. In the first decades of the telephone a number of companies set up such services relaying concerts, plays, occasionally political speeches but frequently church services over telephone networks – telephone microphones would be placed in the church and subscribers might be hotels, where guests could listen using headsets provided in the lobby, or private subscribers who could listen on their telephone at home. The hotel guest might choose a different telephone for a different denomination service, or the home listener could ask the telephone operator to connect to a particular service or event. Marvin lists some of the events on offer: opera from Covent Garden or plays from the Theatre Royal in London, courtesy of the Universal Telephone Company in 1891; subscribers in Rochester, Buffalo and other cities heard a concert from New York City, together with contributions transmitted from Troy and Poughkeepsie; a live description of a baseball game from Chattanooga could be listened to in Nashville in 1884. An early form of teleconferencing also emerged: in 1912, the annual Chicago Yale Club's alumni banquet was addressed by Yale's president by telephone from New Haven (Marvin 1988: 209–16).

So the telephone also had a role as provider of entertainment, a novelty to amuse the well-to-do who were its principal customers. This usage ran perfectly happily in parallel with the steady growth in the numbers of telephones in use for business communication (as anticipated by Bell) and reflected changing social practices of the time: while the telegraph had provided clear evidence of the value to business of rapid point-to-point communication, novel technologies were increasingly being used for entertainment rather than utility. For example, the second half of the 19th century saw the growth of amateur photography, sideshow entertainment at funfairs and, later, the emergence of cinema (Howells 2003). The new technology of the telephone was simply exploited and adapted to meet these different needs, or markets.

A similar pattern of usage befell another invention of the same period, the phonograph, in which a sound is recorded by speaking into a large tube, the sound vibrations making impressions on a rotating cylinder of wax or tin foil. The recorded sound can be replayed by rotating the cylinder which is mechanically connected through a needle to a conical tube which then acts like a listening horn, amplifying the vibrations until they are audible as sound. While at least two engineers and one poet-turned-inventor, respectively, Thomas Edison in the US, Emile Berliner in Germany and Charles Cros in France had all published proposals for a sound-recording device, Edison had a particular view of what the machine would be used for. Having worked closely with Bell on the telephone, developing and improving the microphone, he patented the phonograph in 1877 as an enhancement of the telephone and emphasised its utility rather than entertainment value. His description the following year of its anticipated purpose has a resonance today (Edison 1878: 534–5):

> ...the phonograph will *perfect the telephone*, and revolutionize present *systems of telegraphy*. That useful invention is now restricted in its field of operation by reason of the fact that it is a means of communication which leaves no record of its transactions, thus restricting its uses to simple conversational chit-chat, and such unimportant details of business as are not considered of sufficient importance to record. Were this different, and our telephone-conversation automatically recorded, we should find the reverse of the present status of the telephone. It would be expressly resorted to *as a means of perfect record* [original emphasis].

As well as what we now call the telephone answering machine (or more recently, voicemail), Edison also envisaged a kind of 'audio telegraph'. The phonograph would be used for dictating a message, which could be relayed over the telephone lines to a recording phonograph at the destination where it could be listened to later. Nevertheless, others saw an entertainment opportunity, and once in production the phonograph was also sold for playing music, pre-recorded onto the cylinders, either in private homes or in public places where, like a juke box, a coin inserted in the machine would allow it to be played for a limited period of time. Much to Edison's irritation, who feared this would 'injure the phonograph' and reduce it to 'nothing more than a mere toy', this proved to be a far more profitable use of the phonograph, and its application as a business machine never developed successfully (Flichy 1995: 65). In fact, for business uses, Edison's ideas for the phonograph offered little that the telegraph did not already provide, so its failure to achieve a significant impact is not surprising. In time, the phonograph was indeed coupled to the telephone but, again, for entertainment purposes when, in 1912, the New York Magnaphone and Music Company installed motor-driven phonographs to play pre-recorded music to subscribers (Marvin 1988: 212). This dual use of the telephone is a recurring feature: echoes of the Magnaphone were evident in 1966, when a 'dial-a-disc' telephone service began in Leeds in the UK providing a similar service to telephone subscribers.

While these telephone entertainment offerings reflected the beginnings of the wider use of early communications (and electrical) devices in the home for private consumption, for pleasure rather than utility (Briggs 1977), a more business-oriented service did also emerge. The electric telegraph had become widely used by the press, and by this time essential to their successful operation, and it was no surprise that the telephone also began to be used for the same purpose. It had the advantage of speed over the telegraph, demanding no particular skill of the user, as Bell had earlier pointed out, though unlike the telegraph did not leave a written record of any conversation (despite Edison's efforts). Its advantages were presented in countless marketing enterprises. For the 1892 US presidential election, arrangements were made for returns to be delivered on election night over the telephone system (as well as the tried and tested telegraphic returns used in earlier elections). Telephone companies in New York and Chicago arranged to forward returns coming to them to subscribing clubs and hotels. In some cases the telephone bulletins were received up to 90 minutes earlier than those from local telegraph offices (Marvin 1998: 218). The telephone's value as a speedy deliverer of news was becoming evident. In 1893, a company in Budapest in Hungary began a daily news service delivered over the telephone to subscribers in exactly the same way as other companies were offering music, theatre and sporting events. Telefon Hirmondó ran throughout the day, carrying news bulletins, business and market news, cultural events in the evenings and a children's programme at weekends. Nationally known authors read serial extracts from their latest novels, and the service even carried a time signal transmitted each hour. At its height, Telefon Hirmondó had around 6000 subscribers, predominantly the wealthier members of Budapest society, and was relayed to public spaces such as coffee houses, doctors' waiting rooms and barber's shops (Marvin 1988: 227). This, of course, was a precursor to what we now know as radio – indeed, it was the coming of radio a few years later that caused the end of such services – and it represented one of the first uses of this communications technology where, rather than merely reporting from or relaying live events, it involved the creation of original content designed specifically to suit this new medium. For example, Telefon Hirmondó had its own newsroom with its own reporters. It was keenly observed in the US and Europe, but attempts to emulate its success were limited – the Telephone Herald in Newark in New Jersey modelled itself on its Budapest counterpart, but suffered financial difficulties and closed after just a few months.

Whilst at the time Telefon Hirmondó and the more entertainment based services were novel, useful and therefore successful, they suffered some limitations. As wire-based services, they relied on a physical connection between transmitter and receiver. Stringing up wires across cities is expensive; to do the same in rural areas is more expensive still, where cables might have to be hung over great distances for the sake of connecting just a few homes or businesses. Thus a cable-based service was likely to offer the best return to investors if it sought to install a relatively small, targeted group of subscribers to the various services carried over its lines. The 6000 subscribers to Telefon Hirmondó's service in Budapest, while sufficient for it to be successful economically, amounted to barely one per cent of the city's population, concentrated in the wealthier districts (Marvin 1988: 227). There was little economic reason to try to extend the network into the poorer areas, and it was many decades before the telephone could be regarded as anything like a universal service anywhere in the world.

A second limitation was the restriction on the sound quality. A telephone wire has only a limited capacity for carrying information. Within that capacity, it might be possible to carry a particular number of phone call signals simultaneously – the multiplexing process mentioned earlier in discussing the telegraph. If, however, each telephone call were deliberately restricted in the amount of the cable's capacity it might use, then each cable could carry even more calls at any one time. This means it would be possible to carry more calls over the network with fewer cables, either saving money or increasing the capacity of the network, depending on one's point of view. This had been exactly the intention in developing a harmonic telegraph, and reflected a view of the telephone (held by Bell and others) which foresaw it as a natural development of the telegraph rather than the proto-broadcasting system that Telefon Hirmondó developed. Thus the sound quality of speech and particularly music was intentionally compromised in the technical design of the telephone, a trade-off between quality (of sound) and quantity (of calls) within the network, such design considerations being necessary in all communications systems (Box 1.2). While this sacrifice may have been of little concern to the early customers, who no doubt were impressed to hear anything at all, when radio broadcasting began after the First World War it had far fewer limitations on sound quality. It offered the further advantage of being a wireless technology and thus could be heard by anybody without the need for a physical connection. Telefon Hirmondó and other telephone-based services began to decline and eventually withered in the face of this new development.

Box 1.2 Bandwidth: sound quality vs. channel capacity

Any signal derived from a physical quantity such as sound or an image is made up of a range of frequencies. For example, speech and music contain very low frequency sounds (heard as bass notes) and high frequencies (treble notes or squeaks or hissing sounds), and when a microphone records such sounds, the electrical signal produced will also contain variations in electrical voltage or current at those same frequencies. The range of frequencies that a source produces is referred to as its bandwidth and, in general, the more information contained in the signal, the higher its bandwidth. So video images, with both sound and picture information, produce a greater bandwidth than sound only. Some typical bandwidths are given in Table 1.1 below.

	Typical bandwidth	
Speech	10 kHz	From around 100 Hz to 10,000 Hz
Music	20 kHz	From 50 Hz to 20,000 Hz
Television	5.5 MHz	Standard definition picture; high definition produces a higher bandwidth

Table 1.1 Bandwidths of common signals

To carry electrical signals through wires or over the airwaves, all the frequencies contained in its bandwidth must be carried through successfully, or the missing frequencies will result in the sound or image becoming distorted. Yet wires or the airwaves are limited in their overall capacity, and sometimes the proportion of a signal's bandwidth that is sent through the wire or over the airwaves is deliberately reduced in order to allow more signals to be carried within that capacity. The distortion resulting from this curtailment is considered an acceptable trade-off between the quality of received signals and the quantity or number of signals that can be carried. For example, in the telephone system the highest and lowest frequencies in the speech signal's bandwidth are filtered out, and the only frequencies carried in the wires are those between 300 Hz and 3400 Hz so that the bandwidth carried is 3100 Hz rather than the full bandwidth of speech which is 10 kHz. Telephone speech quality is degraded but is acceptable for its intended purpose; and this deliberate restriction means many more calls can be carried in the wires simultaneously. In comparison, AM radio carries sound at a bandwidth of 4.5 kHz, so at better quality than the telephone, while FM radio uses a bandwidth of 15 kHz, offering high quality audio.

A Note on Frequencies and Units: Hz, kHz, MHz...

The basic unit in which frequencies, or rates of vibration, are measured is the Hertz, abbreviated to Hz, named after the physicist Heinrich Hertz. Higher frequencies are measured in multiples of a thousand (Table 1.2).

1 Hertz	1 Hz	One vibration per second
1 kiloHertz	1 kHz	Equals 1000 Hz
1 MegaHertz	1 MHz	Equals 1,000,000 Hz
1 GigaHertz	1 GHz	Equals 1,000,000,000 Hz

Table 1.2 Frequencies and units

The Telephone and Social Change

The early history of the telephone illustrates how a new technological innovation in communications can often present a number of possible patterns of usage. Just as when the history of the internet is written it is likely to chart a number of prognoses for its development, from early point-to-point communication and file-sharing, through a middle period when it was a kind of publishing and trading forum dominated by business interests to an emerging (so-called Web 2.0) period of user-generated content (alongside those business interests), so the telephone also provoked a similar variety of expectations over a similar period of time. Ithiel de Sola Pool (1983) gathered together a number of predictions about the likely impact of the telephone, many of them contradictory. For example some argued that the telephone would increase the centralisation of businesses and reduce the autonomy of outlying branches (because the telephone now allowed and thus encouraged branch managers to refer to headquarters before making decisions); alternatively, others imagined the opposite occurring as the telephone allowed junior or outlying people to seek information directly from others in an organisation without going through the 'usual channels', perhaps skipping layers in the business hierarchy. Predictions included effects on migration patterns; for example in 1905 it was predicted that the telephone would end the tendency for people to leave farming in the countryside and head for the city. This proved incorrect of course, as did the recurring assumption that an improvement in communications capacity would lead to a more peaceful world. This time it was General John Carty, in the early 1900s, who suggested (Pool 1983: 89):

Some day we will build up a world telephone system making necessary to all peoples the use of a common language, or common understanding of languages, which will join all the people of the earth into one brotherhood. There will be heard, throughout the earth, a great voice coming out of the ether, which will proclaim, 'Peace on earth, good will to all men.'

As well as all speaking the same language, it was assumed too that we would end up speaking numbers in a new way: rather than reading the number 1,336,442 as one million, three hundred and thirty six thousand, four hundred and forty-two, we would read it as a telephone number: 'one double three six double four two'. Again, in these fanciful imaginings we see similarities with the more recent concern in some parts that the abbreviated language used in text messaging on mobile phones or computer instant messaging would render young people forever unable to spell correctly (Thurlow 2006).

For others, concerns were rather more personal. As the telephone spread beyond the wealthy, and coin-operated telephones began to appear in public places, family structures were threatened. There was much discussion in the press about the potential intrusion of the telephone. For example, rules of courtship in well-to-do families would often include a number of social barriers to be breached before young people might be considered ready for introduction. Unsuitable advances might be repelled by the simple expedient of not allowing the two in question to meet. But it was harder to maintain this kind of supervision when the telephone was freely available. Other social conventions were upset, such as whether due propriety was being observed should a written dinner invitation be replied to with a mere telephone call, or how a call should be answered (a simple 'hello' or giving one's name) when one was unsure of the caller's identity. Still other concerns were simply based on superstition, such as the advice that the telephone should not be used by ill people for fear of spreading the disease to those on the other end (Marvin 1988). Telephone companies produced abundant literature seeking to dispel emerging myths and offering guidance in the appropriate use of their instruments, such as speaking 'directly into the mouthpiece keeping mustache [*sic*] out of the opening' (Fischer 1992: 70).

Conclusion: Lessons from History

What do these histories of the earliest electrical devices tell us more generally about emerging communications technologies? In the cases of both the telegraph and the telephone we see some common patterns of development. Perhaps most importantly, both emerged as a process of development rather than as a dramatic flash of inspiration – the term 'invention' tends to imply a 'eureka' moment when the problem was solved or the challenge suddenly met. Of course, there are key dates in any technology's history, and these are often useful reference points: the date of the telephone's 'invention' is often given as 1876, the year in which it was patented, for example. In fact we have seen that the time between initial speculation and realisation of a useable (and marketable) device was several decades in the cases of both the telegraph and the telephone. In between those two end points, there were a number of stages of development. There were technical issues from the outset, and with both the telegraph and the telephone different technical routes were explored by different experimenters, and no particular solution was initially seen as the best, although as time went on one technical system became dominant: Morse's version of the telegraph and Bell's design for the telephone.

In a similar manner, we can think of any changes in social practice connected with each of these new developments as evolutionary rather than revolutionary. Most new technological developments in communications necessarily build upon something that has gone before. Indeed, it can often be difficult for prospective customers to imagine the value of an innovation. For example, the Admiralty in the UK showed little interest in the electric telegraph initially, rejecting a system proposed by Francis Ronalds as early as 1816, because an optical or semaphore telegraphic system operated perfectly well from London to the southern coast (Winston 1998: 22). In France too, the electric telegraph was slow to develop because an even more extensive optical system had been installed. Bell also had to work hard to explain the key advantages of the telephone over its predecessor, the telegraph, while emphasising that it would continue to fulfil all the telegraph's functions. For if a device emerged which did not incorporate some, at least, of the functionality of a previous technology, it would be unlikely to fit well with social practices and conventions that had built up with that earlier technology. Business practices, for example, by the 1870s had become based upon the speed of communication offered by the telegraph – had the telephone, for some reason, not allowed communication at an equivalent or faster speed, it would not have been successful. In fact it did do so, with the key advantage of being operable by non-experts, as Bell pointed out repeatedly. Even so, while the telephone diminished the importance of the telegraph, it did not replace it. Not only was the telegraph well integrated into society and therefore slow to be displaced, it retained some advantages. Some businesses were keen to retain telegraphic communication alongside the telephone as it left a printed record, important in business transactions, for example. More importantly, to transmit a telephone signal down a cable was technically more complex than transmitting a telegraph signal, and this complexity meant that undersea communication was more challenging for telephony. It was not until 1956 that the first submarine telephone cable was laid across the Atlantic, for example, around 90 years after the transatlantic telegraph cable. Thus, for international communication, the telephone was of little value, and the telegraph remained important until well into the 20th century, the two systems operating in parallel. Examples of newer technologies complementing rather than replacing their predecessors recur throughout communications history – television did not, as anticipated, replace radio; nor did the advent of domestic video recorders bring about the end of the cinema.

For similar reasons, both the telegraph and telephone did not initially find an obvious application with the public and were seen as a novelty or even amusing toy. Again, this should not surprise us. Social practices tend to incorporate the utility value of technologies available to it. Before the telegraph, people were used to communication being geographically limited to the distance it was physically possible to cover in a day, and business practice and social interaction worked on that basis. When someone comes along and announces that such intervals can be reduced from days to minutes, it would not be obvious to everyone why this would be a good thing. In most cases, people did not move far from where they grew up, and so while the telephone in principle allowed dispersed families to stay in contact, in fact personal mobility and the consequent dispersal of families happened later as the telephone (and other technologies, such as the private motor car) became integrated into society. It remains true today that new technologies do not automatically offer immediate benefits to users. Comedian Mark Steel, for example, recalls enthusiastic friends educating him on the potential of the internet by explaining helpfully that he could look at a restaurant menu in Malaysia from his home in the UK. As he commented on acquiring a new home computer, 'do domestic owners need 140 typefaces?' (Steel 1998). Of course, some would see the potential of devices like the telegraph from the outset, and indeed act as a catalyst for their development, such as the railway companies which had already been in the business of speeding up communication between places, and naturally enough these were the audiences the telegraph's inventors, and later the telephone's, would target. The early identification of potential markets (accurately or otherwise) is a clear feature of these histories. The competition inherent to capitalist economics would encourage companies to begin to change practices using the new technologies in order to steal advantage over others, who would themselves be compelled to follow suit in order to survive. Only later would wider social practices begin to reflect the new possibilities opened up by the incorporation of new technologies into everyday life, and this could take some considerable time. For example, even by 1975, almost 100 years after it was first patented, only half of the UK's households had a telephone (National Statistics 2002: 156).

More than 30 years later, in most developed countries at least, the landline telephone is now commonplace and taken for granted. Nevertheless, it has continued to evolve beyond a mere speaking machine into a more sophisticated part of our communications networks. Most obviously, the telephone line provides the connection to the internet in most households. 'Smart homes' use sensors to monitor activity in the house, including movement, temperature and use of appliances to enable remote monitoring to provide services such as intruder and fire alarms or care for the elderly and disabled. While these are more part of a digital data network than the telephone system, they nevertheless rely for their operation on a wired network infrastructure installed for the most basic of purposes, carrying the spoken word, over a century ago.

Radio

2

Everyone is familiar with radio, very familiar. In the UK, people spend on average 23 hours per week listening to it, almost as much time as they spend watching television. For many, radio has changed little for as long as they can remember. Station names may change, music styles too, but listening patterns vary little, a typical listener tuning to three or four favourite stations and hearing familiar voices and programmes. Indeed, in November 2006, one of the longest running radio programmes, *The Archers* soap opera on BBC's Radio 4, broadcast its 15,000th episode, having begun in 1951. Those changes that have taken place in radio technology over the past decades have generally been relatively minor modifications, such as stereo broadcasting and the RDS data system seen on car radios. Only recently has the emergence of digital radio presented potentially significant differences in the way we listen to radio.

However, this appearance of continuity and consistency overshadows substantial changes in radio from its earliest days. The notion of radio itself, listening to a variety of sounds delivered through the air from a transmitting station, is less than 100 years old, a different understanding of the term prevalent before that. As we have seen, by the end of the 19th century, two communications technologies were well advanced and dominated all others: the telegraph and the telephone. The telephone was beginning, slowly, to become established as an important means of one-to-one communication, particularly for business purposes, although it also had a significant role as an information and entertainment device. Radio, by which we mean here simply the use of radio waves to communicate between one place and another, was envisaged simply as a way of doing what the telegraph and telephone already did, but without wires. In other words, it offered a key technical advantage – there was no need for a physical connection between transmitter and receiver – but at the same time fulfilled the functions of those systems it was intended to enhance.

In fact, at first, like the wired systems that preceded it, it was technically possible only to use radio for telegraphy rather than telephony, the telegraph's simple dot-dash signal being more straightforward to transmit and understand.

So the self-explanatory term 'wireless telegraphy' rather than radio was used to describe this new system. The existence of radio waves had been known about since the 1880s, when physicist Heinrich Hertz was able to observe the presence of wave energy in a detector which was not physically connected to the wires from which it emanated. Hertz was not surprised at his findings; James Clerk-Maxwell, a theoretical physicist, had calculated in 1864 that such waves should exist in the presence of electricity, but Hertz was the first to declare publicly that they had been observed, and early texts in fact refer to radio waves as Hertzian waves. These were important scientific discoveries, part of the expansion in scientific investigation and experimentation prompted by industrial growth across the world, but at that time neither Hertz nor Maxwell were thinking of the use of radio waves for communication. But it was not long before others did. As word of Hertz's work spread, other scientists quite naturally strove to reproduce the experiments, and refined and improved the techniques. Over the next ten years, experimenters in many countries developed new ways of transmitting and detecting radio waves: Edouard Branly in France, Augusto Righi in Italy, Oliver Lodge in Britain and many others contributed to the scientific study of radio waves. However, Righi's student, fellow Italian Guglielmo Marconi, saw the practical applications of these developments, and was the first to secure a patent on a radio wave detection device on his arrival in London from Italy in 1896. The possibility of using radio waves for communication was recorded in 1892, in an article in *The Fortnightly*, written by Sir William Crookes (Briggs 1961: 5):

> Rays of light will not pierce through a wall, nor, as we know only too well, through a London fog; but electrical vibrations of a yard or more in wavelength will easily pierce such media which to them will be transparent. Here is reached the bewildering possibility of telegraphy without wires, posts, cables or any of our present costly appliances. Granted a few reasonable postulates and the whole thing becomes well within the realms of possible fulfilment.

This account suggests that the technical knowledge and expertise were well developed by the time Marconi turned his thoughts to exploiting its commercial potential. Having failed to secure any backing, financial or otherwise, for his plans in Italy, he travelled to London and met the Chief Engineer at the Post Office, William Preece. The Post Office by this time was responsible for all telegraphic communication in the UK, having taken over all the different private telegraph companies under the Telegraph Act of 1868. Now, the idea of communication without wires was catching on – as well as their absence saving money, as Crookes had noted, the possibility of mobile communication had already been conjectured. A lecture by W E Ayrton to the British Imperial

Institute in 1867 anticipated some now familiar sounding possibilities. He looked forward to doing away with wires (Marvin 1988: 157):

> Then when a person wants to telegraph to a friend, he knows not where, he will call in an electromagnetic voice, which will be heard loud by him who has the electromagnetic ear, but will be silent to everyone else, he will call, 'Where are you?' and the reply will come loud and clear to the man with the electromagnetic ear, 'I am at the bottom of the coal mine, or crossing the Andes, or in the middle of the Pacific.'

Within months of his arrival in England, Marconi was demonstrating wireless communication to the Admiralty. In contrast with their scepticism about the electric telegraph in the 1830s, this time they were interested. For, by this time, navy warships were being clad in iron rather than simple wooden hulls, and were able to sail faster and further and carried long range guns. Their increased size and speed meant that they sailed further apart, and communication by visual means, such as semaphore, became impossible. Wireless telegraph communication became a solution to this problem in the same way that the wired telegraph had become a solution to the railway's signalling problems (Winston 1998: 71).

The first transmitters were simple refinements of the kind Hertz and others had been experimenting with. So-called spark transmitters are formed by connecting two wires to an electrical supply and bringing the ends together so that there is a small gap between them. When the electrical supply is switched on, a spark jumps between the gaps, and this electrical discharge causes radio waves to be emitted around it. Once the electric current is switched off, the waves stop. These waves travel away, or radiate, from the source of the spark in all directions and the energy carried in the waves can cause electrical effects in detectors at some distance. We are aware of this effect: lightning flashes, for example, are effectively big sparks, and we can hear the consequences as interference on a radio receiver. When a fridge door is opened switching on the light inside, or a piece of electrical machinery operated, the sudden flow of electricity can be heard as a buzz or crackle in an audio system or seen on a TV screen. While the first spark radio wave receivers were designed to create an ink mark on a strip of paper treated with chemical, later wireless telegraph operators used headphones which were quicker to translate. The radio waves made a sound in the headphones, and by switching the transmitter electric current on and off for either short or long durations, the dots and dashes of Morse code could be transmitted.

Selling Radio

Marconi was keen to demonstrate the capabilities of his wireless communications, and in December 1901 generated enormous publicity when he claimed to have successfully transmitted the Morse code for the letter *S* from Poldhu in Cornwall across the Atlantic to St Johns, Newfoundland. He had demonstrated that communication by radio waves was certainly possible but, importantly, that those radio waves could also travel beyond the horizon and were not limited geographically. Not only did this demonstrate forcefully the potential of his communications system but it also made him a celebrity of the day, with magazines and newspapers on both sides of the Atlantic covering both the event and the man, publicity which was encouraged by Marconi but criticised by others who suspected his motives. Oliver Lodge, for example, in letters to *The Times*, referred to the 'incautious and enthusiastic manner' of Marconi's announcement, noting that 'hasty and unreserved acceptance of newspaper or any other second-hand statements concerning physical fact is not usual among scientific men'. Nevertheless, Marconi was again celebrated when before long he began to sell wireless telegraph equipment to ocean liners and offered a transatlantic telegraph service competing directly with the submarine cable companies, which had fallen out of favour with the press because of the high costs of sending messages (Douglas 2004: 49). Staging publicity events was but one part of Marconi's strategy in making the wireless telegraph a commercial success. He also attempted to create an effective monopoly by securing patents on his designs in several countries and not allowing other companies using competing equipment to relay messages though his stations and faced numerous court actions challenging his restrictions. However, his challenge to the submarine cable companies faced some limitations. Radio waves are more susceptible to atmospheric conditions than wired systems, but perhaps more significant was the issue of privacy. The wired telegraph was a private messaging device – in addition to the intended recipient, only a few telegraph operators needed to know the content of your message. But the messages carried by wireless telegraph were available to all who cared to listen, and thus the wired systems retained a role in the communications infrastructure. It was to be precisely this ability to eavesdrop on the radio waves that later was to sow the seeds of the idea of broadcasting.

One momentous event that secured the place of wireless telegraphy in the public imagination occurred on 10 April 1912. The world's largest ocean liner, the *Titanic*, hit an iceberg on its maiden voyage from England to New York and began to sink. The role of wireless and its operators became both heroic and tragic. As Douglas recounts, 'As the story unfolded in the press during the next few weeks, the status of wireless and wireless regulation were permanently altered' (Douglas 1987: 227). While most ships by this time were equipped with wireless, it was usual to have just one trained wireless operator. When this operator finished for the evening, no one monitored the wireless signals. The *Titanic* struck the iceberg late at night, when most ships' operators had finished, including all within reach of the *Titanic* with one exception. The wireless operator on the *Carpathia* had indeed finished his shift, but returned briefly to check time signals transmitted between ships, when he heard the distress call. At that point the *Carpathia* was 58 miles away, and by the time it arrived the *Titanic* had sunk with more than 1500 passengers still on board, and only those who had made it into the lifeboats were rescued. Meanwhile, the *California* had been only 20 miles away, but the wireless operator was asleep; the *Lena* was equally close by, but had no wireless equipment at all (Douglas 1987: 228). While the *Titanic's* wireless operator, Jack Phillips, who went down with the ship, was hailed as a hero, so too was Marconi as a saviour of the survivors. But it also became clear how the inconsistency in provision and use of wireless equipment had been responsible for many deaths, and while regulation of radio had been long resisted or fought over, it was now clear that wireless communication was a vital matter and one in need of international regulation. Legislation followed ensuring all vessels had wireless equipment which was to be monitored all the time. Meanwhile, amateur wireless enthusiasts, who had taken to transmitting in Morse code to each other and anyone who would listen, were also seen as contributing to the problem of congestion on the airwaves. If more than one person was transmitting on a particular frequency, the messages could be mutually obscured. From then on, the hobbyists were to be restricted in which frequency ranges they could transmit.

The difficulty was that the lack of wires in this new technology offered disadvantages as well as its obvious advantages in functionality. Wires keep the electrical signals contained within, and stringing up a second wire between two stations, as well as doubling the capacity for signals, also allowed connections to be kept separate. Wireless communication did not allow signals to be contained: if A wishes to signal to B at the same time as C wishes to contact D, their respective messages will interfere unless they use different frequencies to carry the signals. However, given that the wireless system was also cheap in comparison with its wired counterpart, it was affordable to the amateur enthusiasts who got hold of the relatively simple transmitting and receiving equipment and started sending messages for fun. Fascinating technology as it was, this became more and more popular: by 1912 there were an estimated 122 amateur wireless clubs in the US alone, with national and international links forged on the exchange of Morse code messages (Briggs and Burke 2002: 155). With this level of use, there were bound to be high levels of interference as wireless operators attempted to transmit on the same frequencies.

Regulation would go some way to ensuring that certain frequencies were not subject to interference, such as the international distress signal frequency at 300 m, or 1 MHz, a frequency which was not allowed to be used for any other purpose.

The growing popularity of radio transmitting, and the consequent problems with interference, prompted further technical refinement. A spark generator, producing a burst of radio waves, is rather crude even though it can represent the dots and dashes needed for Morse code. It is inefficient in that it generates waves over an unnecessarily broad frequency range, and the limited confinement compounded interference problems. Things got better as techniques were developed to tune the frequencies to some extent, but some important technical developments took place on the journey from wireless telegraphy to radio. Radio as we understand it today is about the carriage of intelligible sounds, speech and music, over the airwaves. Given the gradual replacement of the wired telegraph by the wired telephone towards the end of the 19th century, it is not surprising that those working in wireless telegraphy at the beginning of the 20th century began to imagine a similar evolution. They talked of the day when wireless telephony would be possible: a telephone without wires. For radio waves to carry a sound, however, they must be generated as a continuous stream rather than a simple burst generated by a spark. A Canadian experimenter, Reginald Fessenden, had nurtured the idea of carrying speech for some years, realising early on that to do so would need a continuous wave generator. In 1901 he devised plans for a generator that would operate at '100,000 cycles', in other words would generate radio waves continuously at 100 kHz frequency. This was way in advance of the existing technical possibilities, and he experimented for some years on lower frequency machines. By 1906 he was finally experimenting with high frequency machines and was hoping to transmit a transatlantic voice signal between his stations at Brant Rock, Massachusetts, and Machrihanish on the Mull of Kintyre in Scotland, which he had already been using since 1905 for transatlantic wireless telegraphy. However, on 6 December 1906, shortly before the planned experiment, the 140 m tall Machrihanish tower was destroyed in a storm. Undaunted, Fessenden decided to continue with the plan, and on Christmas Eve he transmitted what has become regarded as the first radio broadcast but now with no means of detecting its reception. His 'programme' consisted of some phonograph recordings, a recital of poetry and his own violin playing. He added: 'If anybody hears me, please write to Mr Fessenden at Brant Rock' (Briggs and Burke 2002: 158–9). He *was* heard: Fessenden had alerted ships' operators three days before (by wireless telegraph) of his intention of a 'special' transmission, so many of Fessenden's unknown audience were listening ready for something but, expecting the usual crackles and buzzes of Morse code, they were startled to hear voices and music.

Fessenden was not aiming to be the first broadcaster, however. He was demonstrating that with continuous wave generation, it was possible to transmit speech and music over a wide area – in other words, the wireless telephone was a possibility. He wrote: 'The chief use... of the wireless telephone would be to take the place of the present long-distance pole lines... which are very expensive,' indicating the driving force behind the experiments, the cost savings offered by wireless technology, just as Crookes had noted in the case of the telegraph (Douglas 1987: 157). The technology was the same, whether for point-to-point communication or for broadcasting, but the notion of broadcasting was then unknown. The main uses for communications devices at the time were for business and occasional social contact, and therefore the most obvious application of Fessenden's work was the wireless telephone. In the same way that the automobile was first described as a 'horseless carriage' – it was a carriage, serving a carriage-like purpose, but with a mechanical engine instead of a horse – so the wireless telephone was simply a telephone without wires. Others experimented with the idea. In 1906 Lee de Forest, an American physicist, developed the 'audion', a triode valve consisting of a glass tube containing three electrodes. This was an enhancement of an earlier diode valve patented two years earlier by Ambrose Fleming, which aided the reception of radio waves; de Forest's improvement also amplified weak electrical signals. He then proceeded to follow Fessenden in transmitting speech and music, this time in 1908 from the Eiffel Tower in Paris in a well-publicised event. Nevertheless, the audience was small, again mainly wireless operators at sea (the principal users of wireless telegraphy, given that wires mostly sufficed for land-based communication). Undaunted, de Forest repeated his broadcast with 'shows' from the Metropolitan Opera House in New York, news bulletins and live election results. While this was reminiscent of the various news and entertainment services offered over the wired telephone line, unlike those subscription-based services the wireless telephone had no revenue-generating mechanism and so had no obvious application as a mass consumer technology. So no one other than wireless operators possessed the means to hear de Forest's transmissions, and wireless telephony remained a system largely of interest only to radio experimenters.

However, the simpler and cheaper wireless telegraph was undergoing a growth in interest from amateur enthusiasts. The 'hams' as they were known eavesdropped on Morse code messages travelling the airwaves, and many transmitted their own for all to hear. Numbers grew rapidly, particularly in the US where, in an attempt to control the airwaves, the Radio Act of 1912 required that all operators obtain a licence. Many amateurs did so, but far more continued to operate without a licence, and a number began to transmit speech and music as the technology became more readily available. The First World War accelerated the process: wireless communication was essential to warfare, and so it resulted in the rapid industrialisation of the manufacture of radio equipment; it increased vastly the numbers of people trained in its use; and thus, at the end of the war, there was a large number of people able to operate wireless technology and also a large quantity of redundant equipment on the market. What emerged was a forerunner of broadcasting and a rather chaotic one. It was a mix of the two-way nature of the wireless telephone and the one-to-many nature of broadcasting. Some, but not all, shared their thoughts with other groups of like-minded amateurs, and would receive signals back, though of course could not confine their transmissions to that particular audience. Others, including commercial ventures such as store owners seizing an opportunity to advertise their products, simply broadcast into the airwaves without too much regard for who might be listening. Listeners got to know who might transmit at a particular time, and 'tuned in' to their favoured broadcasters, though tuning was haphazard and reception often poor. Nevertheless, 'listening in' as it was known became a craze and by the 1920s, manufacturers could not keep up with demand (in the US, Westinghouse alone was selling more than 25,000 sets each month). In terms similar to those applied in recent times to the internet, in January 1923 the *Review of Reviews* claimed: 'The rapidity with which the thing has spread has possibly not been equaled in all the centuries of human progress' (Douglas 2004: 52).

Institutionalisation

The chaotic scenes in the US were repeated in many countries across the world, and governments and radio manufacturers (keen to sell still more sets) sought to bring some degree of order to broadcasting, as it was now reasonable to call it. In the US, following tight control of radio during wartime, in 1919 a company was formed out of manufacturer General Electric and the Marconi wireless company, and called the Radio Corporation of America, or RCA. Primarily established to control point-to-point communication dominated thereto by Marconi, the RCA tried to use its dominant position in conjunction with other manufacturers to control radio stations, but largely failed to do so, the first serious attempt at regulating the airwaves coming with the Radio Act in 1927. In the UK, things were a little more straightforward since, unlike the US situation, the wireless telegraph and telephones were all subject to control by the Post Office, and so it was a relatively simple matter to bring together the leading manufacturers of radio sets in 1922 to form the British Broadcasting Company, or BBC (to become the British Broadcasting *Corporation* five years later). The BBC was instituted as a monopoly: royalties on all radio receivers sold went to the company, as did a half-share of the licence fees paid by anyone owning a receiver, collected by the Post Office. The point of the BBC was to make radio programmes. If radio manufacturers wanted to sell receivers, there needed to be programmes to listen to. The Marconi company had been broadcasting from Essex for a period in 1920 and listeners had become used to the idea of listening in, protesting when the Post Office rescinded Marconi's licence at the end of that year after complaints from the military. Marconi was allowed to resume broadcasting in 1922, before becoming incorporated into the BBC's programming monopoly.

Listening was a solitary and awkward experience at first. Early receivers were crystal sets, in which a piece of crystal acted as the receiver of the radio waves and a piece of fine wire, the 'cat's whisker' was stroked across the crystal to tune in. Weak signals were produced and listening was invariably through headphones. While some receivers were sold with two sets of headphones, in most cases only one person could listen to the receiver at a time. The familiar image of a family group gathered around the radio set as the focal point of the living room only became reality some years later as valve receivers with built-in loudspeakers became affordable – even then, a manufactured, cabinet receiver (as opposed to one assembled at home from a kit) would cost the equivalent of many weeks' wages. Crystal sets, however, were relatively affordable. For example in 1923, a two valve receiver, the Marconi V2, was advertised in *Wireless World* for more than £22 (including headphones) while a complete crystal set such as the 'Fellocryst' could be bought for under £4. By building the set from components bought individually, a home constructor could have a crystal receiver for half that amount. For comparison, the same magazine's situations vacant columns offered an annual salary of £200 for an experienced college teacher, while a 'strong lad' wanting to work in the wireless industry might expect no more than 15 shillings (75 pence) per week (Bussey 1990: 3–5).

Receiver technology was relatively simple by today's standards, because the transmission system was conceptually straightforward. Once the technical difficulties of generating a high frequency continuous wave had been overcome, the waves could carry the lower frequency speech or music signals produced by a microphone in a process known as modulation (described on p. 49). The simplest modulation technique, amplitude modulation or AM, works well over a wide range of frequencies, though its sound quality is not as good as the alternative frequency modulation (FM) that came to be used later on. Early recordings of radio broadcasts give a sense of the sound quality, though the limitations on the fidelity of early recording equipment do not necessarily give an accurate idea of what radio really sounded like in its early years. Most listeners were probably more impressed with the idea of hearing anything at all! The quality of the sound certainly improved as time went on. Two factors affected the audio quality: the intrusion of noise into the signal and the weakening, or attenuation, of the signal's strength. Noise, which is readily defined here as any unwanted addition to the electrical currents in the receiver circuits, is so called because the consequence of electrical disturbance is audible interference or distortion of the sound. Sources of electrical noise include lightning and external switches or machinery as already mentioned but also arise from the various electrical components of a radio receiver. The earliest and cheapest receivers would generally produce more noise than those which were developed later on with improved design and materials. The second factor affecting sound quality is the strength of the received radio signal. The strength of any transmitted signal falls as it travels away from the transmitter tower. So, a receiver at some distance from the nearest transmitter will receive a weaker signal than one close by. To some extent a good receiving aerial can compensate by capturing more of the transmitted signal, and mounting it high on a roof where there are fewer physical obstacles between it and the transmitter helps. Ultimately however, sound quality will suffer if one is not within reasonable range of the transmitter. As broadcasting developed more powerful transmitters were used, together with additional relay stations, ensuring more listeners were able to receive a good signal. Attenuation or distortion is also a product of the quality of the components used to convert sound into electricity and vice-versa, that is, the microphone at the transmitter and the headphones or loudspeakers at the receiver. The best devices would faithfully convert all the nuances and frequencies of speech or music, but the earliest devices would generally not convert the highest and lowest frequencies, reducing the quality of the final audio (and still, today, the cheaper microphones and speakers do not reproduce sound as well as the better quality devices).

Hence, while the press was somewhat indifferent to radio in its earliest days, seeing it as of interest only to enthusiasts, the rapid improvements in quality as broadcasting became established caused them to change, the response becoming one of awe and excitement for the future. For example, on 29 October 1923 the *Manchester Guardian*'s correspondent reported being given a demonstration of radio one year after the beginning of broadcasting, during which he was converted from earlier scepticism to wonder at the 'news from nowhere' (the headline being a reference to William Morris's utopian musings of 1891). He began his account:

In the first part of that year [when broadcasting began] those who from time to time looked into the progress that was being made frequently found that 'listening in' was a dull occupation and that it was hard to understand the enthusiasm some modern Briton, no less than the old Athenian, is ever seeking some new thing. Indistinct speech, blurring away at times almost to nothingness, gramophone records cast out upon space and recaptured with their already doubtful wings still further clipped – these were some of the reports made, and they were true.

During the demonstration, having heard words and music from different stations across the country, his Damascene moment comes as he hears a familiar voice discussing Mozart's *The Magic Flute*.

I took off the headpiece and exclaimed, 'Why, that's Moses Baritz!' [a fellow *Manchester Guardian* music reviewer and early radio presenter]. And so it was. He was talking in Birmingham, and his unforgettable harsh voice, which had addressed me personally the day before, seemed to be coming from a yard away. This was final conviction – to recognise a voice.

There was a similar response in the American press. As with the telegraph and the telephone before it, radio was praised for its potential to unite the nation: in 1924, Waldemar Kaempffert wrote in *Forum* magazine, 'How fine is the texture of the web that radio is even now spinning! It is achieving the task of making us feel together, think together, live together' (cited in Douglas 1987: 306). Otherwise isolated, farmers, the poor and housebound were listed as the main beneficiaries, with free access to the best cultural events and to education, tending 'strongly to level the class distinctions, which depend so largely on the difference in opportunity for information and culture,' according to a 1922 article in *Collier's* magazine (ibid.: 309).

Indeed, universities and colleges were among the first to set up radio stations in the US, and in the UK the BBC sought to educate and inform as well as entertain its audience. Advertising was ruled out of the British radio system from the outset as it was seen as compromising this objective whereas, in contrast, the way in which broadcasting emerged in the US meant that advertising was part of it from the beginning. However, the progressives in that country, who believed that the airwaves were a public resource and should be used solely for the public good rather than commercial gain, battled against commercialisation. While commercial companies began to expand and consolidate their activities in radio throughout the 1920s, a significant movement grew, calling for reform of radio broadcasting and for the reservation of, at least, some of the airwaves' capacity for non-commercial programming (McChesney 1993). Lee de Forest, following his pioneering radio work earlier in the century, came to despise commercial radio so much that he spent some time attempting to develop a remote control device that would allow listeners to mute the radio when the advertisements came on, and turn the volume back up when they ended.

Local, National and International Broadcasting

Such was the anticipation about the potential impact of radio broadcasting, its reach beyond physical boundaries being celebrated for unifying a vast continent like the US, that the possibility of transmitting *beyond* national boundaries was soon exploited. For example, in 1924 the BBC's Managing Director, John Reith, approached the British government to discuss the possibility of launching a broadcasting service to the various parts of the British Empire around the world. Over the next few years, experiments showed that it was possible, although the Empire Service, later to become the World Service, did not begin regular transmissions until 1932.

The technical characteristics of radio waves made possible many different approaches to broadcasting. While, perhaps understandably, the first demonstrations of the capabilities of radio transmission, such as Marconi's original transatlantic Morse message, sought to impress by emphasising the vast distances that could be covered, radio is equally valued today for its local nature. The earliest broadcasts used medium frequency waves (MF, better known as medium wave), which typically carry for several miles, though much further at night (hence the *Manchester Guardian* correspondent was able to hear broadcasts from Birmingham because he was listening in the evening after dark). Other transmissions, using different radio wavebands, travel differently (Box 2.1).

Box 2.1   Radio Waves: bands and propagation

'Radio waves' are part of the whole electromagnetic spectrum, which includes other kinds of radiation, including light rays and X-rays. The section of the spectrum called radio is actually used for all kinds of wireless communication: radio, certainly, but also television broadcasting, mobile phones, satellite navigation, short range communication such as Bluetooth and more. The radio waves are themselves subdivided into wavebands and referred to according to the frequencies they cover (Table 2.1).

Name	Frequency range	Typical application
Very Low Frequency	3 kHz–30 kHz	Radio telegraphy, maritime navigation
Low Frequency (aka 'long wave')	30 kHz–300 kHz	AM radio broadcasting, time signalling

Table 2.1   Radio wavebands

Box 2.1   (Continued)

Name	Frequency range	Typical application
Medium Frequency (aka 'medium wave')	300 kHz–3 MHz	AM radio broadcasting
High Frequency (aka 'short wave')	3 MHz–30 MHz	International broadcasting
Very High Frequency	30 MHz–300 MHz	FM radio broadcasting
Ultra High Frequency	300 MHz–3 GHz	Television broadcasting, mobile communications
Super High Frequency	3 GHz–30 GHz	Satellite communications; microwave communication
Extremely High Frequency	30 GHz–300 GHz	Radar, radio astronomy

Table 2.1   (Continued)

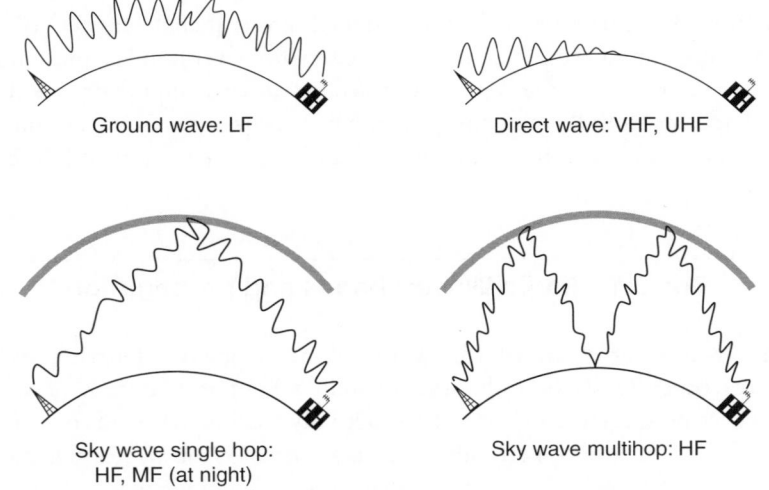

Ground wave: LF

Direct wave: VHF, UHF

Sky wave single hop: HF, MF (at night)

Sky wave multihop: HF

Figure 2.1   Wave propagation

The different bands transmit radio waves differently (Figure 2.1). For example, low frequency (LF) transmissions travel as 'ground waves', bending to follow the curvature of the Earth. So they can travel many miles, beyond the line of sight, and can be used for long distance communication. High frequency transmissions travel in straight lines but interact with a layer of the upper atmosphere, the ionosphere, which refracts them back down to Earth. So, although they travel in straight lines, by pointing the transmitters towards the sky, HF waves can also travel long distances and are suitable for international broadcasting. Medium frequency waves fall somewhere between these two: they bend round the Earth's surface to some extent, with a range of several tens of kilometres, but like HF also refract from the atmosphere so potentially also travel great distances. However during the daytime a light-activated element in the upper atmosphere absorbs MF waves, so the long-distance transmissions only occur at night. Higher frequency transmissions, those in the very- and ultra-high frequency (VHF and UHF) bands and above, also travel in straight lines but do not interact with the atmosphere. Thus their transmission range is limited to little more than line-of-sight, and so FM radio and television, which use these ranges, need a number of relay transmitters to carry signals across the country.

So the first transmitters in the UK, when the BBC began in 1922, were located at London, Birmingham and Manchester, each with a daytime range of around 40 km. Within two years additional transmitters had been installed and 65 per cent of the population was within range. Some of these were regional transmitters, such as Birmingham and Manchester with a 40 km range, but others were 'relay' stations, low power stations transmitting on medium frequency over small areas filling in the gaps between main transmitters. They were linked by high-quality telephone lines to one or other of the main transmitters and did not therefore carry any local programming of their own, merely relaying programmes from elsewhere. This was an economic decision – it was unaffordable to produce programmes for each and every transmitter that was being installed around the country (nine main stations and eleven relays). In fact, as the roll-out of transmitters progressed, all relays were connected to London rather than their nearest regional transmitter. Briggs suggested that it was assumed that listeners in Sheffield would have little interest in programmes from Manchester nor Birmingham, and so London was the default source of programming, even for the relays in Wales and Scotland which spurned regional transmitters in Cardiff, Glasgow and Aberdeen in favour of London (Briggs 1961: 217–19).

Even with this number of transmitters however, 35 per cent of the population could not receive BBC broadcasts, particularly outside urban centres. To consider covering the whole population on the basis of low-power relay transmitters was daunting, and another option was considered. A high-power transmitter located near the centre of the country, transmitting in the low frequency (LF) band, would cover much of the country. LF waves travel by a process of diffraction, that is, they tend to follow the contours of the ground rather than travelling in pure straight lines (as noted above these are known as ground waves). In this they differ from MF waves (which diffract only slightly) and high frequency (HF) waves (which do travel in straight lines). Hence a single LF transmitter could replace a number of MF transmitters (Box 2.2). The new transmitting station, established at Daventry in the midlands, was the biggest radio transmitter in the world and began operation in July 1925. Poet Alfred Noyes wrote a eulogy to commemorate the occasion, such was the sense of mystery and awe (Briggs 1961: 224). At once, coverage of BBC programming was extended to 85 per cent of the British population.

Box 2.2   Transmission Coverage and Frequency Planning

Radio and television services are typically planned to give either local, regional or national coverage. In some cases, radio signals are also intended for international coverage. The range that a signal will travel from a transmitter depends on a combination of its propagation mode, which depends on its frequency band as described in Box 2.1, and the transmitter power. A high power LF transmission will provide a signal of sufficient strength for good reception over a wide area, for example, and so is very suitable for national programming. The direct, straight line propagation of higher frequencies such as VHF limits their range, and so these are suitable for local coverage. By transmitting at particularly low powers, VHF (and other) transmissions can be restricted to very small local areas.

To use the VHF band for national coverage (to take advantage of VHF's better sound quality for example) requires that multiple transmitters be linked together, typically using cables or satellite links, in a large network. Each transmitter then broadcasts the networked programming over its local geographical area. This is less efficient in its use of frequencies than, say, a single LF transmitter, because adjacent transmitters whose coverage areas overlap must use different frequencies, even though they are carrying the same programming. This is because the signals from adjacent transmitters would reach a receiver at slightly different times due to the different path lengths of each transmission and would cause mutual interference. So all transmitters within overlapping areas must be assigned different frequencies, and this is why it is necessary to re-tune a radio while listening to VHF on the move (the RDS system in car radios was designed to automate this re-tuning). The more transmitters that are added to the network, to relay nationwide programming to the deepest valleys and most outlying communities, the more coverage areas overlap and therefore the greater the number of separate frequencies needed. The result of this is that to carry a single station's output on a VHF network might involve the use of several distinct frequency channels, so that, for example, BBC Radio 1 does not have a single frequency assignment but transmits on a range of frequencies between 97 and 99 MHz (Figure 2.2). An alternative approach to broadcasting planning is to provide less high quality coverage in difficult-to-reach areas, thus reducing the number of relay transmitters and using those frequency channels for additional radio stations. There is a trade off between quality, of coverage and reception, and quantity in the number of stations broadcasting.

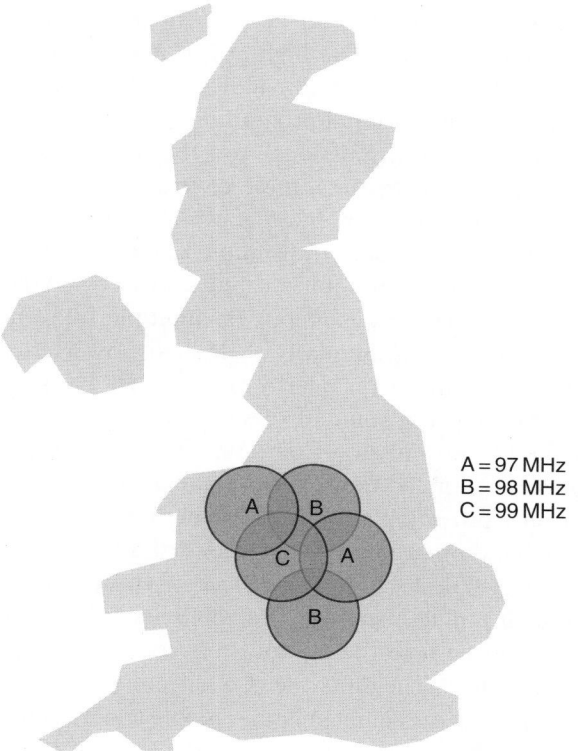

Figure 2.2 Frequency re-use. Transmitters whose coverage areas overlap must transmit on different frequencies, even if they are transmitting the same content. Here, overlapping transmitters are allocated unique frequencies (A, B or C), but where there is no geographical overlap, the same frequencies can be re-used

Where transmitters are geographically well separated (typically by more than a few tens of kilometres depending on the terrain) the same frequencies can be re-used, as there is no potential for overlap between transmissions. This frequency re-use goes some way to making up for the lack of efficiency of transmitter networks.

Of course, this meant that most of the population received the same programming, the national station based in London (carried by wire to Daventry). Meanwhile the regional transmitters in Birmingham, Manchester and so on continued their programmes, so many listeners now had a choice of two programmes. The BBC had long intended that there should be more than one station available, and plans for further development of regional services were explored. No doubt also aware that many listeners were picking up broadcasts from overseas (Street 2006) particularly in the evenings, the Regional Scheme planned for a series of five high-power MF transmitters around the country (more than five were eventually built), which would transmit two frequencies: one carrying the national programme (to provide coverage to those unable to receive the LF transmissions) and the second carrying a regional service. As high power transmitters, these covered a much greater area than the original regional transmitters, most of which closed down. It was 1927 by the time the first new regional transmitter began operation, and receivers were beginning to become more sophisticated. Older crystal sets were not very easy to tune, but the new transmissions on multiple frequencies required a sophisticated level of tuning. Similarly their high power effectively blocked reception of weaker stations on nearby frequencies. Early valve sets could be tuned more precisely, but some of these could only pick up MF transmissions and not the LF transmission from Daventry. While the BBC recognised that many listeners continued to use older equipment, Reith saw the Regional Scheme as not only providing additional listener interest and support for the BBC through its new programming but also in hastening the demise of the crystal set (Bussey 1990: 23). The emergence of cheaper valve receivers and their greater ease of tuning, therefore, presented new opportunities for broadcasters, but at the same time the broadcasters could not immediately render older receivers obsolete. The BBC faced a dilemma: should it have waited until suitable equipment was in most homes before commencing the new transmissions, or should it begin transmissions in the hope of stimulating the take up of new receivers? While this of course was a long time ago, precisely the same issues arise today as analogue broadcasting is slowly replaced by digital transmission.

When the BBC began its high power LF transmissions from Daventry in 1925, it reached not only 85 per cent of the UK population, but of course also many listeners in other nearby countries. Seeking out distant stations after dark, when even the lower power MF transmissions would reach the UK from abroad, had already become a hobby for the enthusiasts, but the beginnings of high power transmissions across Europe threatened to introduce interference and chaotic listening as multiple stations went out on similar frequencies. In the US, in some cases a station would respond to interference from other stations simply by increasing its transmitter power, drowning out the other station (which might be tempted to respond in kind). Long term, this was not sustainable, and in Europe, where transmissions readily crossed national boundaries, regulation of the airwaves had to be not just national but international. A series of international wireless conferences took place almost annually from 1925, and much negotiation and debate reached some sort of agreement by the early 1930s, though international radio conferences continue under the auspices of the International Telecommunication Union (ITU) to organise frequency allocations.

Radio Becomes a Household Item

By the end of the 1920s, the radio receiver was established as a consumer product rather than a hobbyist's toy. This development occurred earliest in the US, which had not (yet) suffered the economic depression encountered in European countries in the early 1920s. Reporting from the New York Radio Fair in 1926, *Wireless World* stated that 'Radio has been elevated from the position of a toy to be occasionally played with...to the status of a real and welcome entertainer' (Bussey 1990: 47). Radio receivers incorporated into fine wooden cabinets were beginning to appear in more and more households, increasingly operated from mains electricity rather than batteries and thus intended to be permanent fixtures, literally part of the furniture. Earlier radios had been cumbersome arrangements of electronic components, headphones and batteries. They had never been portable, of course, in the sense that we use the term today to describe personal audio equipment; but after use it would be packed into its box and put away with its battery until needed next time. Now, however, the radio would have a central place in the household as a source of entertainment and news, and receivers were consciously designed as aesthetic objects. No longer were the components that actually made the radio work on show, but all was hidden behind a stylish exterior. The radio became a desirable part of the modern household, shown off proudly, unlike the telephone, which remained utilitarian, was frequently located out of sight in the hallway, and was available in no colour other than black until the late-1950s (Moore 1989: 242). By the 1930s new materials were becoming available, allowing for mass production. Radio receivers embraced modern design: major manufacturers employed well-known architects to style their radios, which were now available in a variety of colours and levels of finish. For example, architect Wells Coates, most famous for the modernist Isokon building in London, completed in 1934, was brought in by the E K Cole ('Ekco') company. He designed 'a round radio with a body-shell made of Bakelite, simple dials and carefully composed controls: it was a striking design which symbolized the future rather than the past' (Sparke 1986: 28).

A second, important phase in radio design came after the Second World War. The War had stimulated rapid developments in electronics, and in 1947 a device known as the transistor was announced to the world. With dimensions of the order of a few millimetres it was a replacement for the relatively large valves (or tubes) found in receivers up to that point; like a valve, it could be used as part of the receiving and amplification circuits needed to drive a loud-speaker but, importantly, it consumed far less electricity than the valve, and so transistor-based radios were far smaller than traditional household radios and could run off standard, 'dry cell' batteries housed inside the casing. The transistor radio emerged in the 1950s and was truly portable, being marketed heavily as a liberating, modern lifestyle accessory offering music on the move, both inside and outside the home. This miniaturisation also made it more fea-sible to fit radios in cars. At a time when television was taking over from radio as the main medium in the home, this portability gave a new impetus to radio sales. Now the radio could be carried from room to room in the home or, as the advertisements suggested, taken to the beach or into the garden – it became something that accompanied whatever else you were doing. Instead of being a rather central feature of the home, which tended to concentrate listening even if the radio was heard while doing something else, its new role meant it retreated further into the background. Coupled with post-War prosperity and greater personal mobility (people were simply travelling around more) radio programmes began to reflect these new patterns of usage, with a greater number of music programmes (music was more popular generally, with gramo-phone record sales increasing rapidly). In Europe, Radio Luxembourg could be heard in many countries, particularly in the evenings, and was threatening the BBC's audience in the UK. Things got worse for the BBC with the launch of a number of pirate stations, in particular Radio Caroline broadcasting from a ship moored just off the coast. Although it was eventually closed down, by then it had prompted the BBC to change its programming with the launch in 1967 of pop music station Radio 1, going on to employ a number of Caroline's DJs as presenters on the new station. Radio, though it had begun to suffer at the hands of television, was far from killed off and was now on the road to recovery.

Part of this recovery included technical developments in radio transmission. The use of the very high frequency band (VHF), in addition to those bands used since the 1920s, would bring with it more stations, better audio quality including stereo sound long before it became available on television. Trans-missions in the VHF band do not carry over the horizon like LF, HF and, to some extent, MF transmissions but neither do they suffer from the interference experienced on those bands. The use of this additional waveband for radio offered the prospect of many new stations then, but it was also very suitable for a new method of modulation, frequency modulation or FM. This technique was explored in the 1930s when radio was still settling down, and engineer Edwin Armstrong desperately tried to interest the US radio stations in this new system, convinced of its technical superiority over the existing amplitude modulation (AM) system (Box 2.3). Furthermore, its lack of interference and

---

Box 2.3   Modulation

Modulation is the process by which a sound signal (or a signal derived from any source) may be transmitted on a radio wave. The relatively low frequency signal is carried by a higher frequency radio wave, and this radio wave is 'modulated' by the signal in one of two ways: by amplitude modulation (AM) or frequency modulation (FM) (Figure 2.3). A radio tuned to the station frequency receives the high frequency wave and demodulates it to recover the low frequency sound signal.

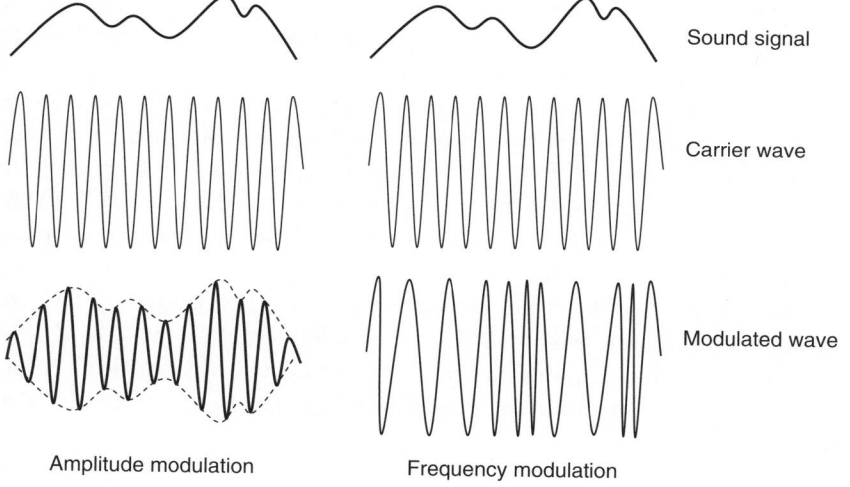

Sound signal

Carrier wave

Modulated wave

Amplitude modulation   Frequency modulation

Figure 2.3 Amplitude modulation and frequency modulation. With AM, the height (or amplitude) of the carrier wave is continuously changed by the value of the sound signal. With the FM technique, the frequency changes in response to the size of the sound signal, so the amplitude of the modulated carrier remains constant

Amplitude modulation is technically straightforward, but signals are susceptible to interference; in contrast, frequency modulation is less affected by interference, but the modulated carrier has a much higher bandwidth than that produced by amplitude modulation.

noise and its better sound could be delivered using lower transmitter power levels, and thus more cheaply. These advantages alone made it seem like an all too obvious successor to AM. However, RCA appeared happy enough with AM radio but, significantly, by this time were also becoming more interested in the prospect of television. FM demands more electromagnetic spectrum than AM for each radio station, so there is a disadvantage, spectrum inefficiency, in replacing AM radio with FM. So while the new VHF band meant more spectrum had become available, that capacity was seen as likely to be more profitably used for television, itself a hungry consumer of spectrum. While the commercial stations were not interested in VHF radio, however, the non-profit stations, mainly educational radio, which had been battling (not very successfully) with the commercial stations over the use of the existing frequency bands, saw the VHF band as a possible solution. In 1945, after much lobbying from all sides (see Chapter 3) the US Federal Communications Commission (FCC) allocated frequencies between 84 MHz and 102 MHz in the VHF band for FM radio.

Meanwhile, in the UK the BBC began experimental broadcasts in the VHF band in 1945. Both modulation techniques, AM and FM, were tried at these higher frequencies, but FM was preferred by the time trials concluded in 1950. The adoption of FM implied a significant investment for the broadcasters to install or convert transmitters, and it was to be another five years before regular broadcasts began. FM also required investment by receiver manufacturers and radio listeners – existing sets were equipped to receive only AM transmissions in the lower frequency bands, and the electronic components for FM reception were more expensive. The listening public would have to be persuaded to pay the necessary premium. The advantages of FM were already being publicly promoted. In the 'Jubilee Issue' of the *World Radio and Television Annual*, published in 1947, an article was entitled 'What is F.M.?' Its careful explanation included a justification for its adoption (Pedrick 1947: 152).

> In their answer, the experts put the emphasis on two advantages: it offers a means of, first, more faithful reproduction of sounds, and secondly, of reducing disturbance by background noise. An incidental fact, but of obvious significance, is that F.M. is really effective only on the ultra-short waves [now known as VHF], which forces attention to them, rather than to the medium waves, for broadcast transmission. This brings into the picture wavebands on which there is no congestion, and so a promise of some relief from the congestion on the existing broadcasting bands.

The difficulties of introducing FM, still unresolved in 1955, were acknowledged in the 1947 article: 'Radio manufacturers have been at work in their research and experimental laboratories for a long time, but there's some way to go before there are sets on the market and transmissions on the air to serve them' (ibid.: 153).

Here we see the age-old difficulty of innovation in a broadcast medium. Given the success that AM radio had achieved, certainly by the end of the 1940s when FM was being trialled, in that most households in countries like the UK and the US had at least one receiver, how were they to be persuaded to buy a new one able to receive FM? Two enhancements appeared to be on offer: better quality reception and possibly more stations. Quality of reception might be important enough if existing reception was poor, but if a listener was used to reasonable AM reception, she might not be too enthusiastic about paying extra to hear the same stations in slightly better quality. After all, the content would be the same. On the other hand, the additional stations might be a greater incentive, depending of course on what sort of stations were introduced. However, for a broadcaster to launch new stations is expensive, in particular when it is clear that at the outset there will be no listeners (given that no one would at that stage have a suitable receiver). For commercial broadcasters in particular, to make such an investment in these circumstances would be a huge leap of faith. All of this is familiar today with the introduction of digital radio: the new digital receivers were sold on the basis of better sound quality to begin with but later on the basis of new stations when better quality did not appear persuasive. Yet in many countries there were no, or only a few, new stations, and so listeners were reluctant to pay the extra for the digital receivers. While the new stations have been pioneered mainly by the publicly funded broadcasters such as the BBC in the UK, commercial stations have been hesitant on the grounds that few receivers have been sold (Lax et al. 2008).

Meanwhile, in the US the move of the educational stations onto FM in the VHF band did not precipitate a rush of sales of new receivers. As Keith notes (2002: 392):

> [FM] was perceived as the province of eggheads and the terminally unhip – the place to tune for Stravinsky and fine arts programming.... Most twenty-year-olds had never tuned to a station between 88 and 108 MHz. Why should they? The cool music and wacky deejays were all over the AM band.

Not until the freeing up of the VHF band in the 1970s following the end of simulcasting (in which the commercial stations broadcast the same content on both AM and FM), a decision which allowed a number of new stations playing rock music albums to draw in listeners, did the take up of FM receivers accelerate. In the UK, the BBC also simulcast its three stations – the Light,

Home and Third programmes – when it began FM transmissions in 1955. The introduction of stereo in 1966 offered a further technical improvement in sound but, again, only to those with suitable receiving equipment, and in this case that was a small, though growing, number of hi-fi enthusiasts. But even by this time, ten years on, more than two-thirds of listeners still had AM-only receivers, so could not receive FM at all, stereo or otherwise (Shacklady and Ellen 2003: 21). One innovation following the advent of stereo FM broadcasting was a number of programmes, usually concerts and operas, broadcast simultaneously on television and radio, so the viewer could have high quality sound with the visual image rather than the inferior sound carried with the TV signal (and listings magazines like the *Radio Times* included instructions for the best audience experience such as turning the TV sound down and placing the radio or hi-fi speakers on either side of the television set). However, FM was slow to catch on – by 1972, 99 per cent of the UK's households were within range of FM signals, yet 60 per cent were still not equipped with an FM receiver (Crisell 2002: 138; Shacklady and Ellen 2003: 21).

In the UK, the increased capacity afforded by the use of the VHF band allowed the BBC to begin local radio stations. The first, Radio Leicester, launched in 1967 and was followed by others around the country. While local radio existed in many other countries, in the UK radio had been national or regional. VHF transmissions suit local delivery particularly as their range is generally limited; however, for national coverage on VHF, this limited coverage means a series of networked transmitters and relays is needed, typically ten times as many as required for MF and LF transmissions. Nevertheless, given the other advantages of VHF, principally audio quality, by the 1990s all of the BBC's local and national stations had migrated to VHF and, in the case of national stations, had largely moved off the MF band. Only Radio 4 remained on the LF band as a simulcast service (where it remains to this day), while a new station, Radio 5 Live, was launched in 1990 on the recently vacated MF frequencies.

The Radio in Everyday Life

As we have seen during the course of the 1920s and 1930s, radio was transformed from being an electronics hobby, explored mainly by enthusiastic men, to occupying a central place in family and domestic life. It was unprecedented in that it either intruded or was welcomed, depending on one's point of view, into the very heart of the household (Moores 1988). Correspondingly, the radio directly addressed its audience, not as a mass but as a collection of individuals. It is regularly observed that we listen as though we are being personally addressed, and the radio forms an intimacy with the listener. At one level, radio has long had programmes that directly express whom they are for: 'Workers' Playtime' or 'Housewives' Choice' for example. But more deeply, the absence of a visual presence allows or, rather, forces the listener to create his own images. In other words, although listening is often characterised as a secondary or background activity because it is often accompanied by some other task, nevertheless we have to work at some level to create the images that the words invoke (Hendy 2000: 115–22). Douglas describes early experiments in the psychology of radio listening, which included (amongst many others) asking subjects to listen to a voice on the radio, or even from behind a curtain, and describe the speaker's appearance, occupation, political affiliation and so on (Douglas 2004: 134). As she argues, 'It is this absence of imagery that is radio's greatest strength, that allows people to bind themselves so powerfully to this device' (Douglas 2004: 28). Or, as the popular saying has it, in comparison with television, 'the pictures are better on radio'.

This was demonstrated famously in 1938, when a radio adaptation of H G Wells's *The War of the Worlds* was presented on CBS on 30 October. Produced by Orson Welles, it was dramatised as a news broadcast reporting the invasion of America by Martians, and its transmission caused panic as listeners believed it was real (despite announcements inserted periodically to explain its theatrical nature). Newspapers reported up to a million listeners panicking and streets clogged as people tried to flee the areas in New Jersey and New York where the aliens were supposed to have landed (Hilliard and Keith 2005: 82). While the newspaper figures were undoubtedly exaggerated, the episode reveals the extent to which the radio had come to be seen as an authoritative source of news. The threat posed to the traditional news providers, the newspaper companies, was recognised early on, and in the UK the Newspaper Proprietors' Association successfully argued for restrictions to be placed on the BBC's reporting of news – no bulletins could go out before 7pm, on the assumption that people would continue to read newspapers for their news. A similar restriction was placed on US radio stations, though generally it was less successful, not least because many of the radio stations were themselves owned by newspapers. Restrictions on broadcasters did not last. In 1926 millions of British workers took part in a General Strike which, amongst other things, halted newspaper production. The transmission restriction on BBC radio was lifted, and news broadcasts kept people informed of the development of the strike (an event which, amongst other things, provoked much debate about the BBC's relationship with the government). While the restrictions were re-imposed after the strike ended, the importance of radio as a news provider had been demonstrated – not only demonstrated, but exploited too, as on 26 May 1926 valve manufacturer Ediswan placed an advertisement in *Wireless*

World magazine proclaiming 'the Nation's Gratitude' to radio. 'The whole nation emerged from industrial chaos with feelings of thankful relief and deep gratitude to Broadcasting. As Mercury the Messenger served the gods in fable, so Wireless served the nation in fact.' The message ended with a reminder: 'The *first* Thermionic Valve was produced in the Ediswan Laboratories' (reproduced in Bussey 1990: 56).

While news reporting restrictions were only fully relaxed by the late 1930s in both the US and the UK (prompted by the outbreak of the Second World War), radio had already begun to demonstrate a new kind of reporting. Two incidents showed the difference between radio and newspaper reporting: in 1936 a fire destroyed the exhibition hall at Crystal Palace in London. It occurred in the evening, after the newspapers' evening editions had been printed but was reported live by Richard Dimbleby down a telephone line, accompanied by the sounds of the fire in the background. Meanwhile, the following year in Lakehurst, New Jersey, the German airship Hindenburg was making its first transatlantic crossing. Herb Morrison, a reporter for WLS radio in Chicago, was recording a report onto a disc recorder for subsequent broadcast, when the airship burst into flames. His reporting of the event as it happened remains poignant today (and can be heard by searching the World Wide Web) and prompted greater use of recording and live radio reporting in the years that followed (Hilliard and Keith 2005: 80). By the end of the decade, radio had established itself as a major source of news. Seventy per cent of US citizens used radio as a primary news source, while 58 per cent thought it more trustworthy than newspapers (even though a third of all US radio stations were owned by newspapers at the time). Radio thus brought a mass-produced version of the outside world into the intimate spaces of people's homes (Moore 1989: 243). Given this embrace of radio as a news source, and particularly given the anxieties in the late 1930s about the rise of fascism in Europe, it is perhaps less surprising that Orson Welles's radio play had the effect that it did in 1938.

In some ways, the way the radio is used today has come full circle. The 'personal stereo' receivers, exemplified in the 1970s by the combined radio and cassette tape-playing Sony Walkman and more recently by mp3 players such as Apple's iPod or phone-based radio, echo earliest listening practices, then necessarily solitary through a single pair of headphones and only later replaced by more open, group listening. Yet, through its portability radio has always retained a facility for private listening. Here, we create an imagined individual world that travels with us, to the exclusion of others. Dependent precisely on the progress made in electronic miniaturisation in the past decades, it is somehow ironic yet a testament to its durability that radio should again become such an individual and personal experience.

Radio Alternatives

If the foregoing has presented a narrative account of radio's development, it should not be assumed that it followed some natural trajectory to the exclusion of all other possibilities. Debates that continue today about how radio might be used for the greater good began in its earliest days. Given that radio began as a means of one-to-one, or perhaps one-to-several, communication, as it evolved into broadcasting, some saw this as a retrograde development. The use of radio for propaganda purposes was noted and exploited in the 1920s but more notoriously in the 1930s. We have already seen that the BBC began considering broadcasting out to its empire as early as 1924 and other countries began international broadcasting in the years following. High frequency, or short wave, transmissions carried 'ideological broadcasting' from the Soviet Union, Germany, and Italy during the 1920s and 1930s, while religious broadcasting, from the Vatican and by an American missionary station based in Ecuador, began in 1931; and evangelical Christian stations continue to populate the high frequency band (Browne 1982: 48–61). Radio was acclaimed for its potential to unify countries, even when the visions of those countries' futures were very different. As the extract from *Collier's* magazine showed earlier (p. 40), American observers hoped that radio would override economic division between the various peoples of the US; meanwhile Leon Trotsky also argued for the unifying potential of radio in consolidating the revolution in Russia. In 1926, he addressed the Soviet Union Congress of the Society of Friends of Radio and described radio as 'the cheapest form of communication'. Appropriately enough, the speech was transmitted as a radio broadcast, and he continued: 'We cannot seriously talk about socialism without having in mind the transformation of the country into a single whole, linked together by means of all kinds of communication' (Trotsky 1973: 259–60). Radio continues today to have an ideological role, at times less benign: Kellow and Steeves give an account of how radio broadcasting was used to foment underlying ethnic division (a remnant of German and Belgian colonial policy) and, ultimately, contribute to the slaughter in Rwanda in 1994 of more than one million of the Tutsi population by Hutu civilians (Kellow and Steeves 1998).

As Trotsky observed, radio is a cheap medium, and this is true of transmission equipment as much as receivers. In comparison with other media (until the recent widespread availability of fast internet connections), radio has been the most accessible communications technology for transmission. Unlicensed, 'pirate' radio stations play a continual cat-and-mouse game with regulators. The German playwright, Bertolt Brecht, lamented the fact that by the 1930s broadcasting had become one-way communication rather than two-way (2000 [1932]: 42):

> ...the radio is *one-sided* when it should be two-sided. It is only a distribution apparatus, it merely dispenses.... The radio could be the finest possible communications apparatus in public life, a vast system of channels. That is, it could be so, if it understood how to let the listener speak as well as hear, how to bring him into a network instead of isolating him. Following this principle the radio should step out of the supply business and organize its listeners as suppliers.

Brecht was not simply idealistic about this – he recognised that the institutionalisation of broadcasting into this one-way medium brought economic benefits to broadcasters. 'But it is not simply our task to renovate the ideological institutions on the basis of the existing social order through innovations. Instead our innovations must get them to abandon this basis. So: for innovations, against renovation!' (ibid.: 46). Just as the broadcast reform movement of the 1930s sought to wrest control of US radio from purely commercial interest, struggles have occurred throughout radio's history in many countries to allow wider access to the airwaves. Sometimes this has been aimed at existing broadcasters. For example, the BBC began to recognise criticism in the 1950s that its radio services could more widely reflect their audience, and, no doubt also aware of the threat of television, encouraged new approaches to radio programme making. Producer Charles Parker collaborated with radical songwriters Ewan MacColl and Peggy Seeger to produce a series of *Radio Ballads*, using tape recording equipment to capture the voices of working class people in their working lives (Street 2004). Without narration, and interspersing monologue with song against natural background sound, these programmes offered a different insight from the more traditional radio of earlier years. The portability of the new tape recording equipment made it easier to capture sounds in this way, although the impetus was also a political desire in some for more diverse cultural expression.

At other times, campaigns for a more representative radio include ambitions beyond influencing mainstream broadcasters' programming. While radio is dominated by a combination of public service radio and commercial radio almost everywhere, a third sector, often known as community radio, has also long been part of the radio landscape to varying degrees in many countries. Often broadcasting over a small area, and thus to a small audience, such stations are characterised by a commitment to some level of social benefit and audience involvement. Commercial success is not the primary aim (and many such stations collapse through lack of funds). Sometimes the goals are overtly political. Downing gives three examples: the rise of radio stations, including the Voice of Fighting Algeria, supporting independence from France in the 1950s; student stations in Italy, most famously Radio Alice, active during riots between police and students at the University of Bologna; and in France, dozens of stations set up in the aftermath of the May 1968 rebellion attempted to provide a voice for the newly politicised (Downing 2001). Well known or, at least, relatively well-studied examples include stations set up by mining communities and trade unions in Bolivia. These small stations were set up in a culture of resistance to the restructuring of the industry by institutions like the International Monetary Fund, assisted by a series of dictatorships and *coups d'état* in that country. These stations allowed ordinary voices to be heard, such as workers, women and students, and the movement continued for around 50 years before beginning to decline in recent decades (O'Connor 1990, 2004).

Elsewhere, and generally more short-lived, similar innovative uses of radio were heard. Kogawa describes the growth of 'mini FM' stations in Tokyo during the early 1980s when as many as 700 stations were set up transmitting at very low powers over a small area, perhaps half a kilometre in radius, from cafes and shops. Customers or passers by would join in the debates. Kogawa describes the process as one of communication rather than of broadcasting (Kogawa 1993). In the US the low power FM (LPFM) movement has had qualified success in lobbying for legislation to permit broadcasts at low transmitter power, finally passed by the FCC in January 2000. Driven by the increasing consolidation of commercial radio in the US following the passage of the 1996 Telecommunications Act – McChesney notes that since the Act was passed, half of the nation's 11,000 stations have changed ownership at least once (2000: 75) – the LPFM movement aimed to increase the number of stations encouraging public participation in radio (or at least to allow those already operating to do so legally). The campaign and ensuing legislation was bitterly opposed by the commercial radio companies' organisation, the National Association of Broadcasters (NAB) and by the public radio organisation, National Public Radio (NPR). Accusations of corrupt practice and illegal lobbying peppered the debate, with successes claimed on both sides (Riismandel 2002; Opel 2004).

In the UK, until recent years there had never been much of a 'third sector' of radio, dominated as it was by public service monopoly by the BBC until the 1970s and since then by an explosion in the number of commercial radio stations, though there had long been a lobby to make provision for such a sector (Lewis and Booth 1989; Lewis 2002). Finally in 2004, the regulator Ofcom invited applications for licences to run small community radio stations, receiving 192 applications in the first year alone, and in March 2008 the hundredth such station went on air.

So radio remains a versatile and pervasive technology in the age of the internet and digital media, technologies which many have claimed would make it redundant. It is a technology that addresses many needs: from hi-fi to 'lo-fi', from local to global, the same technological principles apply, and while the majority of radio use is for traditional, mainstream broadcasting of, usually, recorded music, the examples above give a glimpse of the many different ways in which people have tried to appropriate the techniques to liberate, empower or otherwise enrich people's lives. However cheap and accessible radio may be, nevertheless these alternative voices continue to struggle to be heard. Radio operates within a society in which democratic participation is not privileged above capital accumulation (in other words profit-seeking), and in this sense radio operates like any other medium (Hendy 2000: 198–200).

Digital Broadcasting and the Future of Radio

For many observers, radio today has become something of an anachronism. It remains a mostly analogue technology at a time when other media are increasingly digital; it is linear in that it consists of scheduled programming which the broadcaster, rather than the listener, has decided; further, it remains resolutely an *audio* rather than audiovisual medium at a time when the moving image seeks our attention from more devices in more locations than ever before (such as the tiny screen on an mp4 player or phone to the huge TV projectors in railway stations and city squares). Yet radio remains popular – audience studies in countries across the world show that listening is either steady or increasing.

This characterisation is far too simplistic of course. Radio is part of digital media as much as any other, if not more so in many respects (Lax 2009). Radio is transmitted over the airwaves in digital format alongside analogue in most countries, either as a digital radio network or as part of digital television. It can also be heard on the internet. Many stations also make archives of programmes available on their websites, either for streamed listening or for downloading as podcasts and listening to later. Hence, listening is not determined entirely by schedules. Radio programmes are augmented by links to websites offering more information on programme issues and digital platforms such as DAB radio receivers and digital televisions even incorporate minimal visual information such as scrolling text or basic images. Just as radio has changed over the years as people's listening and viewing changed with the arrival of new technologies, it does so again with the possibilities presented by digital media. Raymond Williams, like Bertolt Brecht, described the beginnings of radio as a technology ahead of its time, in that it was developed before people knew what to do with it (Williams 1990). Radio technology became incorporated into broadcasting not because of some inherent attribute of the technology but because the changes in society, of organisations, families and individuals, created the conditions suitable for a broadcast model of radio. In other words, the technology changes as it is incorporated into society, and it tends to meld with existing technologies and social practices rather than presenting as a single, unified entity for people to adopt (or not); and a similar process can be seen as radio interacts with new digital media today. We will return to the questions of digital broadcasting, internet radio and how technologies are taken up in society in later chapters.

Conclusion

Radio's history illustrates a number of the features we have already identified in the telegraph and telephone but also some differences. Radio (in its earlier wireless telegraph guise) displays the general tendency of a lengthy technological gestation, followed by repeated efforts to identify and realise a market for it. It developed on the back of previous social practices and was valued principally for its utilitarian function, as an aid to communication like the telegraph and telephone but with a lack of wires as its key advantage.

Yet, like the telephone, the technology was evolving at a time when technologies were increasingly finding their way into people's everyday lives and into their homes (not just for communications but also domestic technologies based on electrical power) and while the telephone continued to develop more or less as its original inventors and proponents imagined, radio's use was changed completely following its appropriation by hobbyists and emerging business interests into a novel social practice, broadcasting. There was nothing inherent in the technology that made radio more appropriate for broadcasting than for wireless telegraphy (or telephony); equally, there was nothing in the technology that fundamentally prevented broadcasting becoming the major function of radio many years before it actually emerged in the 1920s. However, once radio broadcasting had become established, it paved the way for future developments: firstly, and obviously perhaps, of television but also, as electronic miniaturisation progressed, of a more intimate and personal audio space which now extends to the popularity of personal audio players. We thus see again how technology can be shaped by changing social forms and patterns of usage but, at the same time, as they develop, those technological capabilities open up new possibilities for social practice.

Television 3

If radio could be claimed, as in the previous chapter, to be a technology developed ahead of its time, television might equally be explained as a technology a long time in coming. Given that in its early days it was frequently described, and sometimes dismissed, as 'radio with pictures', its emergence was a logical consequence of the establishment of radio broadcasting. Yet the ingredients of television are many: viewing moving pictures on the screen of a box with no moving parts is quite a technological achievement, but one which incorporates a host of technical, physiological and social phenomena themselves appreciated and exploited during the preceding decades.

Some of these are obvious: cinema followed fairground entertainments such as the zoetrope in exploiting the latency in our vision to persuade us that a sequence of still images displayed rapidly can be perceived as a moving image; a combination of optical techniques and chemical processes in photography allowed permanent recording of images. These ideas preceded television by up to a century. Other elements of television have more subtle influences, perhaps, but the perception of shape on a screen that is actually made up of discrete dots and lines and the display of colour television can similarly be traced back to the ways in which the limitations of our vision have previously been exploited by artists. For example, the late 19th century technique known as *pointillism* consists of painting with dabs of coloured pigment, while the following century newspapers began to use a halftone printing process for their photographs in which apparent shades of grey were actually constructed from different sized dots of pure black and white; the pop-art of Roy Lichtenstein is well known for its use of coloured dots which, but for their deliberately exaggerated scale, when viewed from a distance would look like continuous colour. Of course, the complexity of this construction is, as it were, invisible to us, and as we watch increasingly high definition pictures on ever-larger screens, surrounded by stereo or multichannel sound, we are to all intents and purposes experiencing all that the roots of the word 'tele-vision' implies: watching events and dramas unfold at a distance.

Television's Origins

The idea of viewing a moving image first emerged in the humble form of a number of 'parlour toys' produced in the first half of the 19th century for the amusement of owners and their visitors. The phenakistoscope and the zoetrope, dating from the 1830s, consisted of a sequence of drawings, each slightly different from the previous one in the sequence, and a mechanism for viewing the drawings in rapid succession. For example, the zoetrope consisted of a drum, with viewing slits cut around its perimeter. A paper strip containing the sequence of drawings was fixed inside the drum, and looking through the slits from the outside as the drum spun, the drawings appeared as a crude moving cartoon image. Of course, the motion is just an illusion – each image is fixed, not moving, yet although we know this we cannot help but perceive the sequence as motion.

This demonstrates a physiological effect which was long thought a consequence of 'persistence of vision', the phenomenon noted by Peter Roget in 1824 that an image remains briefly in our vision for a moment after the source has actually gone. In fact, the perceived motion here involves two factors: firstly, as noted, the viewer is actually exposed to a sequence of *still* images, perceived as motion; secondly, she actually sees each image only momentarily through the viewing slits as most of the time the view is obscured by the drum, yet she perceives continuous and even illumination. The general notion of persistence of vision is inadequate to explain what is occurring here, and more recent exploration has been able to identify the limitations of our perception of apparent motion, each of which is significant in the development of television (Anderson and Anderson 1993; Gregory 1998: 116–18). The first phenomenon, the perception of motion from a sequence of still images, is not clearly understood, but experimental evidence suggests that, provided we see a sequence of images at a minimum rate of about 15 to 20 per second, the motion we perceive appears to be smooth and continuous (in cinema, the standard rate is 24 frames per second (fps), while in television it is 25 or 30 fps). The second effect is the sense of a continuously illuminated view when in fact we are seeing a sequence of on-off images. When the illumination rate is too low, we see flicker and tests show that the 'flicker fusion frequency', the rate at which we stop seeing flicker, is around 50 illuminations per second. In other words, provided a light (or TV screen) is lit up at least 50 times per second, we perceive continuous illumination. So a room lit by fluorescent lights is seen as evenly lit (except when first switched on and the rate is lower while it warms up) and a TV screen or computer monitor, refreshed a minimum of 50 times per second, also does not flicker. However, the flicker fusion rate is higher for very bright illumination or for peripheral vision, so occasionally a very bright screen can be seen to flicker, particularly when we see it out of the corner of our eye.

Developments in photography throughout the 18th century allowed sequences of photographs to be taken in rapid succession. Best known probably are the images of Eadweard Muybridge, who, in addition to changing his name several times and murdering his wife's lover, found time in 1878 to arrange a number of cameras along a track in order to study the motion of a horse. As the horse trotted up the track it triggered each camera in sequence, and the resulting photographs depicted the horse's movement as a series of stills. Subsequently, Muybridge photographed other animals and humans and amassed hundreds of sequences which were studied by scientists and artists alike: for artists were able, for the first time, to see how a horse really jumped over fences and the earlier depictions, with all four legs splayed out simultaneously, were proved wrong (Solnit 2003). Before long, Muybridge was seeking ways of displaying his photographic sequences in a manner similar to the zoetrope. He developed the zoopraxiscope, a device specially designed to project his images, printed onto a rotating glass disc, in sequence onto a screen which he used to illustrate lectures on animal motion. This demonstrated the potential for the public projection of moving images, later to become cinema (Enticknap 2005).

Cinema projects its series of still images by projecting light through a physical medium, film, onto a screen. For each image, or frame, the film has to be held still momentarily so that the image is not blurred on the screen, while at the same time the film reel must be kept moving so that sufficient frames per second can be projected. This was a mechanical process that challenged the earliest cinema pioneers, but the basis of cinema lay clearly in the physical capture of images established in chemical photography. Television drew upon a different set of changes taking place in communications. The idea of sending images over wire cables developed quite naturally out of the electric telegraph as it became an indispensable business tool. Numerous designs of 'printing telegraphs' operated between telegraph offices in cities across the world, though never as extensively as the Morse telegraph. Frequently they were used for sending facsimiles of typed or handwritten text, often for legal purposes where a transcribed Morse message lacked authority, but they were also used for sending crude images. In almost all cases, the devices used a scanning technique to represent the picture as a sequence of lines. The electrical signals from each line were relayed down the wire and reproduced at a similar printing device at the destination. Typically, the source document would be treated with a conductive chemical and then wires drawn across its surface line by line. Where the wire crossed an ink mark, the electric current would change and then change back again as it passed beyond the ink. The electrical signal travelling down the wire to the receiving device would feed a second needle which would stain a piece of paper (also chemically treated to respond to electricity) in accordance with the signal it received. Thus the marks appearing on the destination sheet of paper reflected what the wire at the source document was scanning at that particular time. Though a slow process, gradually a copy of the source document would appear line by line in the receiving office. Thus, quite independently of photography and, later, cinema, ideas were being established that, ultimately, would be applied in television: an image could be reproduced by considering it to be made up of a sequence of lines, which could be transmitted electrically and reproduced provided source and receiving equipment were synchronised (that is, they both started at the same time at the top of the page and also finished each line at the same time).

Given the applications of these devices at the time, it would be faintly ludicrous to suggest that this represented the birth of television – instead, many quite different roles were to be adopted for electrical communication as we have already seen. The telephone eclipsed the telegraph as a point-to-point communications system (though also had its role as an information and entertainment service), while the wireless telegraph also built upon the practices established by its wired forebear. As electrical technology developed, for both communications purposes and to provide power for lighting and motors, it became important to know more about it. Just as electromagnetism was an important subject of study, and a theoretical understanding of the processes was emerging, equally, knowledge about the electrical properties of materials had become an area of interest for scientific exploration. This knowledge was necessary for building electrical equipment, and some insulators, notably selenium, were noted for the fact that their insulating ability varied according to the amount of light falling on it. Conversely, some materials, known as phosphors, had been observed to emit light in the presence of electrical charges. The observation that some materials' electrical properties could be changed in response to light, while others could be made to emit light, prompted further investigation into the fundamental make-up of such materials and by the end of the 19th century, the existence of electrons as electrically charged subparticles of atoms had been proposed by Cambridge physicist Joseph John Thomson. This helped to explain the behaviour of visible rays that a number of scientists had observed in experimental devices known as cathode ray tubes or CRTs. The CRT resembles a large light bulb, a clear glass evacuated sphere with a wire element at one end. Placed between electrical coils it was possible to 'boil' electrons off the element and use the coils to steer them as they passed around the glass sphere. Although this was initially intended simply to find out more about electrons, the ability to steer these 'rays', or electron beams, using electric currents carried in coils was a significant development in the lengthy gestation of television, eventually becoming the basis of an electronically scanned television system.

Meanwhile, other experimenters were taking a different approach to producing television pictures. John Logie Baird was a Scot who moved to Hastings in southern England after the First World War, and he began experiments in television. His approach was based on a mechanical method of scanning the scene. While some considered scanning by CRTs to be a possibility – Campbell Swinton sent a letter sent to *Nature* as early as 1908 suggesting such an approach (Winston 1998: 93) – it was some years before it became possible to build the devices, whereas Baird was applying largely proven technology. Baird's scanning was achieved by spinning a disc based on a design by German engineer Paul Nipkow. The Nipkow disc contained a series of holes following a spiral pattern towards the centre and, when placed between the illuminated subject and a photocell, as it rotated it revealed the subject in a sequence of bright lines scanning from top to bottom: each complete rotation generated one scanned frame. The photocell (a device whose electrical output depends on the strength of the light falling on it) received the variations in the light reflected off the subject as it was scanned. This formed the basis of the television signal, which was transmitted to the receiving device either by wires or radio waves.

To recreate the image at the receiver, a similar disk spun in between a neon lamp and a viewing screen. The lamp's brightness was controlled by the television signal strength and, again, as the viewing disc rotated it allowed lines to be illuminated on the screen. By ensuring that the two discs were spinning in a synchronised manner, the varying intensity of the neon lamp mirrored the light falling on the transmitting photocell, and a crude image was formed on the screen of the subject illuminated at the transmitting device. The number of lines in the scan was determined by the number of holes in the disc, and the number of frames per second depended upon how rapidly it was spun. Baird was able to demonstrate his version of mechanically scanned television to a meeting of the Royal Institution in London on 26 January 1926, the first such demonstration in the world. Just over a year later, in the US, mechanically scanned television carried an address by Secretary of Commerce, Herbert Hoover, in a public demonstration by AT&T on 7 April 1927.

Baird pursued his version of television further still: in September 1927, he demonstrated additional variants of his television idea to the meeting of the British Association for the Advancement of Science at the University of Leeds. The meeting programme announced that 'Television, Noctovision and the Phonovisor will be demonstrated by Mr J. L. Baird of the Baird Television Development Co. Ltd.', before explaining: 'Television may be briefly defined as the transmission of vision by electricity; Noctovision as vision in darkness by means of infra-red rays, and the Phonovisor as an apparatus by which moving images can be recorded on and reproduced from a phonograph record in the same manner as sound.' Baird used standard 10-inch diameter 78rpm wax audio discs and was able to record about three minutes of low frame rate, 30-line video on each disc - and six decades later, in the 1980s, engineer Don McLean used digital restoration techniques to recover the images (McLean 2000). While it might be tempting to marvel at Baird's recordings, at how they were decades ahead of their time (domestic video recording not becoming a reality until the 1970s), Baird's attempts to record video onto a phonographic disc made complete sense at that time. Although radio broadcasting was just beginning to emerge as a new means of bringing audio into people's homes, recorded sound was relatively commonplace (amongst the wealthier at least). Phonographs based originally on cylinders and later on discs had been around since the final decades of the 19th century, and thus it was logical to try to do the same with moving images, particularly as the only other way of seeing the moving image was in the public cinema. However, it was the rapid success of radio broadcasting that turned Baird's and his competitors' minds to the transmission of television over the airwaves, and though he could transmit his own test signals, he spent much time trying to persuade the BBC to allow him occasional use of their radio transmitters to carry television signals more widely. At this time though, the BBC saw itself as a radio organisation, and it was generally indifferent to the idea of television which, apart from anything else, would have been seen as competition for radio listening. Contemporary accounts record this hostility (Robinson 1935: 44).

> Baird quite early had a transmitting licence from the Postmaster-General, and it was possible to pick up his television programmes within a reasonable distance of London if you knew when he was going to transmit, but programmes available to the general public seemed to be impossible owing to the attitude of the B.B.C. and also of the Press. A bitter fight started between the B.B.C. and the Baird Company...

Only when the Postmaster General instructed the BBC to allow Baird regular transmissions could television trials begin. 'On Monday morning, 30th September 1929, Baird stood modestly in a corner of the studio in Long Acre and witnessed the inaugural broadcast of television carried out through the B.B.C. transmitter 2LO for half an hour' (Tiltman 1933: 151). Baird had already been selling his 'Televisor' receiver to the public, and these new regular (although part-time) transmissions meant he could promote it rather more convincingly. However, with its tiny screen and poor image quality – it continued to use mechanical scanning with a light shining through a perforated disc – it remained a plaything for hobbyists (who could buy the Televisor as a kit) or an object of amusement for wealthier households. Elsewhere, similar experiments took place. Mechanically scanned systems were being trialled in the US and in Germany, but interest was growing in all-electronic scanning. In the US, competing electronic systems, based upon CRTs, were being developed by Vladimir Zworykin, working for RCA, and by Philo Farnsworth, who joined the Philadelphia Battery Company, Philco. Before emigrating to the US in 1919, Zworykin had been a student of Russian scientist Boris Rozing, who had pioneered experiments (and secured patents) in electronically scanned television. Another of Rozing's students had emigrated to the UK: Isadore Schoenburg became director of research at Electrical and Musical Industries (EMI) and was working on an electronic system there, known as the Emitron. Mechanical and electronic systems continued to develop side-by-side, and by the time the BBC had begun to take the prospect of television broadcasting a little more seriously (by 1933 it had built a television studio and was making occasional programmes rather than just experimenting), it was still unclear which was to be the better system. The odds had to be in favour of electronics: while mechanical techniques harked back to an older era of steam and heavy engineering, electronics was a relatively novice technology, and the prospects for further, rapid development seemed greater in this field, though clearly this was not obvious at the time (Winston 1998: 107).

1936 and Television Broadcasting Begins – Official!

By the beginning of the 1930s, and probably some years before, it was obvious to most that television was going to become a reality. However, the question was not only when, but also how? Different technical systems were in continual development in countries across the world, with no single system established as a clear frontrunner. This hampered the production of receivers, as manufacturers would be unwilling to back an eventual loser. Equally, there were other technical questions: how would the transmission frequencies be decided upon, and how would broadcasting be organised? Some of these questions were readily answered, others less straightforwardly. In the US, the Federal Radio Commission (FRC) was still grappling with the organisation of spectrum for radio broadcasting and seeking to prevent the establishment of a monopoly among manufacturers of radio receivers; now it was also being confronted with similar challenges in television (the FRC becoming the Federal Communications Commission in 1934, incorporating these new responsibilities). So the FCC was unwilling to agree on a standard for television broadcasting, for fear of favouring a particular manufacturer (all these competing standards of course covered by numerous patents) instead insisting that further experimentation should resolve the issue (Winston 1998: 116). Meanwhile, in the UK the BBC, as monopoly radio broadcaster and experimenter in television, was clearly placed to become the monopoly provider of television services. In 1934, the government appointed a committee chaired by Lord Selsdon to consider the introduction of regular domestic television services. The Selsdon report, published a year later, proposed that the BBC should begin transmissions using both available standards, the Baird mechanically scanned system and the Emitron electronic system. Each would be operated in alternate weeks until the better of the two had been agreed upon. Much was at stake: an agreement on a particular standard would naturally secure one company's future, while simultaneously sealing the fate of the other, and to promote and expand the television service, that standard, once agreed, would have to endure. To attempt to introduce a new standard when a previous one has become established is difficult, to say the least, and has been a recurring challenge in broadcasting, most recently with the introduction of digital transmission. The battle to become a dominant standard is thus commercial (for example the battle for supremacy between VHS and Betamax video recording systems) and also political, as it is often also ultimately a decision taken by governments.

In the case of the UK television standards, it was also a decision based on technology. Although most observers expected the EMI system to prove the best, it was politically expedient to give the mechanical system a chance given Baird's history with the technology and the BBC, but the technical odds were against it. Selsdon had also raised the stakes by stipulating that the minimum picture resolution should be 240 lines per frame, and while electronic systems had already demonstrated this capability, Baird's company battled to improve their system which was still operating its 30-line experimental transmissions. When the BBC television broadcasts began on 2 November 1936, Baird's system had met the 240-line requirement and was used in the first week; but the EMI system by now was capable of transmitting 405 lines and had its first official transmission the following week. The Baird system was easily outperformed by the higher definition Emitron, and the end of mechanically scanned television came in February 1937 when Emitron became the full-time television standard (and 405-line transmissions were only finally discontinued in the UK in 1985). Television in other countries remained largely experimental, and so the BBC was the world's first full domestic service. Even so, transmissions were for just a few hours per day, in the evenings, and initial transmissions covered only a radius of some 50 miles serving viewers in London and the south east of England. Meanwhile, the BBC continued investment in its radio services and, in comparison, television was a minority interest (though of course costing more to run). When television abruptly ended at the outbreak of the Second World War (its transmissions were considered a means for enemy aircraft to navigate their way to London) a total of around 20,000 sets had been sold (Crisell 2002: 78). This compared poorly with the nine million radio licences which had been issued by this time and, with radio transmission coverage extending to 98 per cent of the population, it could be assumed that a number of unlicensed sets were also in use (Briggs 1965: 253). In other words, almost every household in the UK had access to radio and, unlike television, which was dispensable, radio transmissions continued throughout wartime and its role during this period has been widely documented (for example Briggs 1970).

Opinions vary as to whether pre-war television in the UK should be considered a success. While it was a notable technical achievement, and the BBC's monopoly status helped it to be the first to launch, it was limited in its geographical coverage, its audience grew only slowly and it was expensive (the usual comparison is that a television receiver and a small car cost roughly the same). Although costs were reduced as kits and vision-only sets were sold (the sound being picked up on a conventional radio receiver to accompany the images on vision-only television sets), much of the country was still suffering the effects of the economic depression. In addition, the uncertainty in technical standards at the outset (in contrast with radio) may have made many waver at the thought of spending a large sum of money on a potentially redundant technology (as indeed it was after 1939). Much of the content was 'solidly middle-brow and numbingly worthy' according to Robson (2004: 226), while Crisell is more forgiving, suggesting if anything a lack of gravitas: 'While television was new and there had to be more concern with its technical reliability than with its content, some lack of range and seriousness in the latter might be permissible' (Crisell 2002: 79). Other than the efforts of the BBC, most observers (certainly outside the UK) regard pre-war television as an experimental phase, and histories tend to date television's real beginnings from after World War II.

Setting Television's Technical Standards

With the battle between scanning techniques settled in favour of electronic systems, the varying technical standards for television began to stabilise, with two eventual standards in use. In Europe, the picture was made up of the 405 lines per frame achieved by the Emitron system, with 25 frames scanned per second. In the US, the National Television Standards Committee (NTSC) was established in 1940 with eventual agreement between the FCC and television manufacturers, and the standard here was a 525-line picture and a frame rate of 30 fps. These standards persisted for many decades: in the US the frame rate and resolution (number of lines per frame) is still in use, while the European system has been superseded in some (but by no means all) countries by the 625-line system. Otherwise, many of the techniques established in the 1930s continue to dictate how television is recorded, transmitted and received 70 years later.

Scanning

In both the European and the NTSC cases, the picture scanning used a technique known as interlacing. Interlaced scanning involves scanning alternate lines, so the first 'half-scan' covered the first line, then the third, fifth and so on. On reaching the bottom of the image, the scanning beam would fly back to begin scanning the second, fourth, sixth and so on. This arrangement, on the face of it an unnecessary complication, overcame the limitations of the phosphor coatings on the insides of early television screens. The phosphor emits light as it is struck by the scanning electron beam inside the television picture tube. It continues to shine briefly after the beam has moved away but only very briefly. Were the images illuminated line-by-line in strict sequence, first, second, third and so on (so-called progressive scanning), by the time the beam reached the bottom of the screen the top of the screen would have started to dim. By interlacing the scans, the screen was effectively covered top-to-bottom in half the time, giving the appearance of more even illumination. Thus each frame is made up of two 'fields', the odd line field and the even field. With 25 *frames* per second, therefore, the screen is illuminated by 50 fields per second, while in the NTSC system, 30 fps gives 60 fields per second. These illumination rates have the advantage that they also exceed the threshold for the detection of flicker. The different rates in the NTSC and European system are not accidental: with mains electricity having a frequency of 60 Hz (or cycles per second) in the US and 50 Hz in Europe, electronic scanning circuits had to be based on these rates and the standard frame rate for cinema, for example, of 24 fps could not be applied to television. Today, electronics and screen coatings have advanced sufficiently to render interlacing unnecessary, and computer monitors for example do not use it but are instead progressively scanned. Analogue television, however, continues to use interlacing: cameras, production systems and of course all receivers have always been designed for it, and so interlaced scanning remains a legacy from the 1930s (only now becoming obsolete with the introduction of digital television).

So scanning rates based on mains electrical frequencies differ from cinema frame rates. There might seem no reason why this should be important; yet in the early days of television, film was the only medium for recording moving images (magnetic videotape recording being decades away), and so, like radio, most television was live. There was in fact a certain pride among broadcasters in this fact – its 'liveness' differentiated it from cinema, a virtue made of a necessity – but, even so, realistically not all television could be live. Newsreels, as shown to audiences in cinemas, were frequently shown on television. Occasionally, feature films were also shown. This was achieved by scanning the film with a flying electron beam, in a so-called telecine machine, in exactly the same way as a television camera scanned the scene through its lens. In fact the earliest television cameras, in particular those based on mechanical scanning, could only work by recording the scene onto film and then scanning the developed film (some cameras came with on-board processing tanks), so the idea of scanning film for transmission as a television signal was not novel. The discrepancy in frame rates was overcome relatively easily in the European television system. The difference between 24 fps (cinema) and 25 fps (television) is not great, and so by simply running the film through the scanner at 25 fps it would be synchronised with the television signal. The slight speeding-up that resulted in the final viewing was not noticeable.

For the NTSC system with its 30 fps frame rate, the difference was too great to be solved by simply speeding the film up. Instead, each frame was scanned more than once: alternate frames would be scanned twice or three times (that is, on average, frames were scanned two and a half times each), the resulting scans matching the 60 Hz field rate in NTSC. Once again, the slight unevenness in scanning one frame twice and the next three times goes undetected by the viewer. The principle of this system remains in use today and is sufficiently reliable that, until improvements in video recording quality in recent years, much television drama continued to be shot on film and then broadcast using the telecine process.

Synchronisation and blanking

Further legacies of early television technology are found in the detail of the scanning process. When television cameras consisted of a glass tube (the cathode ray tube, or CRT, only finally replaced in the last decade with CCD cameras – see later), the high voltage electric coils would be used to steer the electron beam across the 'target plate' onto which the scene had been focused. At the end of each line, the beam had to be returned to the beginning of the next line ready to start another line scan. Similarly when the beam had scanned the last line at the bottom of the image, it had to be steered back to the top of the image diagonally across the plate. These return times were fast by the standards of 1930s electronics, but were not instantaneous, so in order to avoid scanning unwanted signals on these return paths, the beam was switched off or 'blanked'. Consequently, of the 625 lines in a television frame of today, for example, only 575 lines carry picture information – during the remaining time the beam is switched off. These blanking intervals serve to mark in the camera's electronic signal the end of a line or, with a longer interval, the end of a scanned field. Electronic synchronisation pulses are inserted into the television signal before transmission, and, at the receiver, these pulses are used to synchronise the screen's beam so that it begins each frame's line in the right place and in the right sequence (Figure 3.1).

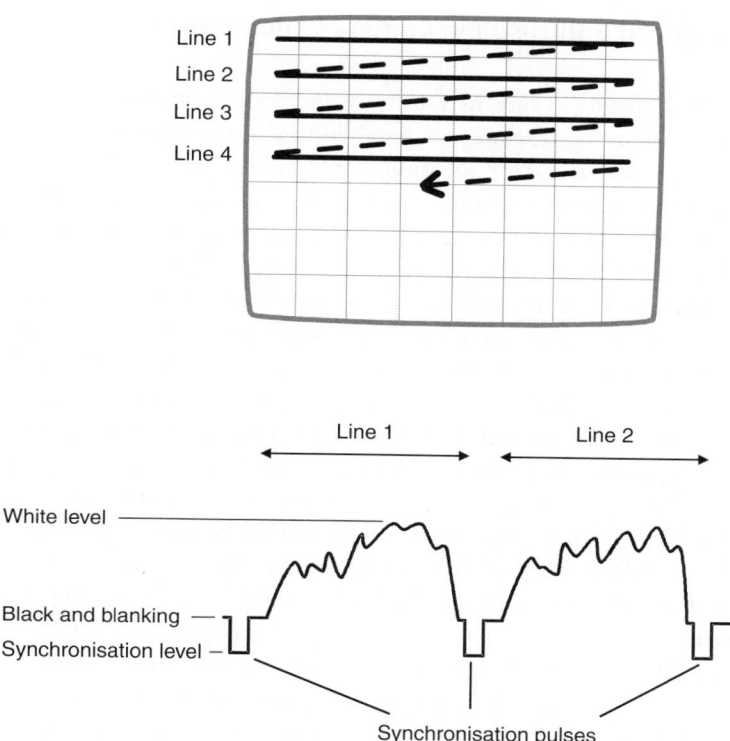

Figure 3.1   Scanning and synchronisation

Once again, more recent electronic systems would no doubt need shorter blanking intervals and more of the 625 lines could be used to fill the screen to give a slightly higher definition picture, but, without changing all production equipment and receiving sets overnight, television sets bought at the beginning of the 21st century must conform to standards established 70 years earlier.

One recent development that did take advantage of the long blanking interval at the end of each field was teletext, introduced in the 1970s, and now an almost universal system for transmitting text and crude graphics over the airwaves for display on a television screen. (Again, this is now being slowly displaced as digital television takes over, but the example serves as a useful illustration.) While the television signal is blanked as the beam is returned from the bottom of the scan back to the top, data in the form of electronic pulses can be transmitted without interfering with the picture, in the same way that synchronisation pulses are added. Teletext data sent during the blanking interval, that is 50 or 60 times per second, rapidly builds up into the text pages that can be viewed on the screen.

Image Capture and Display: Cameras and Screens

Cameras and television screens are the video equivalents of an audio microphone and loudspeakers: they are designed to capture information and allow us to see it at some distant location (and possibly at a different time, but video recording is covered later on). Just as the microphone and the loudspeaker are effectively mirror-images of each other, the camera uses materials which change electrical properties in the presence of light, while the receiver uses materials which emit light in the presence of an electrical stimulus. Early cameras, based on CRTs, have been described above. With their glass tubes containing electron beams and high voltage steering coils, CRT cameras were heavy, power-hungry and occasionally fragile. They also suffered from defects, such as streaking when a pan shot covers a car headlights, and tube cameras have now been replaced by lighter, more reliable charge coupled device (CCD) cameras. A similar replacement process is underway at the receiving end of television: CRT-based screens are being displaced by plasma and liquid crystal displays (LCDs). These offer a number of advantages but, nevertheless, are based on the same principles by which we are able to view moving images on television.

In a number of respects, television mimics the way our eyes enable us to make sense of the world. When we look at a scene, we focus that scene on the retina at the back of our eyes. The arrangement of light sensitive cells on the retina comprises a grid of sensors ('retina' is derived from the Latin word for net) all linked to the brain. Each sensor fires off a sequence of nerve pulses when light falls upon it, with more pulses the brighter the light. There are two types of sensor, rods and cones. Rods are sensitive to the total brightness of light, while cones respond to particular colours of light, some being more sensitive to red light, some to blue and others to green. Shapes and colours are detected, or interpreted, by our brain's response to the nerve pulses from particular parts of the eye: the relative arrangement of rods receiving light and dark helps discern shape, while in the presence of light of a particular colour, some cones respond more intensely than others.

The finite size of the rods and cones means that when two objects are very close together, or are very far away from the viewer (the effect is the same) the objects are focused onto the same parts of the retina and are, in effect seen as a single object – they cannot visually be separated or 'resolved' into two objects. This threshold represents the limit of our 'visual acuity'. On a television screen, provided the lines making up the picture are close enough together, or provided we sit far enough from the screen, we do not see individual lines but a continuous image. In the case of colour, a grid behind the television screen breaks the lines into separate dots of red, green and blue light but, again, we do not see the individual dots of colour but blend them and perceive a whole range of colours depending on the relative intensities of the red, green and blue components. As screens become larger, and thus the lines or dots on the screen more separated, the picture can begin to look less sharp unless we sit further from it. (Computer screens, to which we tend to sit much closer, require a higher resolution than a television, that is, more dots in a given area.) So the definition of a television picture is ultimately limited by its resolution (number of lines), and this limitation is exposed, ironically, by advances in receiver technology such as larger screens. Naturally enough then, television systems with a greater number of lines per frame are gradually being introduced. Known generally as high definition television (HDTV) – as indeed was 625-line television at its launch in the 1960s – the HDTV image is made up of more than 1000 lines (1080 is typical). Available only on digital television broadcasting systems, the novelty of HDTV allows the introduction of a number of other changes in television such as a new picture format ratio of 16:9 in comparison with standard television's 4:3, which was inherited from the aspect ratio of early cinema. Finally, HDTV includes the option of using progressive scanning instead of interlaced scanning resulting, in the right conditions, in a portrayal of motion more akin to that in film.

Audio for Television

Television is an audiovisual medium, but the audio element is often overlooked. Indeed it was often overlooked by manufacturers, and television's sound quality was for a long time poor (other than on the most expensive sets) in comparison with a decent radio receiver, and the simultaneous transmission of music concerts on both radio and television has already been noted, taking advantage of the best of both worlds. The audio part of television has, since the 1940s, been carried using frequency modulation which, as discussed in the radio chapter, offers better quality than the AM alternative. Even so, things improved further for television audio with the introduction of stereo sound in the 1980s, based on a digital process known as NICAM (less well known as 'near-instantaneous companding audio multiplex') and television manufacturers began to include better loudspeaker arrangements in standard receivers. The improvement was also prompted by the new practice of watching cinema films at home on videocassette, sound having long been a valued element of the cinematic experience.

A second cinema technology, surround sound, is also finding its way into television audio. Long available on DVDs, the so-called 5.1 format used in 'home cinema' has a total of six audio channels: three at the front (left, centre and right), two behind the listener (left surround, right surround) and a bass unit (commonly known as a sub-woofer) to receive the low frequency effects audio channel. The emergent HDTV system includes the option of 5.1 audio and in time more and more programmes will be made and broadcast using this format.

Television Transmission and Innovation

While the current period is witnessing a number of technological developments in television, such as the high definition and new audio systems noted above, innovation in broadcasting is a complex process. In the 1920s and 1930s, following radio, television was also naturally planned for transmission on radio waves (the term 'radio waves', confusingly, applies to all electromagnetic spectrum used for wireless communications, radio itself but also including television, mobile phones, radio microphones, satellite communications and more). Baird's trials may well have used the same transmitters and frequencies as the BBC's radio broadcasts, but when television was being established as a full domestic service, additional frequencies had to be used. Television is greedy of radio waves: combining audio and visual information, it has a much larger bandwidth than radio. The European 625-line system has a base bandwidth of 5.5 MHz, while the US system occupies a baseband of 4.2 MHz. Given that the process of modulation increases the bandwidth of the signal, in comparison with radio, a television station requires a transmission frequency channel some thirty times wider, or almost a thousand times greater than an AM radio station. Early decisions on allocating frequencies for television were entangled with demands from the radio industry to satisfy its growth. As noted in the previous chapter, in the 1930s Edwin Armstrong was pressing the FCC to allow FM radio to begin in the US, promising more reliable reception and better sound quality than its AM forebear, and after some delay FM was allocated frequencies around 42 MHz in the lower VHF band. However, in 1945, following much lobbying by television interests, and counter-lobbying and legal challenges by the FM radio proponents, the FCC reallocated FM radio further up the VHF band and used the lower VHF band for television. The tortuous history of this decision reveals the complex mix of technical, commercial and public-interest factors involved and serves as a valuable illustration of the mechanisms by which such developments emerge (Slotten 1996). (Armstrong continued to battle against the FCC and what he regarded as its capitulation to the interests of the big broadcasters, finally giving up the fight in 1954, when he threw himself out of his 13th-floor apartment window.)

In time, transmission and reception at higher frequencies became possible, and television was allocated new channels in the higher-capacity ultra-high frequency or UHF band, leaving FM radio to operate in the VHF band. Even so,

VHF television transmissions continued for many decades and continue today in a number of countries, for a simple reason – the very success of television (and radio) makes it very difficult to bring in changes (such as moving to a new frequency band) when the existing version of the system has become so popular. For example, until 1955 in the UK, when a second television channel was launched, there had been only a single television station, the BBC. When ITV began transmissions, it used new frequency channels which the BBC had never used, and so most television receivers were not set up to receive the new broadcasts. Unless they bought a new television designed for the new channel, viewers had to have their existing set adapted and in many cases buy a new aerial as well, but despite the expense and inconvenience, the new channel rapidly proved to be popular, at the expense of the BBC's audience share (Crisell 2002: 93–4). While this might have been an issue for only a minority of the UK's households in 1955 (when around 4.5 million homes, less than a third of all households, had a set) as television became ever more popular, the introduction of change faced ever greater challenges. So, when 'high definition', 625-line television was introduced to the UK in 1964, 14.2 m homes, 83 per cent of the total, were already equipped with a television receiver which was incapable of displaying the new pictures. While the enthusiast might rush out and buy a new 625-line set, most would only consider a new set when the existing one irretrievably broke down. The audience share of the new BBC2 channel, available only on the new 625-line system, remained low for many years to come.

The new 625-line system promised better quality pictures (a 50 per cent increase in definition compared with the previous 405-line system), but also these extra lines demanded more bandwidth, and so transmission of the new format would only become possible when the migration of television from the crowded VHF waveband to the relatively unpopulated UHF band could take place. The changes required to the transmitter network slowed the roll out of the new service, and BBC2 was in fact the only channel on the new system for some years. BBC1, the new (and obvious) name for the existing BBC channel, and ITV remained on the lower-definition, 405-line system on the VHF band. New sets available after 1964, therefore, were 'dual band', capable of receiving both VHF transmissions for BBC1 and ITV and, with the flick of a switch, also able to show BBC2's higher definition pictures. The flick of the switch actually involved entirely different tuning circuitry, and thus the new sets were more complex than their single band predecessors. This meant that they were both more expensive and tended to be more unreliable, and given that the UHF band also required the use of another new aerial (as had been required with ITV's introduction nine years earlier), the incentive to acquire suitable receiving equipment for the new channel was limited.

More change: The introduction of colour

The coming of colour posed more challenges for broadcasters and viewers. Colour in television is derived by combining relative intensities of red, green and blue (RGB) light emitted from the screen. The varying intensities of each colour across the screen must of course match the combination of colours captured by the camera, and filters are used to capture each colour component. Each filter in the camera (essentially a high grade piece of coloured glass) allows only one colour to pass (in the same way that the cones in our retina respond to only one colour element), so a colour camera contains three separate CCDs (or three tubes in earlier cameras), each generating, via the appropriate filter, the electronic signal for one colour's intensity. So instead of a single television signal produced by a black and white (or mono) camera, a colour camera produces three separate signals. At the receiver, each separate signal controls a separate electron beam (for a CRT receiver) or drives separate colour cells on a plasma or LCD screen.

Technically, this is not particularly difficult – if a mono camera can produce a signal based on the total amount of light falling on different parts of the CCD, a colour camera does exactly the same but with a series of mirrors and filters to produce three signals, the only additional complexity being the need to keep all three colour signals in synchronisation. The challenge is faced when confronted with the more mundane problem of finding space to transmit the signals. Where the black and white television system required the transmission of a single television signal, the colour system would require three separate transmissions, one for each colour. However, the mono signal cannot be done away with – at the outset of colour broadcasting, naturally, almost all television sets in use would be black and white receivers, so those transmissions had to remain in place. Even today, some cheap portable television receivers are still mono, so to transmit colour *and* mono signals implied that four times as much frequency space would be required. Given that there was already pressure on spectrum availability, even on the UHF band, the prospect of allocating 32 MHz rather than 8 MHz for a single television station, or 24 MHz compared with 6 MHz in the US, was one that was not considered an option even at the outset. Instead, some way was needed of including colour information and mono signals together within the existing channel bandwidth of 8 MHz or 6 MHz.

This was essentially an electronic engineering problem and three different solutions were adopted (Box 3.1). First by many years was the NTSC system, devised in 1953 and used in both North and South America. Colour television had been in preparation for many years (experiments in colour were conducted by John Logie Baird and others as early as the 1920s), but the requirement for compatibility with mono receivers concentrated manufacturers' efforts on

Box 3.1   Colour Television Signals

In the 1950s, incorporating the colour information signal into the same bandwidth as already occupied by a mono signal was a technical challenge. The three colour signals, red, green and blue (RGB), electronically separated by the camera's filters, could be re-combined together to reproduce the overall mono information needed by a black and white receiver, but to provide a signal for a colour receiver required colour information to be sent. Humans perceive images as shape, which is derived from variations in brightness as well as in colour, and as movement from differences between successive frames. Through testing human response to different aspects of images it is known that we are not as sensitive to colour information as to overall variations in brightness. So it is possible to project a black and white image, and superimpose rather indistinct and imprecisely defined colour on top, and the viewer will perceive a sharply defined colour image. In electronic terms, a fuzzy colour signal does not need much bandwidth to transmit as a sharp one, since relatively little information is carried.

So the brightness information, known as luminance and given the symbol Y, was transmitted just as it had been prior to the introduction of colour, and the colour information was carried as two 'colour difference' signals, Y-R and Y-B, combined together to make up chrominance, C. The chrominance signal could be carried within the upper frequency end of the luminance signal without causing detectable interference (most of the luminance information is at lower frequencies), and so the transmitted television signal consisted of two components, Y and C. A mono receiver would receive the Y carrier wave (as it had always been designed to do) while a new colour receiver would include circuits designed to receive Y and C carriers, from which the receiver electronics could derive the separate RGB signals.

a number of competing systems. Ultimately, the early introduction of colour in the US resulted in the adoption of a system which turned out to be inferior to the system adopted some 14 years later in Europe (Winston 1998: 120–2). The NTSC system had problems with inconsistent and inaccurate colour rendition, and the abbreviation became referred to by its critics as standing for 'Never Twice the Same Colour', so the two European versions of colour television that emerged were able to benefit from the American experience. The 'phase alternate line' or PAL system was developed in Germany and used first in 1967 in the UK before being adopted throughout most of western Europe. Colour was available only on the 625-line, UHF system, so initially only on one channel, BBC2, and even then only on occasional programmes, the proportion gradually increasing over the following years. In France, a second system was developed at the same time: the *Système Eléctronique Couleur Avec Memoire*. SECAM differed only slightly from PAL in the way it encoded the colour information into the mono signal, but came to be used in France, Russia and the eastern European countries.

In the UK, this ongoing sequence of innovations finally ended in 1969 when both BBC1 and ITV began 625-line, colour transmissions on the UHF band (though of course they also had to continue their 405-line transmissions on VHF for those without 625-line receivers). Now, finally, a television viewer could buy a new, single-standard set and expect to receive all three existing channels in similar definition and in colour, all through a single aerial. While the 1950s had seen one significant change, the introduction of a second channel in 1955, the 1960s had seen a series of upheavals requiring an upgraded receiver to keep up: in 1964, the introduction of another new channel, but only on the 625-line system; the 1967 introduction of colour television; and, two years later, the beginning of 625-line colour broadcasting by all channels. This period saw a rapid growth in the television rental service, where a television would be rented for a monthly payment rather than bought outright, and, while serving the growing demand for television more generally, for many renting rather than buying would be a pragmatic response to a period of regular technological innovation, as the set could be replaced on a more regular basis.

Video and Television Recording

Following such a flurry of activity, the following decades seemed relatively calm. The newly introduced European systems remained in place, while the NTSC format continued in America. Television across the world was now standardised on one of these three formats, and while each was mutually incompatible (a television receiver bought in Europe would not work in the US and vice versa) such was the level of international trade in programmes that it was possible to convert between standards prior to transmission. This introduces one of the major changes affecting both television production and consumption: videotape. The introduction of reliable magnetic tape recording for television lagged audio recording by some two decades, the reason being simply the huge bandwidth of video in comparison with audio. Magnetic tape recording works by dragging a length of tape across a magnetic recording head, the magnetic field in the head being energised by the electronic signal passing through it (Figure 3.2). The variations in the signal are fixed as variations in the magnetisation along the length of the tape, which can be played back later by passing it again over a second head in which an electrical impulse is excited by the movement of the magnetic medium.

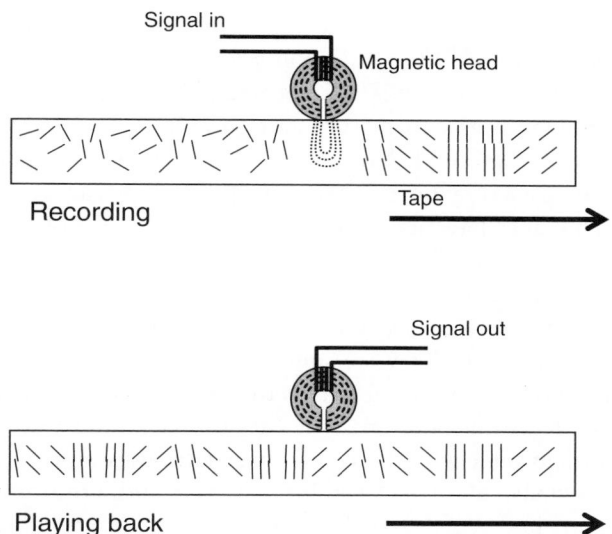

Figure 3.2 Magnetic recording. Recording: the electronic signal passing through the coil generates a magnetic field in the recording head. When the tape (or disk), which is coated in randomly magnetised ferrous particles, passes next to the head the magnetic field leaks out of the gap in the head into the tape, where it magnetises the ferrous particles according to the electronic signal. If the tape is moving past the head fast enough, that magnetised state is 'frozen' into the tape as a linear, magnetic record of the electronic signal. Playing back: the magnetised state of the particles on the tape remains intact provided it has not been exposed to external magnetic fields. When the magnetised tape is passed across the playback head, the moving magnetic field sets up a field in the head, which in turn generates an electric current in the coil. The size of the current depends on the state of the magnetic field in the head, which of course reflects the magnetisation level in the tape. Thus the output electronic signal is a reproduction of the original input signal that was used to record the magnetic track. This recording and playing back principle applies to all magnetic recording (audio and video, tape and disk) although the arrangement of heads and tape or disk transport mechanisms varies

On recording, the more rapid the variations in the signal, the faster the tape has to move in relationship to the head, and the higher frequencies in video mean that the signal can be varying several hundred times faster than in audio. It was simply not possible to move tape past the head rapidly enough for video, so when video recording began to emerge in the 1950s, it was based on spinning drums containing two or more heads passing rapidly across slowly moving tape to increase the relative head-to-tape speed. Not only does this sound more complicated, but it also made for difficulties in tape transport, and early video recording was very expensive, managed with difficulty and consequently unreliable; thus it did not significantly displace live television. Film continued to be the main recording medium, including for newsgathering, and the main purpose of videotape was to 'time shift' programmes such as news bulletins across the different time zones in large landmasses like the US rather than transmit a series of live bulletins repeated at hourly intervals.

As the technology began to mature and become more reliable, its advantages began to outweigh its disadvantages. One obvious advantage was cost: film stock can be used only once, whereas magnetic tape can be recorded over many times. This does have its disadvantages as historians of television have found in later years: television continued to see itself as primarily a live and therefore ephemeral medium, and videotape was simply a useful production tool rather than an obvious archiving system. Many television programmes made in the 1960s and 1970s were subsequently recorded over and lost forever (a fate that became familiar perhaps to many viewers using the domestic video recorders that came later on). The earliest machines stored tape in reels and a breakthrough came when Sony introduced the videotape cassette in 1971 in its U-Matic format, following a similar pattern in audio recording where the Compact Cassette had begun to replace reel-to-reel recorders in the late 1960s. The cassette format made operation easier for professional use and also raised the prospect of a consumer version, and a U-Matic video cassette recorder (VCR) was briefly marketed by Sony from 1972 (mainly to corporate users such as educational institutions) before replacing it with a new cassette format, Betamax, in 1975. With television tuning circuits and timers built in, these VCRs were clearly aimed at allowing viewers to record television programmes for watching at a later time, and were marketed as such, a logical extension into the domestic sphere of the existing timeshifting practice in television production. A year after Sony's Betamax, in October 1976 the Victor Company of Japan (JVC) launched a similar but incompatible video recorder based on its Video Home System (VHS), and the infamous battle between the formats was joined. If VCR use remained restricted to timeshifted recording, then the existence of two (or more) formats would not represent such a problem: blank cassettes were available for both formats, and recording programmes for later viewing was straightforward as the same machine would be used, whichever format it happened to be. Nevertheless, just as Sony had dominated the professional market and thus established its U-Matic format as a *de facto* standard, it expected to do the same in the domestic arena. While developing the Betamax format, Sony had simultaneously approached other manufacturers to seek agreement on developing a common format, which, presumably, they expected to be the Betamax. Given that, for some years, JVC themselves had been manufacturing professional U-Matic machines under licence from Sony, this may have been an understandable assumption, but by the time of these negotiations in 1974, JVC were busy making alliances of their own (Cusumano et al. 1992). In the ensuing years, JVC became more astute than Sony in licensing their system to other manufacturers and persuaded American giant RCA and a number of leading European manufacturers to support the VHS system rather than Betamax. These commercial manoeuvres, rather than any technical superiority, were mainly responsible for VHS being in a commanding position when the point came for a single format to become the universal standard.

From a technical point of view, there was little to distinguish the two formats. While Sony's system initially could only record one hour's worth of television, and thus, crucially, was unable to record a feature-length film, within five months of the VHS launch with a superior two-hour capacity, the Betamax had been improved and also had a two-hour capability. Similarly, as new features such as pause or long play were added to one format, they appeared within a matter of months in the other (Cusumano et al. 1992: 77–8). Where they did differ was in picture quality: it is generally agreed that Betamax offered a superior picture to VHS, a distinction that was clearly not important enough on its own to secure its success in the domestic arena but did help ensure the format's longevity in the professional market, with a number of successors surviving as broadcast formats (Enticknap 2005: 181). What finally saw off Betamax, and more minor competitor formats such as Philips's V-2000, was the rise of a new use for the VCR, for viewing pre-recorded video cassettes.

As noted above, the early uses of the VCR were for recording off-air transmissions of television programmes. As sales of VCRs grew, both formats sold more units, but manufacturers using VHS sold more than those offering Betamax machines. VCR sales began to take off in particular when, in the early 1980s, pre-recorded cassettes of films became available in large numbers spawning the emergence of the video rental store. Between 1980 and 1981, annual production of both Betamax and VHS machines doubled; over the next three years, annual production of Betamax doubled again, while that of VHS almost quadrupled (Cusumano et al. 1992: 54). The VCR was beginning to sell in numbers that would make it 'by far the most widely diffused of the new media technologies' (Winston 1998: 127). Europe in particular began to buy VCRs in huge numbers. With fewer television channels in many cases than in the US, the video rental system offered an attractive alternative viewing option in these countries. In the UK, the relatively high numbers of households with televisions on a rental agreement found it easy to add a VCR to the package, and here growth was highest of all, three times as high as in the US (Cusumano et al. 1992: 85). Once again, JVC and its other VHS backers agreed deals with the leading television rental companies to ensure that the VHS format was supported at the expense of Betamax.

At this point, it *did* begin to matter to the viewer which format of VCR he owned. No longer simply playing his cassettes on the same machine used to record them, he now wanted to be able to play cassettes rented from the local shop, and that shop would need to carry two different versions of every film to satisfy its customers. Equally, the film distributors would need to make duplicate versions of each film in the two different formats. In any system which involves a supply of 'hardware' and 'software' – not just personal computers, but televisions, radios, digital music players and so on – there is a tendency for one format to become dominant and others either to be eliminated or reduced to a specialist or niche market. In some instances, this is enforced by regulations (for instance in broadcasting) or by agreements between manufacturers, while in others it emerges through a process of positive reinforcement as one format becomes more popular (hardware and software suppliers congregating behind that format, as in the case of Microsoft/Intel's supremacy over Apple Macintosh). In the case of the VCR, the latter was the mechanism by which VHS emerged triumphant in the video format war. The video rental outlets began to stock films only in the format that had the highest number of users, VHS, and distributors began to release new films only in that format. Increasingly, Betamax viewers found their choice of films diminished, or even completely non-existent, and this cycle of causes and effects sent Betamax sales into tailspin. By 1988, annual worldwide production of Betamax VCRs was 148,000 compared with almost 45 million VHS, and for every Betamax recorder in use there were nine VHS machines (Cusumano et al. 1992: 54).

In passing, it should be noted that Betamax and VHS were not the only options presented to consumers for watching pre-recorded television or film. Analogue disc systems such as Philips's Laservision disc emerged in the late 1970s as competitors to videotape. The Laservision disc was approximately the same size as a vinyl LP and resembled it further in that it contained video information recorded in grooves on both sides of the disc. While they were initially aimed at the home user market, when take up proved to be minimal they were marketed at educational institutions. Home users were by now used to the idea that their video devices could record from television as well as play films rented from the corner shop, and the prospect of something as large as an LP that could not be recorded onto seemed a retrograde step. Meanwhile, educational institutions were more likely to be ready to pay for pre-recorded material. However, as with earlier attempts to exploit audiovisual services for educational purposes, Laservision attracted some brief interest but was quickly replaced with the by now mass market VHS system.

While Betamax had failed in the domestic market, Sony's various successors to U-Matic remained popular for broadcast production, and the same logic of a single dominant format did not apply so forcefully, as the size of broadcasting organisations meant they would tend to equip for a particular format and stick with it, installing the occasional machine for reading material in other formats. Magnetic recording did not herald the beginning of the use of recorded material for television broadcasting though it did help to increase it. Film had on occasion been used to pre-record television programmes, thus allowing some of the creative possibilities long enjoyed by cinema directors, and film cameras had also been used to record off-air, as it were, live television (by the crude but effective technique of pointing a film camera at a high-resolution television monitor and synchronising shutter and frame rates). So some television output consisted of material recorded previously but not much. This limited use was partly due to a cultural block – as noted earlier, one of television's underlying attributes was its live nature – but also to an economic one, as film stock, its processing and its post-production were expensive and relatively time consuming. Magnetic tape recording was potentially cheaper (though not when it was first introduced) as tapes could be used over and over, but also the results could be viewed instantly, a significant advantage over film. During the 1960s and 1970s videotape became increasingly used not only for editing and post-production work but also for origination. With the introduction of cassette formats, recorders became more compact and thus portable, and later still recording and camera could be combined into a single unit, the camcorder. These found applications particularly in newsgathering, where their relatively compact size (diminished further by the introduction of digital video) and the ability to view rushes immediately both proved to be great benefits and have enabled television news reporting to reach our screens from places that would have proved too inhospitable a few decades ago. The cost advantages of videotape were greatest here too, as in newsgathering the shooting ratio is greater than in other realms, typically as much as 15:1 – for every hour's recording that was actually transmitted, 14 hours remained unused, and thus a large quantity of tape could be re-used.

Videotape also helped establish television programmes as commodities, fixed entities rather than fleeting episodes in a continuing flow of live audiovisual experiences – and moreover, commodities which could be traded. Certainly programmes could more easily be traded between broadcasters but also could now be marketed to the public in exactly the same way as the film studios were doing with movies. Once Hollywood distributors realised that far from killing off the audience for its films, video could provide another income stream (which now provides significantly more income than cinema screenings) then television programmes could also be seen in the same way, with drama series in particular sitting on the shelves in the rental shops for popular consumption at a time suited to the viewer.

Other Developments in Television Technology

Rather less significantly than the videocassette recorder, but also contributing to a new way of using the television, teletext was introduced in the mid-1970s. Beginning with trials between 1972 and 1973 in the UK, teletext's data signals are transmitted during the signal blanking intervals where picture information is not being sent. Storing the data briefly in the television receiver allows the viewer to call up pages of text and graphics containing information such as news updates, traffic information, weather and so on. Following the growing adoption of remote control devices for television sets, without which teletext would not be a practical proposition, the television receiver became further removed from the linear, live stream of scheduled programming that had characterised it up until that point. Instead, it could be seen more as an information resource, one with which the viewer interacted, that interaction meaning rather more than simply changing channels. This changing perception was enhanced, of course, by the emergence of the VCR in the same decade.

To receive and display teletext information, a receiver must have the appropriate decoding circuits, and so once again initial adoption was dependent upon the rate at which households replaced their sets (though adapter boxes were available for those who were keenest). With its tradition of renting television sets, the UK once more had one of the fastest growing rates of adoption of teletext, though by 1990 just a quarter of households had access to a suitably equipped receiver (Crisell 2002: 215). The BBC's service was known as Ceefax, while ITV named theirs Oracle, and both offered the same sort of information although ITV, as a commercial broadcaster, carried advertising on its pages. With the almost-simultaneous launch of two-way information services such as Prestel in the UK or Minitel in France, teletext came to be regarded as part of the beginning of a new era of widespread public access to information, in particular in conjunction with the expansion of cable television networks that was taking place in many European and American countries. Talk of new communication highways – or, in Amsterdam where cable networks were well established, canals seemed a better metaphor – prefigured much of the fevered debate that arose with the emergence of the internet some twenty years later, including concerns about access and the gap between the 'information-rich' and 'information-poor' (Parker and Dunn 1972; Smith 1972; Aumente 1987; Brants et al. 1996). Some anticipated that, with cable and satellite connections, television would become merely one part of an augmented public sphere, with access to information from multiple sources and interactive, two-way communication between citizens. However, this was barely realised, and instead, as we will explore in the next chapter, these new physical communications channels enriched our lives mainly by offering a huge expansion in the number of television channels available to paying householders.

Conclusion

Television was conceived early in the 20th century as a natural enhancement of radio and after the Second World War rapidly eclipsed radio in the popular imagination. Television receivers became the focal point of many a living room, occupying (literally) the position held by radio during the previous decades. The BBC was funded through a *television* licence, implying its radio services were a secondary bonus, and certainly the bulk of that revenue was spent on television rather than radio. Most national newspapers had (and still have) television critics, while few cover radio programming in the same way, and a similar emphasis is to be found in academic research. Ostensibly serving the same function as radio, bringing an external world into the home but this time with pictures, it did not, however, replace radio as completely as many had once imagined. Radio became something quite different from its previous guise and in so doing also differentiated itself from television. Its portability and increasingly secondary nature imbued it with a potential accessibility and intimacy with its listener which television has not been able to emulate.

Television has not changed in form to the same extent over the years – it is remarkable in fact how similar television watching is today to its earliest days. Despite the introduction of video recording and the multitude of channels on offer through new platforms, much television watching remains a passive (or 'lean back' as the marketing industry has it) activity. Scheduling remains important, despite those predicting its irrelevance two decades ago in the face of the VCR's timeshifting capabilities. Despite claims of 'dumbing down', a comparison of schedules over the decades shows much of the fare on offer to have changed less than is often suggested. This resilience might be attributed to the way in which television suits its audience. It is easy (some would complain, too easy) to 'consume' television, and rather more demanding to interact or create one's own schedules through timed recordings, although that facility is there when needed.

These observations suggest that one should be cautious in predicting how readily changes in social practice (in this case television watching) might result from the introduction of new technologies. There have indeed been significant changes in television technology, none greater perhaps than the emergence of satellite and cable systems in the 1980s and, now, the adoption of digital systems. These technological developments are accompanied by political and economic changes in the television industry, but it is uncertain whether they are to prove any more effective than previous innovations in changing fundamentally the ways in which television is viewed in the future.

Communication Channels and Delivery Platforms

4

For the first four decades of television's existence, and for the whole of radio's, we have thought of them principally as terrestrial services, that is, they are delivered to us by broadcasters who transmit signals from the top of a hill or a tall building over the airwaves mainly by ground or direct waves (see Chapter 2) to our receiving aerials. Since the 1980s, however, we have become familiar with additional ways in which such signals may be delivered to our homes. Cable and satellite distribution offer alternative paths, with distinct implications for the kinds of services we may receive. In particular, as we shall see, the advent of widespread cable systems prompted speculation about an imminent information-rich society, bringing about cultural, political and economic transformations. That such visions failed to materialise, and that only 20 years later has it become reasonable once again to consider such possibilities, is perhaps surprising; however, that this scenario has now been delivered in most homes not via the new cable networks but instead via the humble, hundred-year-older telephone wire is quite remarkable.

Overview of Delivery Systems

The term 'delivery systems' here is understood as the means by which information represented in electronic signals may be carried from one place to another, and since we are considering electronic communication, this is further understood to mean instantaneous communications. So we are not including the physical transport of electronic data in say a CD-Rom sent through the postal service, though in some situations that might be a perfectly suitable delivery system. Instead, we are exploring here the delivery methods available for carrying electronic data, telephone conversations, radio and television programmes, in other words telecommunications and broadcasting.

Terrestrial radio waves

To establish communication by radio waves, as Marconi realised over a hundred years ago, is relatively straightforward. For widespread coverage, a transmitter generally needs to be mounted as high as possible (on top of a mast, itself constructed on high ground ideally), and the receiving aerial should also be placed as high as possible, on a roof if it is to receive television broadcasts, for example. (Not all radio wave transmission is expected to travel long distances however – sometimes, radio waves are used to cover small areas such as wireless internet networks, or wireless mobile phone headsets, such as those using the Bluetooth system. In such a case, the emphasis is on convenience, communicating without wires.) For distant communication, one of the key advantages of radio waves is, of course, the lack of the need for physical infrastructure. As the accounts of the attempts to lay the first transatlantic telegraph cable indicate, the costs saved by using radio waves are enormous and make it feasible to communicate to areas which would never be economic to serve with wired connections. The reverse of this universal coverage is that signals cannot be confined. For broadcasters, this is not a drawback but is the essence of their activity, to send signals to as many as possible. For other applications, for example, mobile or cordless phones, the potential 'leakage' of signals is one to be guarded against and, while digital coding techniques generally now protect us well, earlier analogue calls have been prone to interception, including on occasion by tabloid journalists.

Broadcasters and telecommunications companies plan appropriate geographical transmitter coverage by the selection of sites, transmission power and appropriate frequencies (see Chapter 2). While broadcasting consumes a lot of power (a single main radio transmitter might use 250 kW, equivalent to 100 kettles boiling continuously), just a few transmitters can cover a large number of people. For example, 40 of these high-power transmitters or so might be enough to provide FM radio to around 90 per cent of the UK population (some 50 million people). This makes terrestrial transmission a relatively cheap way of providing one-way services like broadcasting – once the initial main transmitter network is in place, the audience can grow as it acquires receiving equipment at no additional cost to the broadcaster. However, this arrangement still leaves around ten per cent of the population unable to receive signals, and they tend to be those who live in remote areas or in difficult terrain, such as at the bottom of a steep valley. To increase coverage further, a broadcaster must install additional relay transmitters, which run at low power over a small area, filling in the gaps in coverage. Naturally, each of these will bring coverage to a far lower number of people than the main transmitters, and so this begins to increase transmission costs for terrestrial broadcasters. It is sometimes estimated that the costs of transmitting to the final ten per cent of a country's population is greater than the cost of the first 90 per cent. For example, the BBC's 40 or so main FM radio transmitters are augmented by a total of almost 200 relays to provide coverage to 99.5 per cent of the UK population. These transmitters are linked by a combination of land-based lines and line-of-sight microwave links (small dishes mounted on masts transmitting a highly directional beam of super high frequency radio waves to receiving dishes on adjacent masts). So costs are related to the levels of coverage required, but the absence of any physical link can make terrestrial networks relatively easy to install.

Cable networks

In almost complete contrast to terrestrial radio transmission, cable networks do require a physical link between source and destination. Moreover, they can readily enable point to point, two-way communication, and the signals are not broadcast to all within range but confined to the physical medium itself. As we have seen, the first networks, the telegraph and telephone, found their main applications in point-to-point communication, but early attempts at providing entertainment and news services were successful in the absence of a cheaper alternative. Only when radio communication and, later, broadcasting emerged did the difference in costs between cable and terrestrial transmission methods become decisive.

Even so, cable had a role. Terrestrial transmissions are susceptible to geographic factors (as radio waves are blocked by or reflected off hills and tall buildings, for instance) which can cause poor reception. Equally, distant transmissions on nearby frequencies can interfere with the station being listened to (and the degree of interference is also increased in certain atmospheric conditions). In contrast, cable can be screened almost entirely from interference, and as signals weaken with distance from their source, they can readily be amplified. So when, in the earliest days of radio, listeners in the south east of England, for example, experienced interference from stations broadcasting in continental Europe, a number of companies offered cable alternatives. These companies would install their own high-quality receiving aerial and then relay the signals down wires to subscribers' homes, in many ways mimicking the pioneering telephone entertainment services of the late 19th century. As radio grew in popularity, so too did these relay stations, even more so when they began to add to the two existing BBC relay stations by carrying some of the continental stations, which were proving increasingly popular with those already able to receive them. Between 1929 and 1935 these 'Re-diffusion' companies, as they came to be known, increased in number from 34 to 343, with subscribers increasing from 8592 to 233,554 (Street 2002: 42–3). Thus the cost of installing cables and making physical connections to homes becomes sustainable when the service offered is sufficiently attractive to persuade people to pay a subscription for something otherwise available for free over the airwaves, an economic argument that proved compelling once more when, in later decades, cable re-diffusion of television services again offered viewers better reception.

The physical connection between transmitter and receiver gives cable a further unique advantage over radio wave communication, and that is the ability to allow a return path. The receiver can respond to the originator of the information. For television services, in principle, rather than relaying the same suite of television programmes one way to all subscribers (literally, 'broadcasting'), each could be offered an individual service. Of course, this is exactly how the telephone worked from its inception, and the strength of the wired connection became greater as the network itself grew in size. After all, a telephone is not much use if you and only a few others are connected to the network. So a network's functionality (and its appeal to new users) increases exponentially as it grows, a network externality in economic terms. However, in contrast to radio communication, the costs of adding new members to the network continue too as more infrastructure is required. The additional costs of serving dispersed communities, such as those in rural locations, are increased even more than for terrestrial transmission, and so cable networks tend to be developed first in urban centres. The spread of telephone lines to the most outlying parts of some countries, particularly industrialised countries, has only been achieved by regulation obliging the large telecommunications companies to offer a 'universal service', meaning that they were obliged to connect all households to the network for a similar charge to the subscriber; the companies installing cable television networks in more recent years have not been placed under equivalent obligations, and so these services remain concentrated in urban centres and are rarely available to rural dwellers.

Satellite transmission

Essentially a satellite is a straightforward relay device for communications signals. The very first communications satellites (*Telstar* was launched in 1962, *Syncom* in 1963) were intended to relay telephone calls and a limited number of television channels from one side of the world to another, in a similar manner to the way in which a network of terrestrial television or radio transmitters relays programmes across a country. The difference of course is the distance involved, and the first satellite links were transatlantic, connecting continents separated by thousands of kilometres. Transatlantic telephony had worked successfully since the 1920s using radio links, following early attempts by Marconi and Fessenden in 1906, and this relied on low frequency terrestrial radio waves bending round the surface of the earth. Such calls were of very poor quality and connection was unreliable, and the wired, electric telegraph remained important for intercontinental communication. An improvement came when the first telephone cables were laid in 1956, with some difficulty, across the ocean floor connecting the two continents. Again, their capacity was limited (initially to a total of 36 two-way calls), as was their quality, and the beginnings of satellite transmission promised a rapid expansion in international communication. For television, however, the potential for live or near-live transmissions from the other side of the world was to be a momentous occasion in broadcasting history.

Whether telecommunications, television or radio, an Earth station aims its satellite transmission, the uplink, at the orbiting satellite. Circuitry within the satellite receives the signal, shifts it to a slightly different frequency and transmits back the downlink to a receiving Earth station. The downlink can be a spot-beam, intended to be received over a small area, or a wide beam, covering countries or whole continents. In 1945, scientist and novelist Arthur C. Clarke conceived of satellites each covering approximately one third of the Earth's surface; in his arrangement, three satellites between them could provide real-time communication between any two places on the planet (other than the polar regions, where coverage is less straightforward). *Telstar* and *Syncom* differed from each other in one important aspect: *Telstar* was intended to circumnavigate the Earth in an elliptical orbit, 5600 km above the Earth's surface at its highest point, while *Syncom* (or *Syncom* 2 to be precise) was the first 'geostationary' communications satellite, launched into a much higher circular orbit almost 36,000 km above Earth. Sitting in orbit this far out, the gravitational pull of the Earth on the satellite is such that *Syncom* and its geostationary successors circulate round the Earth once every 24 hours. Since the Earth also rotates at the same speed, from the point of view of someone standing on Earth, and more importantly from a satellite Earth station, the satellite appears to be stationary. This makes it a relatively easy job to point the Earth station's dish at the satellite for the uplink and to have fixed receiving dishes for the downlink. It also means that the satellite is 'visible' to the transmitting and receiving dishes 24 hours per day. Satellites like *Telstar*, launched into lower orbits, have to circulate at higher rates and so are visible from the ground only for a few hours per day as they pass over. Not only does this mean that they can only be used for part of the day (or, alternatively, must be supplemented with additional satellites spaced evenly round the orbit so that, as one disappears, the next appears in view) it also adds the complication that the Earth station dishes for uplink and downlink must themselves move to track the satellite as it crosses the sky. While this is quite possible for point-to-point communication, it would not be feasible for domestic television reception – here the geostationary satellite is essential as it allows fixed position receiving dishes.

Finally, the different altitudes of geostationary and the lower orbiting satellites have other consequences. The huge distance in the signal transmission path of a geostationary orbit (72,000 km for the combined uplink and downlink) introduces a noticeable delay between transmission and reception. Even though the radio waves travel at the speed of light, it takes one quarter of a second to cover that distance. This may seem small, and is irrelevant for one-way communication such as television pictures beamed to household receiving dishes, but for two-way communication, such as telephone calls or live television link-ups and two-way interviews, the delay occurs both ways and can make conversation a little difficult. Satellites orbiting much closer to the Earth only have a much shorter transmission path, and so the delay can be almost eliminated, and the shorter distance has the further advantage that lower power levels are needed for the uplink and downlink, so smaller dishes can be used (the bigger the dish, the more energy is 'scooped up' to provide a clear signal). Despite these disadvantages however, the geostationary satellite is favoured for its constant visibility and cost savings in comparison with the multiple satellites needed to provide continuous communication in low orbits.

Broadcasting and New Distribution Technologies

Since Marconi's successful application of radio communication, terrestrial transmission has served broadcasters across the world. Following the initial experimental period, the use of different frequency bands and transmitter configurations have allowed radio to serve a multiplicity of needs, from national, regional and international broadcasting in the early decades, followed by more local services in later years. In addition, the quality of audio and video delivery has increased, with the introduction of colour television and stereo sound in both television and radio. Thus terrestrial transmission has evolved to the point where it serves populations of diverse sizes with a variety of content.

Nevertheless, the emergence of alternative delivery platforms for broadcasting has altered not just the ways we receive programmes but has also been part of a change in the public role of broadcasting, especially television. For telecommunications (that is, telephone and data communications) the deployment of different transmission techniques, initially cable but also radio communication and more recently the satellite link, could be characterised as an evolutionary and managed process of incorporation of complementary technologies. This is in large part explained by telecommunications historically having been recognised as a public utility, much like power or water supplies, and therefore in almost all countries the telecommunications industry was incorporated as a government-controlled monopoly like those other services. Broadcasting has never been seen in quite this way, although a 'public service' role has always been acknowledged. Thus broadcasting has always been allowed, partially at least, to be a commercial undertaking, and in fact this has been encouraged as an important competitive element with the public service institutions. (In recent decades, of course, telecommunications industries across the world have equally become commercialised and subject to market competition.) Since the 1980s, in particular, the commercial role of broadcasting has come to the fore as new technological possibilities have been seized upon by broadcasters principally as ways of competing for a greater share of the audience.

This is not to suggest that commercial competition is the only mechanism by which new technologies can be introduced, although as we have seen in previous chapters, intensely competing commercial interests lay behind early developments in both radio and television, and the earliest cable networks also had commercial aims at their heart. However, the launch of communication satellites was not a commercial endeavour but a military one. With the USSR launching the first orbiting satellite, *Sputnik*, in October 1957, three months ahead of the US, commercial questions were put aside. Nevertheless, television companies were amongst the first to exploit their ability to transmit reliable, live signals across the Atlantic. Between 1959 and 1962, the BBC had used undersea telephone cables for the transatlantic exchange of programmes, although their limited capacity meant live programming was impossible. With each minute of programme material requiring more than one and a half hours to transfer, this was a slow, but ultimately effective, way of transferring programmes. The first satellite link ups, carried via *Telstar* in 1962, were also for studio-to-studio transmission, with programmes being re-broadcast over each country's terrestrial network, either live or recorded for later transmission. However, as it was real-time transmission, live link ups inevitably followed. The first transmissions later that year were a cause for commemoration within the television industry, with live pictures from the US shown in 16 European countries. The geostationary *Syncom 2* relayed extended coverage of the funeral of John F. Kennedy in 1963, while Crisell suggests that the first 'global' event transmitted live in countries around the world was the 1968 Mexico Olympics. In July the following year, an estimated 600 million people, one sixth of the world's population, simultaneously watched live pictures of the Apollo moon landings (Crisell 2002: 128).

If satellite's beginnings were in point-to-point communications between individual broadcasting companies, a simultaneous development was opening up television broadcasts to a wider population. Cable television networks emerged to fulfil a similar need as had the radio relay exchanges in the 1920s. When the FCC had finished allocating terrestrial television frequencies in 1952, most attention (and frequencies) had been given to urban centres, and some 15 per cent of US homes were unable to receive any television at all. Enterprising television store owners in these areas had begun to erect receiving aerials on high ground and towers, in order to feed the signals via cable to their stores so as to show off television at its best; subsequently they extended these cable feeds both to customers who had already bought sets and to those who might buy. As with the earlier radio services, people were willing to pay for improved reception, and before long new stations were being added to the service, for instance television channels being broadcast locally, but also channels from nearby cities, which were effectively available only via the cable network (which would install a sophisticated receiving aerial beyond the reach of individual householders). By 1952, the FCC's frequency allocations had long been seen as unsuccessful, and around a hundred of these community antenna television (CATV) networks were running in towns and cities across the country (Gomery 2006a: 23). With the addition of exclusive new channels, the cable networks went from a position of making up for the shortcomings of the terrestrially broadcast networks to one of offering twice or three times as many channels as could be received with a simple television aerial. Over the coming decades FCC regulations held back the expansion of cable, but by the 1970s it was relaxing its grip and a market for non-broadcast programming, aimed at the cable companies, was opened up. In 1972, Time Incorporated launched the Home Box Office (HBO), showing uncut films without any advertising, relayed to CATV companies who then made it available to its customers for an additional subscription. As the demand for HBO grew it effectively became a national network, just like the existing terrestrial networks except that it was only available on cable. This was the beginning of a period of rapid growth in these so-called cable network stations, which now include familiar names such as CNN, and by 2005 cable television was available to 96 per cent of US homes, with 80 per cent signed up (Gomery 2006a: 25).

HBO had initially used terrestrial microwave links to deliver its programming across the country to the cable networks. This line-of-sight technique limited its coverage and in 1975 it booked space on RCA's *Satcom 1* satellite. With its wide beam downlink, HBO immediately became available to CATV networks across the whole country. Other channels followed this distribution path and the number of cable network channels grew dramatically. Towards the end of the 1970s, the terrestrial networks also began to use satellite to link up its transmitters instead of the combination of landlines and microwave links, and satellite became an indispensable link in the transmission chain of all broadcasters (also coming to be used for national radio networks such as Radio 5 Live in the UK). As satellite reception equipment became more widely available, some enterprising viewers put their own dishes up in their back yards and received HBO's and other cable networks' programming more-or-less for free, following the logic that radio waves travelling through the air were there for the taking just as broadcast terrestrial transmissions were. HBO's view was different: having decided this constituted 'signal theft', but also having failed to dissuade the thieves, it proceeded to become the first cable network to encrypt, or scramble, its transmissions. The inevitable lawsuits followed but, ultimately, HBO's view prevailed and scrambled transmissions are now the norm for subscription-based satellite television services.

What the signal thieves had established, however, was that there was a potential market for direct home reception of satellite television signals rather than reception via a cable operator, and the direct-to-home services began to emerge in a number of countries, notably the UK. Though well established in the US, cable networks were in variable degrees of development in European countries. While they were well established in a few countries, in others they had only begun to develop very slowly, and so in their absence direct broadcast satellite (DBS) services stood a reasonable chance of success. Nevertheless, they faced some technical difficulties. Just as terrestrial broadcasting suffered the vagaries of weather and topography, so too did satellite services. Poor weather, rain or snow, could impede the signals, and the receiving dish needed a clear 'view' of the orbiting satellite, unobstructed by other buildings or trees, for example. Given that the first DBS satellites used transmission frequencies within the super-high frequency (SHF) range known as C-band, which was also in use for microwave systems on the ground, to avoid interference they had to operate at low power, and this required large receiving dishes to gather enough power to provide decent reception. Typically, depending on where you were in the continent, a dish might need to be two metres or more across, and so, given the other constraints on positioning, reception by home-mounted dishes was not straightforward. Thus, as in the US the previous decade, most early deployments of DBS television in Europe were to supply the emerging cable television operators. By 1989, however, satellites were operating in a different frequency band, the Ku band, and could operate at higher power so that dishes could be as little as half a metre across. These were much easier to mount on individual homes, and the higher power meant reception was generally better; the DBS market began to take off. The main operator, Sky TV, part of Rupert Murdoch's News International, secured exclusive rights to key sports events and launched movie channels, helping to bolster the success of the service. Sky's launch in 1989 of its DBS service beat its main UK rival, British Satellite Broadcasting, to market by a year and within another year

Sky had taken over BSB's remnants to become, as BSkyB, the UK's only major satellite television operator (BSkyB reverting to the name Sky when it launched digital services in 1998).

Like the cable services before it, BSkyB grew only slowly, its main customer base being amongst sports fans and, to a lesser degree, film enthusiasts. With more than 99 per cent of the UK population having been served with good quality reception since the introduction of 625-line UHF services in the 1960s, one key advantage of cable reception was eliminated. Equally, the four UK terrestrial channels already on offer were felt by most to offer adequate choice in programming, including advertisement-free public service television, so some of the unique features that made satellite and cable appealing in the US were absent. So, despite the increased number of channels on offer on these new platforms, terrestrial television remains the dominant way of receiving television signals in the UK.

The Wired Nation: Cable Communications

As we have noted, cable television networks and cable radio networks developed principally to offer better reception of broadcast programmes and, as they evolved, to offer additional channels to those available on terrestrial networks. However, from the 1970s, cable was also viewed as a key element of a wider communications infrastructure, with origins in data communications as much as in broadcasting. Until this time, telecommunications and broadcasting were considered quite separate spheres: telecommunications was about point-to-point communication, while cable television (and radio) systems confined their activities to carrying programmes.

Telecommunications evolution

Telecommunications in the early 20th century consisted of the telegraph and telephone. More and more businesses began to use these systems as they evolved, the telegraph having the advantage of leaving a written copy of the communicated message, while the telephone did not require a skilled operator. At the end of the Second World War, a further development combined these distinct advantages into a new network based on the teleprinter exchange or Telex service. A teleprinter terminal looked like an electric typewriter with a telephone dial on the side, and by connecting it to a similar device over the Telex wire network, an operator could type text on the typewriter keyboard and the words would be typed out simultaneously on the remote receiving machine. Pre-War prototypes had used the existing telephone network but by the end of the War it was clear that Telex would need its own dedicated cables.

By 1954, all lines in the UK used dedicated cabling, and over the following seven years subscriber numbers grew from 1700 to more than 8000 (Barton 1968: 4).

A Telex terminal could be operated by anyone who could type, and terminals began to appear in public places such as hotels. As might be imagined, they were used extensively by journalists working in the field to send copy back to their newsrooms, but soon Telex became an important business tool when near-instant text-based messages needed to be sent, including overseas as the network became international. Telex continued to grow until the mid-1980s, by which time it was widely used with, for example, 185,000 subscribers in Germany in 1988, and Telex interfaces were being installed in office computers so that the computer terminal also operated as the Telex machine, the computer screen replacing paper. While progress was being made on developing a successor to Telex, known briefly as Teletex, the fax machine was also being developed and, with its easy connection to the existing telephone network rather than a dedicated network, the fax machine was rapidly adopted and Teletex development ended. The scanned pages of a fax machine could transmit text, like Telex, but also graphics (including, importantly, handwritten signatures) and from the late-1980s the fax became a standard piece of office communication hardware or software, as it also became incorporated into computers (Jeppesen and Poulsen 1994).

While the fax machine, as its name suggests (fax being short for facsimile), would send a graphical representation of the message content, including text, the telephone network was being explored further in the 1970s for data transfer, this time in a two-way communication system known generically as videotex. Appearing first in the UK with the brand name Prestel, videotex was developed by the then nationalised telephone company (later to become British Telecom, or BT) and was envisaged as a data system for use both in business and at home. Emerging at almost the exact same time as the television data system, Teletext, Prestel's distinction was that it was a two-way system, and so the viewer could also respond to information, booking theatre tickets or making financial enquiries, for instance. This was not quite computer-to-computer communication: the terminals were 'dumb', there simply to display information as it was sent down the line, requested by the user at the keyboard, connected to the telephone line via a modem. The first services required dedicated terminals, increasing the cost of subscription, but within a few years televisions could display the data via an adapter and in 1986, ten years after its initial trials, Prestel had 65,000 terminals in use, split more-or-less equally between businesses and home users (Aumente 1987: 30). A similar service in France, Minitel, was more closely allied to the telephone, with combined devices incorporating a telephone handset and small display screen, and one of the first services available was an electronic telephone directory. Indeed, by offering low cost (or free) terminals with the advantage of a bigger elec-tronic directory than its paper counterpart, Minitel became widely adopted, with more than a million subscribers by 1985 (making Prestel's numbers look rather puny) and, unlike the UK service, continued to grow into the 1990s with six million subscribers in 1993. The differences in how these two appar-ently similar systems fared is explained by a number of factors including a rather more *dirigiste* approach on the part of the government in France in comparison with increasingly market-oriented telecommunications policies in the UK, which included the privatisation of BT in 1984 (Cats-Baril and Jelassi 1994; Case 1994). Indeed, such was the success of Minitel amongst the public as well as businesses that it was seen as hindering the adoption of the inter-net: in 1997, by which time the internet was familiar to many, there were almost 15 m Minitel users in France compared with just 1m internet users (Webster 1997).

Cable television as an 'information utility'

With these data communication developments happening at the same time as cable television networks were expanding rapidly in North America and some European countries, it should not be surprising that many saw the potential for the cable television infrastructure to be used for far more than one-way transmission of programming. From the earliest days of cable, it was anticipated that 'television' could become an 'information utility', pro-viding 'access to all available public information about society, government, opportunities, products, entertainment, knowledge, and educational services' (Parker and Dunn 1972: 1395). Writing in 1973, Raymond Williams antici-pated some of the potential uses of cable television, including: news, weather and traffic information; shopping services; educational services; information from libraries; newspapers 'faxed' to the screen; public meetings and online voting (Williams 1990: 137). For these writers, the hope was that such systems would provide more equitable access to information for individuals, and that more groups would have the opportunity to provide information over such networks, including 'alternative' television programming under the 'access' requirements imposed on cable television companies by some regulators (Kellner 1985).

In the 1970s, however, cable television infrastructure was constructed from copper co-axial cable (similar to that used to connect a television aerial). This has a limited capacity, typically a few tens of analogue channels, and so the potential for carrying additional alternative television channels and two-way text and video information was limited, more so given the desire of the cable operators to offer as much popular programming as possible for which they could charge subscription fees. However, by the end of the 1970s a new cable technology was emerging, based not on copper wires and electrical signals but on optical fibres carrying light pulses. Optical fibres were heralded as a breakthrough in communications technology. They are tiny in comparison with co-axial cable (the fibre itself the diameter of a human hair, though the protective cladding results in a diameter of a millimetre or so); their channel capacity is measured in thousands rather than in tens; they are resistant to corrosion and to electrical interference, unlike copper; and the base material, silica, is cheaper (Li 1978). Commenting in the *Library Journal* on the potential for 'a bright information future' based on optical communication, James Rice welcomed a future of person-to-person and business videophone conversations, delivery of educational programmes, community surveys and polls, before adding in parenthesis a note of caution appropriate perhaps to his readership (but also anticipating a later debate): 'With optical communications, the entire 30 volumes of *The Encyclopaedia Britannica* can be clearly transmitted in a tenth of a second (copyright laws permitting)' (Rice 1980: 1137). By the beginning of the 1980s, the deployment of this new technology was suggesting that some of the wider expectations of the cable networks might finally be fulfilled.

The hopes that high capacity optical communications would see a flourishing of public access to information and exchange was voiced most loudly by activists and liberal commentators. For business leaders and the conservative governments coming to power in the 1980s (most notably those of Margaret Thatcher in the UK and Ronald Reagan in the US), the main advantage of fast communications was the competitive edge it offered business corporations over those relying on copper telephone lines. As Sussman notes, in the 1970s policy makers 'began to take cable seriously, some imagining that the system of delivery could be made to serve educational, public information, social, and cultural interests, as well as expanded commercial users', but over the following decades cable companies managed to free themselves of any obligations beyond the mere provision of commercial television (Sussman 1997: 118). In the UK, the government established the Information Technology Advisory Panel (ITAP) in 1981 to consider the mechanisms by which the country could be wired up as a communications grid, based on optical fibre systems. While one option would have been to charge the state-owned telecommunications monopoly British Telecom with the task, this was instead seen as an opportunity to bring commercial competition to bear on BT. The resulting legislation opened the market to commercial companies, who would bid for franchises to install and operate a cable network on a monopoly basis over a given area, typically a town or part of a larger city. These companies would bear the full cost of installing the network, but with a monopoly of provision for 15 years, they could eventually expect to see a return on the investment. The opening paragraph of ITAP's report, *Cable Systems*, indicated how companies were to be enticed (ITAP 1982: 7):

> Modern cable systems, based on coaxial cables or optical fibres, can provide many new telecommunications-based services to homes and businesses. The initial attraction for home subscribers would be the extra television entertainment channels. However, the main role of cable systems eventually will be the delivery of many information, financial and other services to the home and the joining of businesses and homes by high capacity data links.

So to attract potential network operators (and customers) the focus was to be the provision of television rather than telecommunications, and the cable companies would charge subscribers for these services, as was happening in the US. Just as satellite was beginning to deliver multichannel television in Europe, it was anticipated that similar demand for cable television would ensure that, almost by stealth, the UK would become a wired nation with the most modern telecommunications infrastructure.

To assist in the process, there would be no regulation on cable television content. Beyond restrictions on political bias and minimum standards of decency, cable could carry whatever it wished, with no minimum requirements in terms of news provision, drama or current affairs, such as those that applied to the existing terrestrial, public service television broadcasters. The same deregulation was also applied to DBS satellite television and marked the point at which UK television was most clearly to be seen as a commercial commodity rather than a public good.

This was far from a free market, however. Globalisation was not a word that tripped off politicians' tongues in the 1980s in the same way it did 20 years later, and in the hope of bolstering home industries, franchises could only be awarded to European-owned companies (non-European investors limited to a non-controlling interest). Equally, while BT was not allowed to become involved in the cable television business, cable franchise holders were not to be permitted to offer telephone services, the government recognising that BT's statutory obligation to provide universal service (even when uneconomic) meant that open competition from cable companies could severely damage it financially (no doubt, the government was also wary of limiting BT's appeal ahead of its imminent privatisation). With this measured but earnest commitment to minimal regulation, it was anticipated that the cable industry would flourish. Hollins suggests that ITAP members felt that cable 'was as inevitable as information technology itself' (1984: 57), while the Information Technology Minister at the time, Kenneth Baker, addressing the 1982 Edinburgh International Television Festival suggested, 'I am an optimist. I believe that we will have the whole nation cabled from Land's End to John O'Groats within ten years' (cited in Murphy 1983: 129). The expectations for cable, then, were in no doubt.

Unplugged: The Unravelling of Cable in the UK

Come 2008, more than a quarter of a century after Baker's speech, both Land's End and John O'Groats remain without cable services. The growth has been spectacularly slow in comparison with expectations and has now all but stopped. On paper, certainly, initial interest was high. After eleven pilot franchises had been awarded in 1983, the following year the Cable and Broadcasting Act established the Cable Authority to continue the process, and by the time the Authority became incorporated into the Independent Television Commission (ITC) in 1991 it had awarded a total of 135 franchises covering 70 per cent of the UK population, or almost 15 million homes. However, although this number of franchises had been awarded, only around 30 were actually operating by this time, with fewer than one million homes passed by cable; the other franchises remained at the planning stage. Further disappointment for the industry emerged when fewer households than expected opted to take the service. 'Penetration rates', the percentage of those able to take cable services (because it runs down the street in front of the house) who actually do so, hovered at around 16 to 18 per cent. Fortunes changed for the better when two of the few restrictions on cable companies were lifted. Parsons and Frieden explain succinctly (1998: 310):

> The United Kingdom has become a favorite location for cable television investment by U.S. companies, primarily because of the favorable economic and regulatory climate. The nation still has relatively few broadcast television options and cable television operators have the option of providing both cable television and telephone services. The United Kingdom was the first country to permit cable operators to provide telephony.

By 1988, when it was clear to the Cable Authority that most interest in cable franchises was coming from North America, the restriction on foreign ownership of cable operating companies was circumvented by various legal manoeuvres in the full knowledge of the Authority and the government (Goodwin 1998: 65). The restriction was formally rescinded in the 1990 Broadcasting Act, in which the limitations on cable companies operating full telephone services were also relaxed. Telephone services proved to be particularly attractive to customers, and thus the prospects for the cable industry looked a little brighter. The number of operating franchises began to increase (though it still didn't match the 1991 paper figure of 135 until the end of the 1990s) and so did the penetration rate to an eventual steady rate of about one in three (about a quarter of those taking *only* the telephone service). As interest rose, franchises began to be traded: Williams reports, 'In 1993 40 per cent of the industry changed hands as acquisitions and mergers changed the pattern of ownership' (1994: 26). By the end of the decade, however, the growth began to end when around half of the country's homes were passed by cable, concentrated naturally enough in urban centres. Penetration rates remained unchanged and so, since 2001, cable connections have stabilised with around one in eight of all UK households connected to cable television, and an additional third of that number connecting for telephone and, increasingly, internet access alone. These three million or so cable television subscribers are, however, dwarfed by the 19 million receiving multichannel television via either satellite or digital terrestrial routes.

How might we account for the poor performance of cable, a technology believed in the 1980s to be ready to propel the UK into the information age? Much of that expectation was based on the experiences of the US where, as we have seen, cable expanded dramatically throughout the 1980s. However, much of this growth was based on an already-established cable industry that had developed to fulfil a market gap: initially, improved reception, later providing additional content and advertisement-free, subscription television. In the UK, advertisement-free, public service television was already the norm and was universally available. Meanwhile, multichannel television had arrived first with satellite, and so for many, rather than wait for the cable companies to install the infrastructure, a slow and costly process, satellite was available earlier. Finally, a complex and at times farcical franchise-awarding process created expectations that could probably never be fulfilled. For example, the process of competitive bidding for franchises produced some bizarre contests: prospective franchise holders were required to bid an amount of money to win the franchise, an amount which would be paid annually to the ITC. Hence, one would expect some careful judgements and costings to result in similar bids from competing applicants. Some of the more interesting results for franchises awarded between 1995 and 1998 are shown in Table 4.1.

Naturally enough, before long many of these franchises were sold on or handed back to the regulator; for example US Cable returned the Shrewsbury franchise to the regulator in 1997 without building any network, while Convergence handed back its Taunton and Bridgwater licence within three months of it being awarded. By the time the ITC was incorporated into communications regulator Ofcom (Office of Communications) the UK cable network was dominated by two companies, ntl and Telewest, these two themselves merging in 2005 before being rebranded as Virgin Media in 2007.

Franchise area		
Carlisle Awarded 1995	One bid only	US Cable £1
Chichester & Bognor Awarded 1995	Sussex Cable £252,907	Nynex £9.14
Shrewsbury Awarded 1995	US Cable £497,280	SBC CableComms £1000
Canterbury & Thanet Advertised 1996	No bids at all	
Isle of Wight Awarded 1997	One bid only	Utility Cable/Fortuna £101,910
Taunton & Bridgwater Awarded 1997	Convergence Cable £426,027	Telewest £1001
Dumfries & Galloway Awarded 1998	One bid only	US Cable £11
N Wales & S Cheshire Awarded 1998	Metro Comms £258,408.00	Cable & Wireless £17.17

Table 4.1 Examples of cable franchise bids. *Source*: Independent Television Commission

Conclusion: Competing Platforms

Take a typical house in a typical industrialised country, and there are probably three ways by which television signals may be received: by terrestrial reception, direct reception via home-mounted satellite dish or by cable. At least two of these are probably available to most of the remaining, 'atypical' homes. One might think it odd then that all offer essentially the same services (a collection of channels offering niche, scheduled programming) when each has some physical characteristics which make it uniquely placed to offer something different. For example, in telecommunications, the particular strengths of terrestrial communication (via microwave link) and satellite are used to complement the original, wired telephone network. Similar unique characteristics of each platform might also apply in broadcasting: terrestrial transmission, with its network of transmitters, can readily be configured to offer localised or regional services, as well as networked national services; satellite is best placed to offer national and international programming, while cable clearly can deliver highly specialised services on a two-way basis. Though a rather simplistic notion, nevertheless it is instructive to consider possible alternative uses for these distribution platforms.

The technique of terrestrial radio wave communication is of course used in all manner of ways in addition to broadcasting, and thus already serves a variety of needs for short range and longer range communication.

Nevertheless, of the portion of the radio spectrum allocated for radio and television broadcasting, that part devoted to national broadcasting is increased, some would say disproportionately, by the obligation for universal service. To reach 99.5 per cent of the population with good quality national radio (FM) and television signals needs a lot of relay transmitters each with its own allocation of frequencies. Advocates of small-scale and community radio have frequently observed that such stringent requirements reflect a particular view of how broadcasting is to be organised (favouring established institutions like the BBC and larger commercial companies) and has the effect of limiting the use of the radio spectrum by local broadcasters (Lewis and Booth 1989: 21–9). While local and regional broadcasting certainly does exist, its scope could be widened if, for example, satellite transmission were used for national and regional programming to replace many of the frequencies currently used by terrestrial transmission.

In a similar vein, community television activists in the 1970s campaigned for access to the emerging cable systems. While the earliest cable systems did fill the gaps missing in terrestrial coverage in some countries, elsewhere, such as in the UK, there were no such gaps to fill. Nevertheless, cable has been seen essentially as no more than an augmentation of the existing, one-way broadcasting system, with only limited acknowledgement of the opportunities for local and community services presented by its inherently local physical nature (Hollander 1992). So while bids for the UK's cable franchises in the 1980s were not *required* to commit to community services, it was clear to an astute bidder that it would be wise so to do, and most did (Hollins 1984: 284). However, promises of studio facilities and community training for locally originated programming subsequently failed to transpire, as the cable network is used essentially to offer the same fare as provided by satellite and terrestrial television, competing with both merely as alternative platforms in the same market.

So, have the new television broadcasting technologies, satellite and cable, eclipsed the old terrestrial system in countries like the UK? Certainly they offer more channels, and each offers technical advantages to broadcasters. However, as these platforms emerged, the advantage the terrestrial system had was that it already existed, and the installation costs had been paid for many years previously in the public service era. That the traditional terrestrial channels remain the most watched in all homes, including in those with satellite and cable services, says far more about the content than the delivery technology. Moreover, while purely in terms of numbers of channels, in the 1990s terrestrial television certainly began to look distinctly limited with its choice of just four or five, a decade later all that has changed with the advent of digital broadcasting.

Digital Signals and Digital Broadcasting 5

Digital technologies have been used by broadcasters for decades, but only with the launch of public transmissions, of digital radio in 1995 and digital television in 1998, did all links in the chain from production to reception finally become digital. Although the beginnings of digital transmission were greeted with much excitement, justifiably in many cases, the inclusion of the transmission link was merely a further development in a longer process of digitisation of communications technologies, for the process of representing analogue quantities in a coded, digital form has its theoretical origins in the 1930s, and its practical realisation has been in use in telecommunications since the 1960s. If it is possible to carry analogue electrical signals from transmitter to receiver by either terrestrial, satellite or cable channels, then it is also possible to carry information in digital form by the same routes. Hence the beginnings of domestic digital broadcasting occurred more-or-less simultaneously on all three platforms, joined more recently by an additional platform where digital television is provided over a broadband internet connection based on asymmetric digital subscriber link (ADSL), although this only has a minor share of the market.

As with all major technological innovations, digital broadcasting was heralded with much hyperbole. Digital radio was classed as the biggest change since FM, for example, while the change in television was described as a 'revolution' leading to 'a multimedia information superhighway' (Hood and Tabary-Peterssen 1997: 85). While much of this talk was certainly based on the technically feasible rather than the magical (as it occasionally sounded), such views failed to identify the more immediate and prosaic consequences of digitisation for listeners and viewers, which were an increase in the number of channels available on the various platforms and a potential increase in quality of both sound and pictures. In essence, these advantages derive from the ability to perform complex mathematical operations on digital data (using computer processing) that are not possible with analogue, and digital technology's superior resilience to the noise and interference that can affect electronic signals. These two attributes alone lie behind much of the change in television and radio anticipated by digital media observers, and so it is useful to demystify the technology to understand quite how such changes are brought about.

Analogue and Digital Signals

The electronic signals used in analogue systems vary in size, or intensity, to reflect precisely the varying state of the physical phenomenon they are intended to represent. So the electrical output from a microphone (measured in one of two electrical quantities, its voltage or current, depending on design) should change in a way which faithfully reflects the pressure variations on the microphone diaphragm resulting from the changing sound. Similarly, the electronic signal produced by a video camera should go up and down in accordance with the changing levels of illumination on the CCD target as the image area is scanned. Loud sounds produce big signals from a microphone and quiet sounds produce small signals, for example. In an analogue device, then, if it were possible to measure the electrical signal at any part of the system, it would be possible to deduce something about the level of sound (or illumination) that produced it.

In a digital system, in contrast, there is no direct relationship between the size of the electronic signal and the physical quantity producing it. A digital electronic signal can only be in one of two states: a high value or a low value, conventionally labelled one and zero. (In practice, in an electronic device, the two values could represent different voltage levels, typically, 3 V for a 1 and 0 V for a 0.) So the state of the electronic signal is continually changing, like that in an analogue system, but in this case only between these two conditions. So, whereas an analogue electronic signal can adopt any value (within the equipment's operating limits) representing the continuously changing nature of sound or light, the digital system has to represent changing physical phenomena differently. It does this by using a coding system known as pulse code modulation (PCM), developed theoretically and understood as early as the 1930s. In the PCM technique, a sequence of digital signals are used in combination to represent differing levels of sound or light: a sequence of digital signals, even though each one individually can only be a 1 or 0, can in combination indicate a number of different values. Sometimes this range of values is extremely limited: for example, if there are only two digital signals in the combination, there are only four different ways in which they can combine (00, 01, 10 or 11). These individual digital signals are referred to as bits, from *bi*nary dig*its*. So the example here is of a 'two-bit' digital system, which can only represent four different levels of light or sound – it would probably not be of much practical use given the near-infinite variation in those two quantities to which our human senses are susceptible. But more bits in the combination increases exponentially the number of values that can be represented.

Digital signals representing analogue quantities: Quantisation

It may (or may not) help to imagine a typical living room in a house, illuminated by a number of lights (a ceiling light, table lamp, a couple of wall lights and so on). Each light individually can only be switched on and off, that is, it can only have two light levels. However, in combination, a number of lights can illuminate the room in a broad range of ways, from all lights switched off (darkness) to all lights switched on, with a number of variations in between – in fact, with four lights, 16 different combinations would be possible giving 16 levels of room illumination. Yet, each individual light itself could only be 'definitely off' or 'definitely on', 0 or 1. More lights still in the room would increase further the number of different lighting settings available – each additional light doubling the number in fact. Once a sufficient number of lights had been added, quite subtle variations in the overall lighting level would be possible by switching individual lights on and off, and ultimately this fine variability would approach the range of lighting levels offered by a single dimmer switch, which is an analogue device.

Returning from the (increasingly unsustainable) analogy to a real digital communications system, combining larger numbers of bits together allows such fine distinctions in sound or light levels to be represented that our senses cannot distinguish between this digital variability and that of an analogue system. Certainly, like four light switches, if only four bits were used for the codes, meaning only 16 levels of sound were available in the digital system, this would not produce good quality audio. The digital system would have to allocate all possible sounds to one or other of these 16. The process of allocating recorded sounds to one of a limited range of possible levels is known as quantisation (Figure 5.1). Ascribing all sound signals picked up by a microphone to just 16 different quantisation levels would in effect mean changing the analogue signal slightly from its measured value to match the quantisation level, producing quantisation error in the signal. On reproducing the sound at the receiver, it would be distorted, and this is known as quantisation distortion. To get decent quality digital audio, higher numbers of bits must be used in the coding process to allow far more quantisation levels. For example, the coding used in digitising sound for CD recordings uses a combination of 16 bits rather than the two or four in the examples above, and this allows for a total of 65,536 different quantisation levels to represent the sound at any one time. Although this is still a finite number, with this range of sound levels available at any instant in a digital CD device, it produces sounds indistinguishable from the range in an analogue device (as we know from experience in playing our CDs).

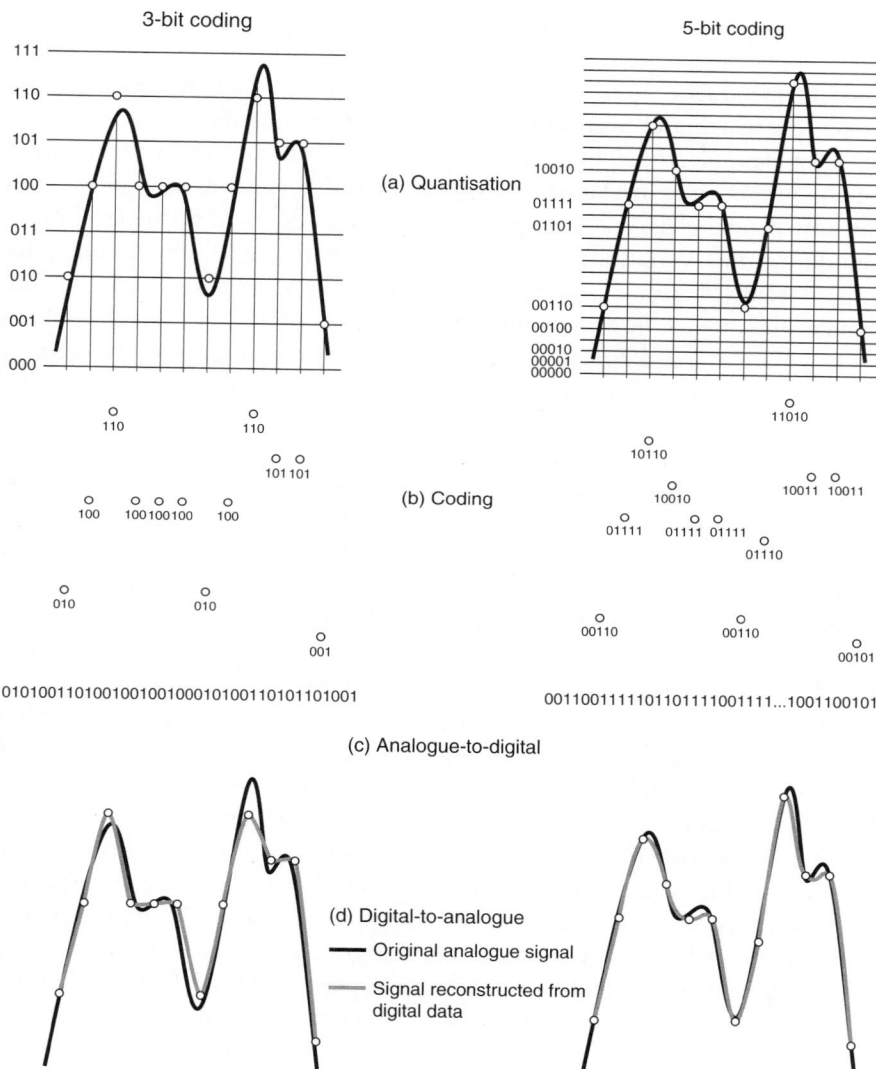

Figure 5.1 Quantisation and errors. (a) The analogue signal is measured at regular intervals and rounded to the nearest quantisation level. 3-bit coding allows for eight quantisation levels while 5-bit coding allows 32 levels. (b) Each quantisation level has a unique binary code. (c) The digital code for the analogue signal is simply a sequence of 0s and 1s. 5-bit coding generates more digital data than 3-bit for the same analogue signal. (d) On converting back from digital to analogue, 5-bit coding gives more accurate reproduction, that is, less quantisation error, because of the higher number of quantisation levels available, although more bits would give better accuracy still

Measuring the analogue variation: Sampling

The CD introduces the second aspect of converting an analogue quantity such as sound into a digital electronic representation (and sound probably makes for an easier example, though the same principles apply to any analogue quantity). Again, an analogue instrument such as a microphone seems straightforward: not only can its electronic output level go up and down with the level of the sound (or rather variations in air pressure), but it also works in real time, that is, its output (electronic) matches the input (air pressure) exactly, and as one changes the other follows suit immediately and continuously. Such simplicity is not possible in a digital system. Here, instead of continuously monitoring the sound in real time, the intention is to produce a rapid sequence of coded combinations of bits representing the changing value of the sound in digital form. So the sound is measured repeatedly at rapid intervals, each measured value being quantised and coded into its appropriate combination of 1s and 0s. This repeated measurement of the sound signal is known as *sampling*. Again, it might seem that this is an inferior practice compared with analogue, but provided the sampling rate is high enough, that is, the sound is measured frequently enough, we do not notice any gaps. The example of CD audio is again helpful: here the sound is sampled 44,100 times per second, and even those with the best hearing cannot tell that this is not continuous sound.

It is possible to derive mathematically a minimum value for this sampling frequency in any system. The most rapid changes in air pressure (staying with the example of sound for now) occur at the highest frequencies, a high note played on a violin, for example, at around 20 kHz (which actually exceeds the threshold of hearing for most people, who can only hear up to around 15 kHz, a limiting value which reduces as we age). Swedish-born American physicist Henry Nyquist showed as early as the 1920s that to sample a frequency such as this without losing any information, the sampling frequency should be at least twice as high. So the CD-audio sampling rate of 44.1 kHz is comfortably above the Nyquist minimum and is chosen to ensure all audible frequencies are captured in the sampling process. Put the other way round, Nyquist's theorem means that any given sampling rate used in the digitising process will limit the maximum frequency that can be converted to half the sampling frequency (Figure 5.2).

Analogue to digital conversion: ADC

Why is this complication necessary? The two techniques of sampling and quantisation together comprise the process of analogue to digital conversion (ADC). The input to the ADC system is an electronic signal (for instance from

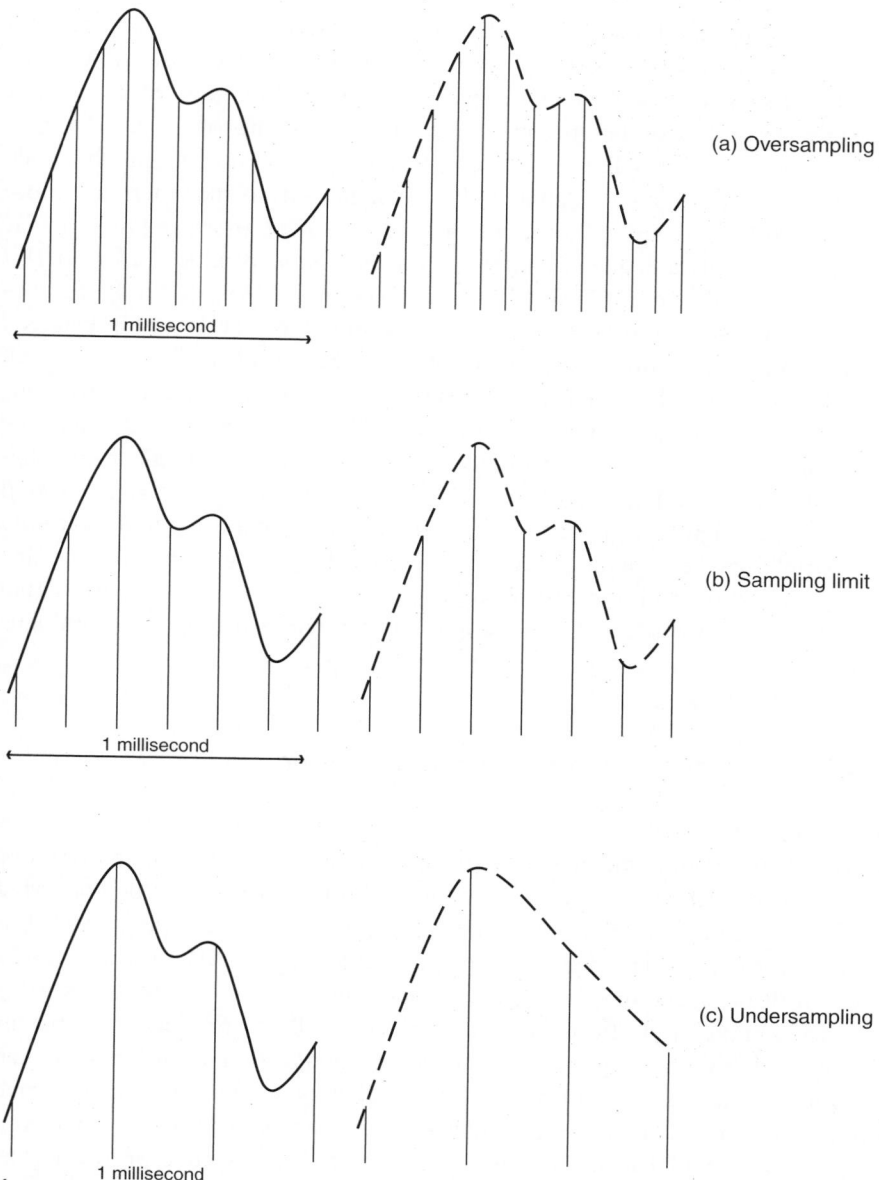

(a) Oversampling

(b) Sampling limit

(c) Undersampling

Figure 5.2 Sampling rates. The sampling rate must be high enough to capture the variations in the signal. (a) Here, 12 samples are taken per millisecond, easily capturing all the changes in the signal. (b) Six samples per millisecond is just enough to capture these variations. (c) Three samples per millisecond is too low a sampling rate to capture the fast variations in the signal. The highest frequencies, or fastest changes, will not be captured at this rate. The slower, lower frequency, general variation is caught, but the higher frequency detail is lost

a microphone, tape head, or camera), which is continuously varying according to the loudness, brightness or so on. What emerges from the ADC stage is a rapid sequence of data pulses representing combinations of 1s and 0s. In the case of CD audio, for example, this long string of 1s and 0s consists of groups of 16 digits for each sample, representing the 16-bit code for the state of the sound signal at that moment. Given that there are more than 40,000 such samples for each second of sound (the sampling rate is 44.1 kHz), the data sequence, known as a *bitstream*, produces $16 \times 44,100$ bits each second, around 700,000 bits per second (700 kbps). Unlike the signal in an analogue system, however, there is no obvious relationship between the emerging bitstream signal and the state of the sound. However, when all that data is decoded at the receiver, what the listener hears is the continuous sound made up of a sequence of over 40,000 sounds per second, each one corresponding to one of the 65,000 different sound levels available to the digital coding system. The advantages of converting the original analogue signal into a digital signal are essentially two-fold: in this digital form, it is readily compatible with computer processors allowing it to be manipulated in various ways and, in addition, the absolute 'on/off' (or 1/0) nature of the signal means that it is not affected by noise and interference as readily as an analogue signal.

DAC: A note on converting back to analogue

These advantages of digital signals mean that as far as possible the information being communicated through the system should remain represented in digital form. However, ultimately the electronic signal must be converted back into the physical quantity that was originally digitised, that is, sound or visual information. The digital to analogue conversion (DAC) is, naturally, a reversal of the ADC process in which each combination of bits representing a coded sample is in effect decoded mathematically to produce a particular signal level (that is, a particular electronic voltage or current) which then produces sound or light through a loudspeaker or screen. Once again, each sample is decoded in sequence and so, in the case of CD audio for example, a stream of 44,100 signal values are generated each second producing the varying signal levels matching the analogue information source. Ultimately, then, as Figure 5.3 shows, the concept is no different from the standard input-output model, and the ADC and DAC processes are simply employed to ensure that all electronic signals in the system are digitised and remain in digital form as much as possible, in order to benefit from its advantageous qualities mentioned above and described in more detail in the following paragraphs.

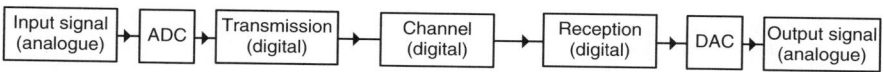

Figure 5.3 Input–output sequence: analogue and digital

Advantages of Digital Signals Explained

The requirements of our standard communications system are to convey information from source to destination, faithfully and efficiently. Faithful means without unacceptable degradation in the quality of the received information, while efficient relates to the amount of bandwidth required for the communication to take place. We have seen how there is often a tension between the two: AM radio produces poorer sound quality than FM, for example, but is more efficient in that it requires less bandwidth. Using digital signals addresses this tension: it has the potential to increase both the quality and efficiency of communication, although there remains a trade-off between the two.

Noise immunity

A distinct advantage of digital signals is that they are not affected by noise and interference in the same way as an analogue signal. Noise is a permanent feature of any electronic system, and in an analogue system, the noise signal is manifested as unwanted sound such as hiss or rumble in an audio system, or fuzziness or spots on a television picture. Interference is usually an occasional problem, perhaps heard on a radio when other stations transmissions are increased in relative size (such as on AM at night) or from external electrical sources such as during thunderstorms. Interference on a television picture is often caused by reflected signals and seen as shadowing or ghosting of the image. In these analogue systems, the unwanted signal is added to the wanted signal and produces audible or visible effects in receivers, because analogue devices are designed to accept electronic signals of all values. Thus it is not easy for the analogue electronic system to distinguish the original information signal from the additional noise.

A digital device is designed instead to work with signals of quite definite values. Here, the signal oscillates between two distinct levels, perhaps 3 V and 0 V, for example, for the 1 and 0 of a digital system. In this arrangement, the electronic circuits in a receiving device must identify the incoming signal merely as a 1 or a 0 and can have some latitude in making that distinction. Thus even if noise or interference distorts the signal level to some extent, it is still possible to identify it accurately as either a 1 or a 0 and thus to receive the intended information exactly and precisely (Figure 5.4). Only

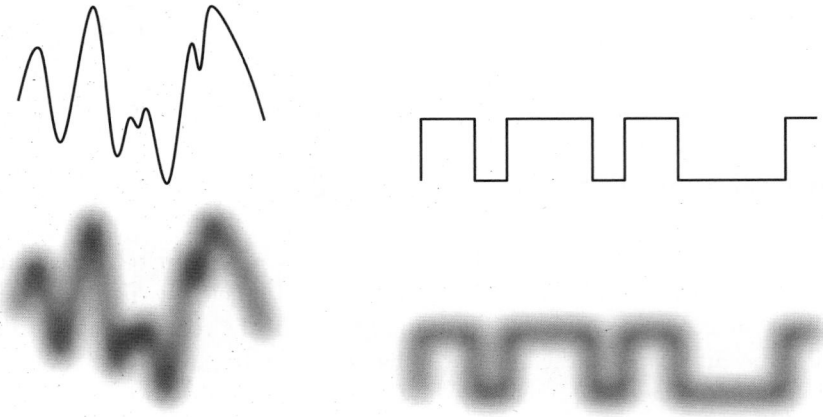

Figure 5.4 Effects of electronic noise. Noise is present in all signals, both analogue and digital. If the lines representing both signals are drawn as blurred lines to represent electronic noise, it can be seen that detail is lost more quickly in the analogue signal; the digital signal is still easily read as a 1 or 0 despite the presence of the same amount of noise

when the noise becomes very large in relation to the information signal will it become impossible to distinguish a 1 from a 0, but these levels of noise would already have completely masked the signals in an analogue system. So although noise occurs in digital systems just as it does in analogue, the integrity of the information signal is retained, a quality sometimes referred to as noise immunity.

The distinct nature of the electronic signals in a digital system also make it possible to 'clean up' signals at different stages in the communications system by generating new 1/0 pulses rather than simply relaying them on through the system. In an analogue system, noise is tackled by amplifying the signals as a whole, the desired information signal and the unwanted noise (as they cannot be distinguished), at various 'repeater' stages in the communications chain. While this should help to separate the information and noise signals by boosting the information the most, the noise continues to increase as it passes through the system. In a digital system, the intended value of the information signal is known precisely – it must be a 1 or a 0 – even in the presence of noise. In this case, rather than boosting both information and noise signals at a repeater stage, completely new, precise pulse signals are generated to replace the 'noisy' ones, and these can travel on through the system until noise becomes a significant concern again. In this way, by the time the digital signal reaches the end of the transmission chain, it is more or less as 'clean' as the original, since noise picked up on the way has been removed. The integrity of the signal is thus retained, and the signal power levels used can generally be lower, whereas in an analogue device continual boosting is needed to keep the information signal above the noise level.

The practical consequences are that electronic noise and interference, though still present in digital devices, do not produce perceptible consequences (unless the noise is substantial). A CD will play high quality audio even if its surface is dirty, whereas finger marks or dust on an analogue tape or vinyl record can produce audible distortion. In broadcasting, good quality sound and pictures may well be received from digital broadcasts in the kind of poor reception conditions which would cause unacceptable distortion to an analogue trans-mission. Further, because digital systems regenerate new, clean data rather than simply amplifying all signals, any copies made of digital signals (for example from CD to computer, or vice versa) are as good as the original. In comparison, copying an analogue tape to another tape produces notice-able degradation (known as generation loss), as the existing noise is copied with the desired signal and new noise is added in the copying process. Dig-ital copying is sometimes known as 'cloning' (because the copy is a newly generated replica of the original) and the possibility of creating copies of digital information in as high a quality as the original has of course caused problems for the music and video industries, who now face a problem of piracy many degrees more challenging than in the days of analogue piracy, when copies of video and audio tapes were invariably of relatively poor quality.

Error detection and correction

The quality of a digital signal is not guaranteed, however. As we have seen, the value of a digital signal remains distinguishable in the presence of quite large quantities of noise and interference, but equally once it gets to the level where noise can corrupt the signal, digital data can immediately be rendered completely useless. For in a coded system, the corruption of a single piece of data in a bitstream changes its meaning completely: two coded samples 11010 and 01010 mean quite different things even though just one digit has changed. For digital broadcasting, therefore, while digital signals *can* improve quality in conditions of poor reception, signals can equally be lost very easily when reception is marginal, as the loss of a relatively small quantity of data means the receiver is silenced or the screen goes blank! Given that terrestrial and satellite transmission are both affected by atmospheric factors such as air temperature and humidity, in certain circumstances when reception *is* marginal the receiver can be as prone to distortion (albeit of a different kind) as an analogue device, despite some of the myths about digital quality.

To a large extent, this susceptibility of digital data to corruption is ameliorated by the application of computer-processing techniques. Error correction methods are available, which enable the receiving device to check whether the digital samples have been received uncorrupted. Just as digital signals have been used as the basis of computing since the Second World War, when communications signals, including radio and television, are converted to digital format, they too can be processed mathematically using computing techniques. Error detection methods involve adding extra data to the bitstream which can be used by the receiver to ensure that there has been no corruption of the data between transmitter and receiver. This is known as adding redundancy as the extra, redundant data contains no information about the desired signal but is there merely to enable its accurate transmission. A relatively straightforward illustration of adding redundancy is known as parity error detection. Here, a single digit is added to a binary code for each sample before transmission, its value chosen to ensure odd or even parity, that is, the sum of the digits is an odd or even number. The receiver checks that all the samples received contain the correct parity before discarding the parity bit and recovering the original code. If a sample were received with incorrect parity, it would indicate that the code had been corrupted between transmission and reception, and this particular sample would be rejected by the receiver (Table 5.1).

						Parity bit added at transmission (redundant)	Parity check at receiver (sum of all digits)	Action at receiver
Sample A								
Transmitted	1	1	0	1	0	1		
Received	1	1	0	1	0	1	Even	Accepted as correct
Sample B								
Transmitted	1	0	1	1	0	1		
Received	1	0	1	1	0	1	Even	Accepted as correct
Sample C								
Transmitted	0	1	1	0	0	0		
Received	0	1	1	0	1	0	Odd	Rejected (code has been corrupted between transmission and reception)
Sample D								
Transmitted	1	0	1	1	1	0		
Received	1	0	1	1	1	0	Even	Accepted as correct

Table 5.1 Parity error detection identifies corrupted code received in Sample C (assuming 'even parity' system)

This example is of limited value as, should *two* bits become corrupted, parity would actually be restored, and the receiver would accept the corrupted sample. In practice then, this only offers minimal error detection, and more advanced techniques allow the precise digit in the sample that has been corrupted to be identified. Once this is done, the receiver no longer need reject the corrupted sample but can actually correct the error by reversing the value of the corrupted bit (in a binary system, if a bit is known to be incorrect, then logically its correct value is also known). Hence more sophisticated processing allows for error *correction* rather than error detection, though this usually means adding more redundancy. In general, the better the error protection required, the greater the redundancy that must be added; of all the data on a typical audio CD, for instance, as much as one third is redundant, that is, it contains no audio information but exists solely to enable errors to be detected and corrected. So the resilience of audio CDs is not just because of the inherent noise-resistant nature of digital signals but also because when errors do occur they can be corrected, to the point that audio CDs have been observed to play even after a hole has been drilled through them (try this at your own risk)!

Clearly, such error detection and correction techniques, based on computer processing, are not available to analogue systems, which means either that digital systems are more reliable and produce better sound and vision or, alternatively, to produce the same quality of sound and vision as an analogue system, digital hardware can be designed to less demanding specifications resulting in faster processing and, in theory, cheaper manufacture (in practice, cost savings are often outweighed by the additional functionality built into digital devices).

Digital Consumers: The Compact Disc

Digital technologies remained the province of professionals until the late 1970s, when the first digital consumer device was developed. Based on a similar laser-reading technique developed by Philips for its laser video disc, the audio compact disc, or CD, differed in that its data was stored and read in digital format. Launched publicly in the early 1980s, it was intended to replace the 12-inch (or 30 cm) diameter vinyl LP record, its advantages being its resistance to wear and tear, the ability to skip tracks and its compact size.

Like an LP, the CD contains its information in a spiral track which contains microscopic undulations: depressions, or pits, separated by flat areas known as lands. This physical nature of the storage medium means CDs can be mass produced quickly in a stamping process similar to vinyl, but the metallic layer containing the data in the form of a series of depressions, or pits, is encased in clear plastic to protect it. Reading the data is by means of an optical semiconductor laser, a novel electronic device in the 1970s that produces a finely focused beam of light which is reflected differently as it passes over the pits of the spinning disc: where the laser passes over a pit the reflected light is detected as a series of 0s, depending on the pit's length, while over a land it registers 1s. The use of a laser means there is no physical contact between the disc and the reading head, and thus no wear; in theory a CD should last for many decades. With its sampling rate of 44.1 kHz and 16 bit coding, as noted earlier, each second of audio generates over 700 kilobits of data, or twice as much for the two tracks in stereo recording. Added to this is up to a third as much data again in the form of redundancy, and despite the fine nature of the tracks on the disc (about 1 micrometre, or 1/1000 of a millimetre wide) the 120mm diameter CD can hold just over one hour of audio.

For the recorded music industry, the CD offered a welcome shot in the arm. Sales of vinyl LPs had been falling towards the end of the 1970s, partly because pre-recorded cassette tapes were being bought in increasing numbers, but the music industry suspected that recording of LPs and cassettes onto blank tape, that is piracy, was also suppressing sales – though convincing evidence for this is hard to find. The fact that the CD and its playing equipment could not record was a reassurance to the industry, but initial sales of CD players were slow (Winston 1998: 135). The increasingly popular cassette tape players *could* record, and the recordings were portable thanks to new personal audio players such as the Sony Walkman, launched in 1979; meanwhile, for those who already owned vinyl LPs and record players the advantages of CD players were perceived as marginal, while popular speculation raised questions about the longevity of CD discs (Horstmann and MacDonald 2003: 320). So despite the technical superiority of digital technologies, other factors influenced consumer adoption of the new format. However, with the music industry keen to speed the transition from LP to CD, more and more CDs were released as LPs were withdrawn, and increasingly people who had seen no need to buy a CD player began to feel they no longer had an option. Thus, while in 1984 just 800,000 CDs were sold in the US in comparison with 200 million LPs, by 1987 sales were more-or-less even at 102 and 107 million, respectively. By 1995, the transition was complete: just 2.2 million LPs were pressed while over 700 million CDs were sold. Winston describes this process as a 'curious history which, on its face, would appear to be a completely effective manipulation of the market by a few international communication conglomerates' (Winston 1998: 135–6). Hence, by the mid-1990s, more than half of all households in the UK (59 per cent in 1996) had acquired a digital consumer item, for many their first and the beginning of a gradual process in which most consumer audiovisual equipment has migrated from analogue to digital operation.

Bit Rates and Data Reduction

So if the CD signified the beginning of domestic digital environments, it was still a number of years before its video counterpart, the DVD (strictly 'digital versatile disc' but commonly 'digital video disc') made its appearance in 1995. At the same time, although the CD had introduced the idea of digital audio into everyday life, radio broadcasting (and television) remained resolutely an analogue audio medium. The explanation for this limited influence on domestic technology is both technical and political, the former relatively straightforward. The example of the CD demonstrates the enormous quantity of data produced by the ADC process: each second, 1.4 million bits of data are produced from a digitised stereo sound source, before redundancy for error correction is added, a bit rate of 1.4 Mbps. To transmit this quantity of data over airwaves would typically require a transmission channel bandwidth of 1 MHz or more (depending on the modulation technique). In comparison with the 250 kHz needed for a stereo FM radio broadcast, this is not only inefficient but in practical terms a non-starter given the existing constraints on radio spectrum. For television, a similar calculation based on digitising the standard definition number of lines using 10-bit sampling produces a theoretical video bit rate of as much as 270 Mbps which would require a bandwidth vastly in excess of the current 8 MHz (PAL) or 6 MHz (NTSC) allocation for analogue television. The sheer quantity of data produced by digitisation made it impracticable to put video onto a CD-like disc and for broadcasting over the airwaves would imply severely restricting the number of channels on offer. Given that one of the claimed advantages of digital broadcasting is an *increase* in the number of channels, something else must be going on.

There are some obvious ways in which the volume of data produced by digitising an analogue signal can be reduced. The quantity of data is a product of two factors, the sampling rate and the number of bits used in the coding. Lowering the sampling rate would result in a reduction in data produced, but (following Nyquist's rule) at the expense of limiting the range of frequencies that can be converted. In audio, this means that the high notes would be lost, while in television the resolution would be degraded. The alternative of reducing the number of bits used in the coding process produces a disproportionate quality sacrifice for the quantity of data saved. For example, if audio was sampled with 8-bit coding rather than 16, it would reduce the quantity of data produced by a half, but the number of quantisation levels available would reduce from 65,536 to just 256, a dramatic reduction in sound quality. A further option in television is to reduce the frame rate: reducing frame rates from the standard 30 or 25 to, say, 15 or 12.5 again would reduce the data by a half but is then below the threshold for acceptable representation of motion. Needless to say, then, the consequent effects on sound and picture quality mean these crude approaches to data reduction are not acceptable (certainly in order to maintain broadcast quality), and more sophisticated techniques have been developed.

Commonly referred to as data compression (or simply 'compression', though this term also has another meaning in audio) the aim of data reduction techniques is to reduce the quantity of data produced by digitisation without causing an unacceptable loss in quality of picture or sound. Numerous international standards have been approved by the ITU, and in broadcasting these have been developed by the Motion Pictures Experts Group (MPEG, pronounced 'em-peg'), a body of engineers drawn from academic and industry institutions. While these techniques are inevitably mathematically complex, the principle of the processes is relatively straightforward and is based on mathematical modelling and subjective testing of the limitations of human perception. The subjectivity involved explains why the intention is to avoid *unacceptable* loss in quality, and there has been some debate about what does constitute acceptable quality. An understanding of the principles of data reduction goes some way in illuminating the debate.

First, however, it should be noted that there are some methods by which data can be reduced without any implications for quality. So-called lossless compression involves looking for patterns such as repetition within the bitstream produced by digitisation and eliminating data by sending the repeated pattern just once, with additional information about the number of repetitions. For example, consider an image in which a third of the scene was made up of blue sky, all of the same colour. An analogue image scanning process would send signals from all 200 or so lines in sequence (625-line system), and all those covering blue sky would contain the same information. A digitised version of the same lines would contain the 10-bit codes for the samples of the first pixel and, obviously, the same codes for the next pixel and so on for thousands more pixels (note: when analogue video is digitised, the sampling process effectively converts the continuous lines of analogue signals into a discrete series of pixels, hence reference to 'lines' in analogue and 'pixels' in digital). Logically, sending the codes for the first pixel alone, together with additional coded data specifying the number of following pixels that should contain the same data (that is, the same colour), would save an enormous amount of data. The receiver would then receive both the coded samples from the first pixel and would recreate the next few thousand based on the same information, according to the instructions sent with the pixel data. Provided the receiver is able to process the instruction codes, no visual information is lost, and the resulting picture would look the same as if the data had been sent separately for each individual pixel.

This technique is more appropriate to certain kinds of scene, principally those in which there are broad blocks of the same colour (animation is one example) but in all images there is a degree to which information is repeated from pixel to pixel. So this technique, known as run length encoding, is used as far as possible, potentially yielding an uncompromised result. Such lossless techniques, however, can only produce so much reduction in data, as most scenes will include perhaps subtle but nevertheless real variations in tone and brightness, and thus only a limited amount of repetition, so the capabilities of lossless methods can soon become exhausted.

At this point further techniques are employed. These rely on the limitations of our perception and mean ignoring or, effectively, eliminating minor changes in brightness or colour (or sound in audio data reduction). Thus if there were just small variations in the hue of the blue sky in the example above, it might be possible to ignore those differences and treat all the sky as being the same blue, which then opens up the possibility of further data reduction based on the run length encoding technique. This is 'lossy' compression in that the original image can never be fully recovered or recreated at the receiver – some information is permanently lost (discarded is actually a better word, as it is a deliberate rather than accidental effect) and the resulting image (or sound) will be different from the original. The idea, though, is that this difference either is undetectable, that is, below the threshold of perception, or is at least acceptable, and viewers and listeners do not perceive any reduction in quality. Similar variations relying on perceptual limitations include limited sensitivity to colour variations, exploited in colour television (see Box 3.1), which means that fewer quantisation levels (and therefore bits) need be allocated to certain kinds of colour variation than to others. Such thresholds are deduced from empirical, subjective studies (that is, from listeners' and viewers' responses to laboratory controlled tests) and can be defined mathematically and incorporated into complex, lossy data reduction algorithms. These algorithms, or sets of logical rules, are performed (using computers) on the array of data emerging from the digital signal derived from the sound or image; such algorithms, which were first developed for still images by the Joint Photographers Experts Group (JPEG – 'jay-peg'), are widely used in electronic imaging. Once again, the ability to process digital audio and video data by computer makes sound and vision amenable to such data reduction techniques, but while some of the basic methods have been known since the 1950s, only in the last decade or two have computers become powerful enough to prompt the development of ever more sophisticated techniques. JPEG data reduction has the facility within it to choose the level of compression, with the lowest levels of compression offering the highest quality output, typically offering a reduction in data to around one-tenth or even one-twentieth or the original amount. Choosing higher levels of compression reduces the amount of data still further, but image quality can begin to suffer, and artefacts such as pixilation or poor colour rendition begin to become noticeable. Again, then, we note that there remains a tension between quality and quantity of data in the digital world just as in the analogue.

Video compression

The same JPEG still image data reduction method can obviously be applied to each frame in a sequence of video, but further reduction can be obtained by looking at variations between successive frames, so-called interframe compression. Just as intraframe compression, described above, can economise on data by seeking repetition from pixel to pixel within the frame, if the same pixels are unchanged over a number of frames, there is no need to send the data for those pixels from successive frames. In combination, *intra*frame compression (sometimes referred to as spatial compression) and *inter*frame compression (or temporal compression) can produce dramatic data reduction rates, standardised as a set of MPEG formats.

So interframe compression extends the techniques of intraframe compression to sequences of frames. Where there is repetition between frames, lossless compression is possible, but equally when there are subtle variations between frames which would go undetected by the viewer, lossy compression can be employed effectively discarding such differences. A further stage of lossy interframe compression is interpolation between frames. In many cases, a sequence of frames from a section of video will only change in a particular part of the frame. For example, a bird flying across the sky for a second or so will contain perhaps 20 frames with essentially the same background, and only the pixels representing the bird will change from frame to frame. The changes between two adjacent frames will be small indeed. Provided the data is sent for, say, the first, seventh and 13th frames, linear interpolation can be used to reconstruct the missing ten frames in a process known as motion compensation (Figure 5.5).

One consequence (of many) of this temporal compression is that processing the predicted frames inserts a delay in the transmission-reception chain. Irrespective of the decoding of the compressed data, if the second or third frame in the sequence cannot be reconstructed until after the next I- or P-frame has been received, the full pictures can be displayed in some cases only after a second or two have elapsed after transmission, a delay which is clearly noticeable when comparing television side by side on digital and analogue receivers.

As with intraframe compression, some kinds of video sequences are more amenable to interframe compression than others. Frames within sequences with lots of movement or action, such as sport, will be less easily predicted than slower paced pictures such as news or nature programmes, where the differences between frames will be less. However, different levels of data

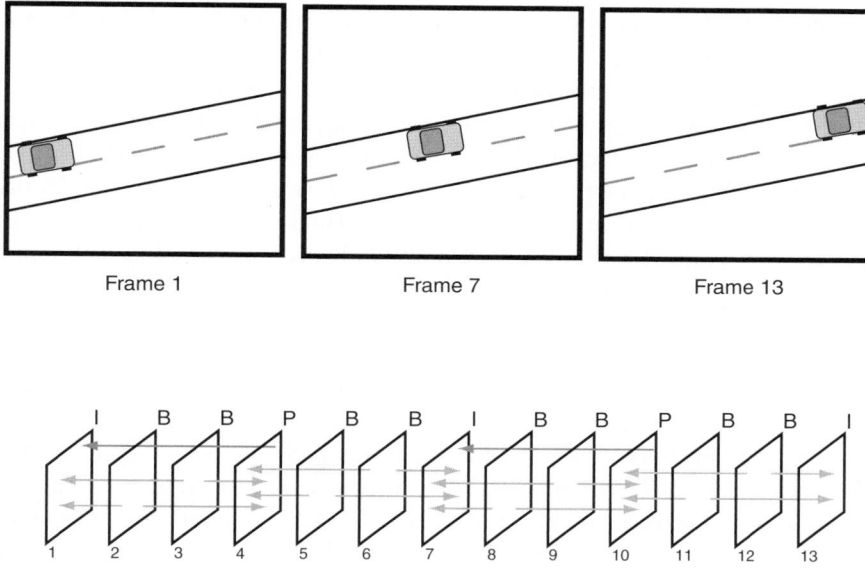

Figure 1

Frame 1   Frame 7   Frame 13

Figure 5.5 Motion compensation (see Benoit 1997). An aerial shot sees a car cross the scene from left to right, taking around half a second, or 13 frames. Rather than transmit all 13, motion compensation allows ten of these to be recreated at the receiver by predicting them from the remaining three. Some frames, the 'intra' or I-frames, are sent in their entirety, and remaining frames recreated from these. 'Predictive', P-frames are interpolated entirely from I-frames, interpolating the location of pixels representing the car (and any other changes) from the previous I-frame, while 'bidirectionally-predictive' B-frames use both the previous and next I and P frames to establish the location of the car. The frames are thus generated at the receiver out of sequence (frame 2 in this example cannot be recreated until frame 4 has been predicted from frame 1) and must be re-ordered before display

reduction can be applied by broadcasters at different times, depending on the programming, and in general, using the full capacity of MPEG interframe and intraframe compression, it is possible to reduce the amount of data in a digital television bitstream from a figure vastly exceeding the existing analogue bandwidth to one in which around six digital television signals may be carried within a single 8 MHz channel. Thus the quantitative advantage of digital signals, an increase in the number of channels, is delivered.

Audio compression

A moment's reflection will reveal that there is no equivalent in audio to the video data reduction techniques based on pixel repetition. Audio information consists of continuous variations (based upon the vibrations of air molecules) and without this, there is no sound. A different approach to data reduction is taken in audio. First, however, it should be noted that the situation is not quite so critical in audio; as with analogue technology, digitising audio produces far less data than video, and so in considering how to reduce the data in a television signal, for example, most effort is devoted to the visual element rather than the audio. Nevertheless, as the earlier example shows, the quantity of data produced in CD audio is far in excess of that which can be transmitted over the air within an FM radio channel, and so data reduction techniques are certainly required for radio broadcasting. The techniques used are based upon psychoacoustic modelling, analysis of the elements of sounds in terms of how we hear them. Again, the idea is that some components of sound can be removed without us noticing they are not there. For example, slight variations in sound may be below the threshold of hearing; similarly some high frequency sounds may be at the limit of hearing and, if accompanied by other frequencies, may be discarded. A further phenomenon, based upon subjective testing of listeners, is audio masking: if there is a loud sound followed in short succession by a quiet sound, the quiet sound can be removed and we do not hear the difference. Perhaps more counter-intuitively, if a quiet sound *precedes* a loud sound, again the quiet sound can be eliminated. Already, it can be seen that in audio any data reduction is lossy; there is no real scope for lossless compression.

Applying these techniques can result in reductions in audio data of a factor typically between five and ten, without producing noticeable change in audio quality, and this method, based upon the MPEG Layer II standard, is used in both the audio in digital television broadcasting and in digital radio broadcasting.

Problems can arise if lossy compression techniques are employed repeatedly. For example, a piece of video or audio might be compressed for storage or carriage purposes, and then the data might subsequently be expanded or 'uncompressed', that is, the data file might be opened up for further editing or other processing, before being compressed once more for storage. Given that at each stage some data is discarded, the effects of each successive compression-expansion cycle can build up to the point where the missing data becomes noticeable. Such 'digital artefacts' become visible in video as pixilation or blockiness, or the occasional blip or burble in digital audio. In general, the preferred option is to use lossless compression as far as possible during production and post-production so that lossy compression is only applied at the final storage or transmission stage. However, for video certainly, with its huge volume of uncompressed data, this is frequently not possible, and even within the camera there may be some low-level lossy compression in order to capture enough footage on the camera's storage medium. Digital audio recorders frequently allow uncompressed recording, but of course this limits the recording time available on the device. So, despite the advantages of digital signals, an increase in the quantity of information we might wish to store or transmit is at the expense of a possible reduction in quality. The sort of decisions which had to be made to balance competing quality-quantity demands in early analogue standards are, therefore, also necessary in the establishment of digital formats.

The Introduction of Digital Broadcasting

Managing the transition from analogue to digital broadcasting is a mammoth challenge. As we noted in Chapter 4, the sheer success of radio and television in its analogue form creates difficulties that would not arise in a niche market. When most homes in countries like the UK have at least two television sets and a handful of radio receivers, sensible politicians would be very wary of pronouncing an end to analogue broadcasting. Yet the ultimate goal is just that, implying that all of these receivers will in time have to be replaced, or adapted, with digital equipment.

It is in terrestrial broadcasting that the challenge is greatest. For one thing, with many governments, as in the UK, having eradicated most regulations that might have applied to satellite and cable television providers there would anyway be only limited scope for intervention in these sectors, and here implementation of the transition has necessarily been left to the operators themselves. Moreover, in many European countries only terrestrial broadcasting reaches almost all the population: the scale of the challenge faced by satellite and cable companies is a lesser one on the basis of a smaller customer base alone. The reverse applies in the US, where most households receive their main television service through cable and satellite and, ironically, the prospect of securing a digital transition in terrestrial television faces challenges due to its relative insignificance. Terrestrial television, however, stands to benefit most from conversion to digital transmission, allowing increases in the number of channels from single to mid and ultimately high double figures, beginning to approach the multichannel offerings of cable and satellite services. For radio, where analogue listeners can already typically choose from between ten and 20 stations – and, of these, most of the time an average listener selects just two – the advantage of the increased number of stations offered by digital transmission has proved less compelling.

The technical design of the digital broadcasting system implies a quite different structure for terrestrial transmission. In analogue broadcasting, a television channel or radio station is transmitted on a particular frequency channel over a particular area; the same content is then networked around the country to give national coverage where desired, using different frequencies in adjacent areas to avoid interference. A broadcaster is then allocated a number of transmission frequencies for that networked coverage, the allocations being made by a regulating body such as Ofcom in the UK or the FCC in the US. The introduction of additional channels can only be achieved by spectrum planning to ensure that new frequencies are available for the area where the channel is to be available. In other words, the broadcaster has a direct relationship with the transmission process, in effect an 'ownership' of a frequency channel, and indeed for radio stations the transmission frequency becomes an important part of its identity. The analogue broadcaster carries out the transmission, including building the transmitter network (although this is often subcontracted to a transmission company), and it is the broadcaster who is responsible both for maintaining the service on air and for its transmission quality.

All this is changed in the digital system. Rather than allocating a single station or channel to a single frequency, the most widespread digital broadcasting systems bundle a number together onto each frequency channel. In the case of the digital video broadcasting (DVB) system adopted across Europe, this bundle of television stations is transmitted within a frequency channel (known as a multiplex) which is 8 MHz wide, equal to that used in analogue transmission. For the digital audio broadcasting (DAB) system used in most countries around the world, the multiplex is 1.5 MHz wide, around six times wider than the frequency channel allocated for a single FM station in the analogue world. (Some countries, notably the US, have adopted standards other than DVB for television, while the US and a number of other countries are using or considering systems other than DAB for radio. These differences are covered later in this chapter.) Because of the data reduction processes applied before transmission, a DVB multiplex can typically carry six television stations, together with a number of radio stations and some data associated with the programme (for on-screen displays and so on), while a DAB multiplex can carry up to ten radio stations in varying degrees of audio quality. Under this arrangement, it no longer makes sense to allocate a whole multiplex frequency to a single broadcaster, since the multiplex would need to be occupied by several television channels or radio stations rather than just one; effectively then, under the digital system, broadcasters' twin roles of content creation and of transmission are separated, with the introduction of a third party responsible for transmitter operation, the multiplex operator.

Alongside this change in the organisation of broadcasting, the new digital transmission systems introduced other changes. Like analogue broadcasting, the digital signals are transmitted from an array of transmitters around the country, in most cases sharing the existing analogue transmission sites. The television multiplexes in fact use unused frequencies within the existing allocation for analogue transmission, while the DAB radio transmissions were allocated new frequencies within the so-called Band III of the VHF segment previously used for 405-line television (the UK was initially allocated a 12.5 MHz segment between 217.5 and 230 MHz, but this was augmented to 19.5 MHz following international agreements at the Regional Radiocommunications Conference in 2006). The transmission patterns are essentially unchanged then, and by choice of transmitter sites and power, coverage patterns could be tailored to national, regional and local coverage in exactly the same way as in analogue transmission. For nationally networked coverage, or larger regions, one advantage offered by digital transmission is that there is no need to use different frequencies in adjacent transmission areas; using the same frequencies in a so-called single frequency network does not cause interference as it does in analogue, and this results in greater efficiency in the use of frequencies. For local coverage, it remains necessary to use different frequencies in adjacent areas in order to carry different programming, and so the efficiency of the single frequency network facility is diminished as the transmission areas get smaller.

So digital transmission techniques offer greater efficiency in usage of frequencies, and this, together with data reduction techniques, offers greater capacity and thus the opportunity for more television and radio stations. The composition of the multiplex capacity can also be varied by the operator so that at different times additional stations can be included on a temporary basis, with no changes needed at the receiver. For example, the BBC operates a sports station, Five Live Sports Extra, on a part-time basis to cover particular sports events, in addition to its permanent stations. The radio receiver simply adds this station to its menu list without any action by the listener. Hence the operation of the digital transmission multiplex introduces structural changes in broadcasting, the separation of content creation and transmission and the need to share multiplex capacity with other competing broadcasters potentially having significant economic and political consequences.

Why Digital Broadcasting?

Governments seeking to introduce digital terrestrial broadcasting have had to consider how to manage the introduction of this new organisational arrangement. In addition to the regulatory and licensing arrangements, migration to digital broadcasting requires broadcasters to prepare to begin digital transmissions, manufacturers to build and sell digital equipment and consumers to then buy it in sufficient numbers. Some of the decisions to be taken include the following: should coordination between broadcasters, multiplex operators and manufacturers be left to the market or should government intervention kick start the process? Should new licences for the new channels be given to existing broadcasters or to new entrants? Should they be sold to the highest bidder, or given away with obligations attached? Who should operate the transmission multiplexes? Who should pay for consumers to upgrade their equipment (Galperin 2004: 16)? None of the answers to these questions is obvious, although most countries recognise the need for some level of intervention to achieve the necessary coordination to resolve the traditional chicken-and-egg situation: broadcasters, particularly commercial broadcasters, are reluctant to begin digital transmissions when there is no audience; manufacturers equally would not wish to begin manufacturing new, unproven equipment if retailers and, ultimately, consumers are not likely to buy it; meanwhile, consumers of course will not buy the equipment, and so retailers will not stock it, while there is either only minimal digital programming to be received or even none at all.

Despite such difficulties then, digital broadcasting was seen as important enough by governments around the world to adopt intervention strategies to begin the transition and, given that when digital broadcasting was being developed during the 1980s and 1990s, political consensus was (at the level of rhetoric at least) against intervention in markets, the question arises as to what was the motivation for making an exception here. Certainly broadcasters themselves were not the leading drivers towards digitisation, despite any technical benefits it might offer (after all, there is no obvious reason why existing broadcasters would welcome the addition of new, competing channels). Galperin suggests three principal motives for governments to develop digital broadcasting: to provide a boost to the domestic consumer electronics industry, a belief in the idea of an imminent 'information society' and increasing demands on the radio spectrum (Galperin 2004). The first of these reflects a number of trends during the 1970s and 1980s. European consumer electronics (CE) manufacturers had lost considerable shares in global exports to Japan and the newly industrialising countries (NICs) of South East Asia, and it was believed that in developing digital broadcasting as a European project, and thus requiring consumers to replace all analogue reception equipment, they would create a huge boost to the European CE sector, which could then take a lead in the global market. This was explicitly acknowledged in the proposal form for the European Union's Eureka 147 project under which the DAB system was developed (Eureka 1986):

After agreement of this [DAB] standard, the path will be opened up for the European entertainment electronics industry to stimulate a virtually saturated market with new products for car and domestic audio broadcasting units. In turn, this will encourage considerable innovation from European microelectronics manufacturers. The drawing up of a new digital audio broadcasting standard will therefore provide a long term counterbalance to the increasing dominance of the countries of the Far East in the consumer electronics sector.... As a new means of radio distribution the DAB system opens up new broadcasting markets in terms of coverage and services (e.g. operation of conditional access services) and even more important new markets for professional and consumer equipment. There is a good chance for worldwide adoption of these innovative systems. Due to the incompatibility with the existing systems (AM, FM) consumers have to obtain new receivers and broadcasters new transmitter networks.

This incentive to develop digital broadcasting was less keenly felt in the US, where the CE industry had long been relatively minor, and there was thus inevitably a huge trade deficit in CE goods, more than $10 billion in 1988, for example (Galperin 2004: 30). However, the second factor, a belief in the imminence of an information society, was a driver on both sides of the Atlantic. The prospects of an information-rich society, with greater equality and opportunity brought about by telecommunications, had been debated with the expansion of cable television systems, particularly in the US but also elsewhere such as in the UK (see previous chapter). By the late 1980s, it was clear that cable television had not brought about the plethora of services that had been anticipated and, in the UK at least, take up of cable television remained low. The digital signals used in DVB would naturally be more compatible with other data-based services, and so digital terrestrial television offered a new opportunity to realise some of the promise that cable had failed to deliver. With a 99 per cent take up of analogue television, a switch to digital would eventually ensure universal provision, and so, by 1990, George Gilder could publish a book with the title *Life After Television*, while Humphreys and Lang later echoed the sentiments of many in suggesting that 'digital television is therefore likely to be one of the cornerstones of the "Information Society"' (1998: 10). Digital television became part of the mix that generally heralded the new 'information superhighways', and initiatives to steer developments were established both in the US and in Europe, the Clinton administration setting up the US Information Infrastructure Task Force in 1993, while the European Commission established a working group under commissioner Martin Bangemann, which reported the following year. This notion of an information society is discussed further in Chapter 8.

The third incentive, the pressure on the existing radio spectrum, derives from the goal of switching off analogue broadcasting completely when migration to digital services is complete. In the UK, for example, it is anticipated that when analogue television is switched off, 112 MHz of what is considered the spectrum of 'most value' will be freed up for other uses, including mobile communication (Ofcom 2006a: 18). (In comparison the VHF spectrum freed up by switching off analogue radio in favour of DAB would be of little value as it has less favourable propagation characteristics and lower capacity.) Given that in a competitive auction in March 2000 five mobile phone operators bid £22.5 billion for UK spectrum licences for third-generation mobile services, almost five times as much as had been anticipated, 'value' in this context represents a significant potential windfall for the government.

Overall, then, even if broadcasters were not initiators of the drive to digital broadcasting, governments (and the electronics industry) had enough reasons to press ahead with its development.

Digital Terrestrial Broadcasting in the UK

In the first years of digital broadcasting, the UK had the highest levels of digital television take up in Europe, based largely on early conversion of existing analogue satellite viewers and later on significant growth in digital terrestrial television (DTT). The US followed with slightly lower levels of digital television, but here digital terrestrial viewing was a tiny proportion with most digital television delivered via cable and satellite. The UK has so far then been most successful in rolling out digital terrestrial services. Radio has been less successful than television everywhere, but again the UK, along with Denmark, also has the highest take up of DAB radio.

What lay behind this relatively rapid take up? In August 1995, the government published a White Paper outlining its plans for digital terrestrial broadcasting (DNH 1995). There were slight differences between the proposals for television and for radio. For television, six frequency channels would be available to carry the multiplexes, and it was estimated then that each multiplex would have the capacity for three television channels. The single frequency network arrangement meant that in many places 18 television channels would be available instead of the four (or in some areas five) on analogue services, though not all multiplexes would be able to cover the country equally because of frequencies already in use for analogue television. Conditional access mechanisms were to be permitted so that subscription services were to operate on terrestrial television for the first time, though of course these were already in operation on satellite and cable. The biggest change, however, one that caused the most protest from existing broadcasters, was the arrangement for operating the multiplexes, that is, running the digital transmission networks. As outlined above, the multiplexes in the digital broadcasting system would necessarily be run by a third party, but the White Paper proposed that licences to run the multiplexes would be awarded by the regulator, the ITC, to commercial organisations which would operate them on a for-profit basis, charging broadcasters for carriage of their content. Beyond minimal regulation in terms of decency and political bias, the ITC would not be able to dictate which channels the multiplex operators chose to carry. Rather than arranging for the regulator itself, or the broadcasters, to run the multiplexes, these new multiplex operators were to occupy a position similar to satellite television providers such as BSkyB or to the cable television companies, which did not originate their own programming but contracted with providers for carriage.

While there were provisions within the proposals that guaranteed carriage of their existing terrestrial channels on the digital multiplexes, the incumbent broadcasters would still need to pay commercial rates for this carriage and, encumbered by their public service obligations, this rankled given that the multiplex operators were to be permitted to carry any additional programming without restriction in the same way that satellite and cable services were largely unregulated. This in many ways satisfied the free market urges of the Thatcher government – all three platforms, terrestrial, satellite and cable, would now operate on the same basis, and the historical association of terrestrial television with universal free public service provision was to end. The public service broadcasters were of course free to contract with the multiplex operators to carry any additional channels they might want to launch but would have to compete with any other content provider. In a notable but paradoxical concession to the public service broadcasting principle, the BBC was to be allocated its guaranteed space on the multiplex which had the largest geographical coverage, while ITV and Channel 4 would be on the multiplex with the next largest coverage. Thus there was an emphatic rejection of the incumbent broadcasters' original proposals that they should each be given their own multiplex: with only six multiplexes available, allocating one multiplex per broadcaster would mean that the whole of digital terrestrial broadcasting would be in the hands of just six broadcasters, and moreover each broadcaster would have three television channels at its disposal. This would not have gone far enough for the government in opening up terrestrial television to full and open competition, with a plethora of new entrants competing for audiences, and so the model adopted was that which had already been pursued in satellite and cable television. Thus there was a clear implication that the introduction of DTT would represent a radical overhaul of the broadcasting industry in the UK, given that at that time terrestrial television was by far the dominant platform (of the 24 million households in the UK in 1995, cable had only one million connected, while BSkyB had just over three million).

Things were slightly different for radio. There was still to be a new tier of organisation, the commercial multiplex licence holder, who would be broadly free to contract with whichever radio stations they wished, but this time the BBC was given control of its own multiplex, again the one anticipated to have the greatest geographical coverage. As a national radio broadcaster, with an existing suite of five radio stations, it made sense for the BBC to have control of its own multiplex (five stations were enough to almost fill the multiplex, although more were added later). The BBC had already begun experimental DAB transmissions, the government noted, and more so than in television there was a clear distinction between the public service radio output of the BBC, with an emphasis on speech and arts programming, and commercial radio, which was dominated by mainstream pop and rock music formats. So the BBC had its secure place in digital radio, but commercial radio was to be given a boost too. There was also to be another nationally networked multiplex to carry commercial radio, while four of the remaining five digital radio multiplex frequencies were to be configured for local transmission, reflecting the tradition of local radio in analogue broadcasting (the use of the final multiplex frequency remained undecided at that point). Given the need to operate adjacent local multiplexes on different frequencies, this arrangement meant that a typical listener would receive stations via two national multiplexes and two local multiplexes (though some would only receive one local multiplex, while a few might be able to receive three). With each multiplex expected to carry five or six radio stations, it was expected that most listeners who switched to digital radio would receive about half as many stations again as analogue (in practice, multiplexes are now carrying eight to ten stations, so doubling the number of stations available to many listeners). With the exception of the BBC multiplex, all multiplexes were to be operated by commercial companies in the same way as digital television, with space being guaranteed on the national commercial multiplex for the three existing UK-wide commercial stations, while the BBC had reserved space on the appropriate multiplex for its local radio stations. Otherwise, regulation was again minimal, and radio stations would need to engage in commercial contracts with their local (or national) multiplex operator for carriage of their broadcasts.

By the time these proposals contained in the White Paper became legislation under the 1996 Broadcasting Act, little had changed. Despite the protests of existing broadcasters, the commercial nature of the multiplex licensing system was largely to remain, although the BBC was now given control of its own television multiplex, with ITV and Channel 4 to jointly run the second multiplex. Channel 5, which was about to launch as a new service on analogue terrestrial television, was awarded half the capacity of the third multiplex, leaving three and a half multiplexes unallocated, which the ITC was charged with advertising in open competition. It was now estimated that each television multiplex could carry six rather than three television channels, making a total of 36 available in much of the UK and so, following digitisation, terrestrial television's capacity would be dramatically expanded, by a factor of more than seven. Of course, the same data compression techniques used in DTT can be used on the satellite and cable platforms, allowing similar rates of expansion, and by March 1995 BSkyB's David Elstein had announced at an industry conference the broadcaster's intention to offer 100 channels in 1996 on its proposed digital satellite service, rising to 200 within a year. So DTT would never compete with digital satellite on channel numbers alone, but terrestrial would now look more like a multichannel platform than before. The expectation was that a new operator running the remaining DTT multiplexes as a pay-TV service would offer a credible alternative to BSkyB, whose dominance of the UK pay-TV market at that time was of concern to the government.

However, the transition to digital TV was not to be a smooth one. BSkyB's announcement of its imminent launch of digital satellite services proved to be ambitious, although it concentrated the minds of the terrestrial broadcasters. The ITC awarded the licences for three of the DTT multiplexes to British Digital Broadcasting (BDB), owned by two existing ITV companies, Carlton and Granada, with programming to be provided under a contract with BSkyB (the remaining half multiplex was awarded to S4C Digital Networks, a subsidiary of the company which ran the analogue terrestrial Welsh language channel). The assumption was that by awarding all three licences to a single company, moreover a company with a pedigree in television and thus access to a vast archive of programming assets with which to fill the capacity, DTT would be in safe hands, and the government could begin to envisage a full transition to digital television in the UK. In 1999, the Culture Secretary Chris Smith announced the criteria for switching off the UK's analogue terrestrial television services: (1) the digital terrestrial service should match the coverage of analogue, that is, 99.4 per cent of the population, and (2) that 95 per cent of households should be equipped to receive DTT transmissions (though with 75 per cent of households owning two or more television sets, it was unclear how *well* equipped a household would need to be to qualify). A tentative estimate was that these conditions might be met between 2006 and 2010. BDB launched its service, called OnDigital, on 15 November 1998, six weeks after BSkyB had finally begun its own digital satellite transmissions on 1 October, while the existing terrestrial broadcasters also began by the end of that year.

The battle over the award of the multiplex licences to BDB in 1997 was just one part of the wrangling over DTT. So-called conditional access (CA) systems, the means of encrypting digital television signals so that some channels could only be viewed by subscription, was another. As the leading player in the pay-TV market, BSkyB dominated the CA systems in use in the UK. The government's expectation had been that all CA systems would be interoperable so that a customer could use a single digital television receiver or set top box to receive signals over all three platforms, changing whenever desired. The BBC and other terrestrial broadcasters were concerned that as it was clear BSkyB would be first to launch a digital service, its CA system would become the *de facto* standard and that this might favour its own channels at the expense of others, so they urged the government to agree on a different, common standard. By 1998, however, the government had changed (Tony Blair's New Labour government having been elected in May 1997) and BSkyB (whose parent company, News International, owned two daily UK newspapers which had backed New Labour in the election) was allowed to launch its service with its own CA system. OnDigital's boxes used a different system, and so it was clear that, unless viewers were to have piles of different set top boxes surrounding the television set, they would be most likely to opt for the services of just one platform. Locking the viewers into their particular service became the main marketing strategy of digital broadcasters, and early in 1999 BSkyB began to offer customers free equipment (dish and decoding box), theirs to keep after 12 months, provided it was connected to a telephone line (to allow a nascent, limited but potentially revenue-generating interactive television service to be provided and viewing habits to be monitored). OnDigital was forced to follow suit in offering the loan of a set top box for no charge in return for a new subscription, thus losing money initially on every new subscriber. Compounding this were reports, accurate in most cases, of poor DTT reception and freezing screens – as noted earlier, adding redundancy to digital signals protects them against corruption and poor reception but at the expense of reduced multiplex capacity, and OnDigital had tried to squeeze as many stations as possible into its multiplexes, economising on the error protection data. Churn, the term used to describe the rate at which new subscribers to a service cancel a few months later, was particularly high for OnDigital, reflecting dissatisfaction with its service. Even a rebranding as ITV Digital could not reverse its fortunes, and in April 2002, having bid rather too much for the rights to show football matches, the ITV Digital service ended and BDB went bankrupt. By this time, ITV Digital had 1.25 million subscribers (against satellite's 5.8 m), and while they could no longer watch ITV Digital's services, they could continue to use their boxes to watch the free-to-air digital services simulcast by the incumbent broadcasters, including the new digital-only channels provided by the BBC. In fact, the set top boxes did not belong to the subscribers but had been loaned to them by ITV Digital, and the administrators requested that its ex-subscribers return the boxes. Needless to say, it is understood that very few did so.

This unravelling of plans for the transition to digital television required urgent remedial action. For the New Labour government, significantly more so than for the Conservative administration that preceded it, digitalisation was part of the 'modernisation' agenda, and Britain was to become a world leader in digital television and digital communications more generally (Freedman 2003). The ITC was asked to re-advertise the multiplex licences and to award them within six weeks (Galperin 2004: 224). There were two main contenders: one, bizarrely, from another alliance involving Carlton and

Granada (the owners of the collapsed ITV Digital) and a second from a consortium of the BBC, BSkyB and transmission company Crown Castle, bidding under the name Free-to-View. This was to be a largely free-to-air service, with the possibility of an element of subscription, and thus did not pitch itself as a direct competitor to BSkyB's satellite service but instead played on the tradition of terrestrial television as a free service. Viewers would need to make a one-off payment to buy a set top box (or a new, digital television set) and that would be it. The ITC, which had been accused of being over-cautious in awarding the original licences to BDB in 1997, now could be forgiven for being ultra-cautious (in addition to the demise of ITV Digital, the collapse of the original analogue satellite competitor to Sky, BSB, was also within recent memory), and when the award was made to what became known as Freeview, few were surprised. With a high number of viewers at its October 2002 launch, thanks to the legacy of hundreds of thousands of ITV Digital set top boxes still in people's homes, the service proved an attractive, subscription-free alternative to satellite (cable services by this time had long ceased to expand their coverage, and so subscription numbers had reached a plateau). From early 2003 onwards, it has grown faster than both satellite and the stagnated cable services, and at the end of 2007 9.6 m UK homes had Freeview reception equipment (a digital television or a set top box), just a few more than the 9.4 m satellite households, while an additional 5.7 m Freeview boxes were in use in a growing trend, where they are used for secondary television receivers in homes which already had cable or satellite services to the main television (Ofcom 2008). In total, by this time just short of 22.2 million UK homes, or 87 per cent of the total, were equipped for digital television in one form or another, and the government's revised schedule for switching off analogue television transmissions became one of a gradual transition to all-digital broadcasting, region by region, between 2008 and 2012.

Digital radio

So much for digital television, but what about the frequently overlooked state of digital radio? As noted, the UK is considered to be as much a success story for digital radio as for digital television, though the story is a little different. Nevertheless, as outlined earlier, the plans for digital terrestrial radio, based on the DAB system, were similar to those for terrestrial television, an array of multiplexes each carrying a number of radio stations, one to be operated by the BBC but the others to be licensed to commercial companies to contract with radio stations to carry their services. The main difference is that some of the multiplexes were configured to cover local areas only, to carry local radio stations, reflecting the geographical differences between television and radio. It should be noted of course that DTT can also carry localised television programming by broadcasting different content from particular transmitters so that regional news programmes, for instance, can be heard in their appropriate areas; however, most television is planned on the basis of national coverage, whereas analogue radio in the UK consists of a mix of national and local coverage, the BBC dominating national radio and commercial radio mainly serving local areas.

Along with broadcasters in a number of other European countries, the BBC began trial transmissions of DAB services in September 1995, days after the government had published its White Paper. However, only a few transmitters were operating, no commercial receivers were available on the market, and of course there were no listeners, although newspaper reports heralded this new age in radio broadcasting. Here then, as so often in its technological history, radio was ahead of television in introducing innovation, but the real beginnings of DAB in the UK came when the licensing mechanisms introduced in the 1996 Broadcasting Act were put into practice, and the first DAB multiplex licence, for national coverage, was advertised to potential bidders. This time, the bidders were expected to pay a cash sum for the licence, as well as be judged on criteria which included commitments to promoting the take up of digital radio and the introduction of innovative services. In the event, there was only one bid for the licence, from a consortium known as Digital One, the biggest and controlling partner in which was GWR, one of the biggest companies in UK analogue commercial radio, owning a number of stations across the country including national station, Classic FM. The licence was awarded in October 1998 and it began broadcasting a year later, carrying simulcasts of the existing three national commercial services (Classic FM, Talk Radio and Virgin) together with two new stations, adding another four over the next few months. By this time, five local multiplexes had also been awarded, but it was estimated that the number of receivers sold were fewer than 3000, and so in comparison with the estimated 100 million analogue receivers, by the end of the 1990s DAB was still only for enthusiasts.

Further licences for local multiplexes were awarded, and by the end of 2003, after the first phase of the licensing process, a total of 48 multiplexes were in operation, two national and 46 local, meaning that around 85 per cent of the UK population was able to receive DAB signals, in most cases, as anticipated in the 1995 White Paper, the two national multiplexes and one or two local multiplexes, offering a total of between 30 and 40 stations. However, sales of receivers failed to match this growth in signal coverage and broadcasters who had taken the plunge into DAB services were beginning to doubt whether DAB would succeed. Certainly, one former Director of Radio at the BBC had his doubts: 'My experience of digital radio development over the past five or six years has been of jam promised for tomorrow and thin gruel arriving today.

Initial optimism has turned to cynicism. I certainly take rosy future projections, so often proved inaccurate in the past, with a handful of salt' (Bannister 2001). One of the biggest difficulties was perceived to be the high cost of receivers in comparison with their analogue counterparts and little overt commitment to producing DAB receivers from the leading electronics manufacturers. In a joint venture, Digital One and technology company, Imagination Technologies, developed a receiver which retailed at £99 on its July 2002 launch, less than half the price of existing receivers. At the same time, the BBC added five new stations to the digital simulcasts of its five national networks on its multiplex, including BBC7, a speech-based station consisting mainly of archive recordings of comedy and drama programming but with some new material. BBC7 proved popular with the demographic group most likely to buy a digital radio (middle-aged, middle-class, with disposable income), and sales of DAB receivers began, belatedly and steadily, to increase. A further factor was the availability of these new stations on the digital television platforms: BSkyB, the cable companies and Freeview all carried radio stations, in addition to television channels, and these included BBC7 and the other digital-only DAB stations, public and commercial. Audience research figures showed that in 2006, 39 per cent of the population had listened to digital radio stations through their digital television at some time, prompting some at least to go and buy a DAB receiver in order to be able to hear them elsewhere in the home. Finally, broadcasters and multiplex operators began to feel a little more confident about its future, although that confidence was shaken in early 2008 by the decision of the biggest UK commercial DAB operator, GCap, to pull out of all its digital commitments. Few by now denied that the growth of digital radio had been far slower than many had originally anticipated and certainly slower than the growth of digital television: at the end of 2007, just 22 per cent of UK adults had a DAB receiver at home compared with the 87 per cent of homes with digital television receivers, although that level of ownership was a significant increase on the figure of 16 per cent a year previously (Rajar 2008). However small, this represented the highest level of digital radio ownership in the world, if the ability to receive radio through digital television is not counted.

The reasons why the UK should have these relatively high levels of ownership in comparison with other countries, cannot be explained precisely as the result of any particular factors, but some differences clearly had some effect (Lax et al. 2008). The licensing arrangement in the UK followed previous patterns for television in adopting a minimal regulation approach. Further, commercial radio was favoured in the allocation of multiplexes. The allocation of one national multiplex for commercial radio meant that the BBC no longer dominated national radio in station numbers alone (still less so with the award in 2007 of an additional national commercial multiplex in a second phase of licensing), while the increased capacity for local radio services was occupied entirely by commercial radio. Deregulation of radio had already begun in the analogue sector in the 1990s and was extended in the digital sphere. Whereas in the analogue system, the Radio Authority had regulated frequency allocation and content, its role in digital radio was limited more-or-less to awarding the multiplex licences in a similar manner to the ITC in television. Content was now hardly regulated at all, and restrictions on licence ownership were relaxed in early 1999. As the multiplex licences were advertised, one by one, theoretically in open competition to all, two thirds of them were uncontested, receiving only one bid. In all cases, the licences were awarded to companies comprising one or more of the five largest commercial radio groups in the analogue sector (with some minor, non-radio partners). The commercial companies operating the multiplexes were themselves owners of significant numbers of radio stations, and these tended to be the ones they carried on their respective multiplexes. Thus through awarding the licences for this novel tier in the structure of radio broadcasting to the dominant commercial radio companies, the balance between public service and commercial interests has shifted significantly in the digital sphere towards the latter (Lax 2007a). Further incentives for commercial radio companies to invest in DAB included 12-year extensions to their analogue broadcasting licences, of great commercial value when analogue listening remained a far higher proportion of listening than digital and looked likely to do so for many years to come. With this unique combination of regulatory (or deregulatory) mechanisms, these incentives encouraged commercial radio to invest in and promote DAB and, together with the BBC's commitment, helps to explain the UK's leading position in digital radio.

Digital Broadcasting in Europe and in the US

Television

The detailed account above of the ways in which digital television and radio have emerged in the UK suggests a number of possible reasons why it has the highest numbers of digitally equipped households in the world. However, the wide variation in different countries across the world equally suggests that there is no simple explanation of digital take up. For example, some countries have almost no penetration of digital television. Homes in Germany and the Netherlands, for example, have traditionally received television through simple cable relay systems, and these are analogue. With a relatively high number of free-to-air channels available (19 in Germany), and thus limited numbers of homes paying for subscription television, it is less easy to convert to digital reception equipment than in, say, the UK where a relatively high number of pay-TV subscribers means the platform operators can subsidise receiving equipment in the expectation of recovering the cost through subscription revenues. This does mean that it is relatively unchallenging to switch off analogue *terrestrial* television in favour of digital, as so few homes are affected, and in Germany, where only 2 per cent of households rely on analogue terrestrial signals, the switchover process is expected to be completed in 2009, three years ahead of the UK (Ofcom 2006b: 102–3). In the US all analogue transmissions, upon which 5 per cent of households are dependent for their television, is planned for switch off on a single day in February 2009. Where analogue terrestrial television remains the principal means of reception such as in France, Italy and Spain, the roll out of digital terrestrial television will necessarily be key to an eventual all-digital service and, as in the UK, strategies to encourage take up have been deployed. In general, DTT has evolved to become a free-to-air system. The UK collapse of ITV Digital was not a unique event: in the same year, Spain's Quiero TV company, a similar subscription-based DTT system, also went bankrupt, and DTT in that country is now mainly a free service.

In the US, where for many years the majority of homes have had some form of subscription television through either cable or satellite, the transition to digital reception has involved all platform operators. Satellite television is now all digital, with two providers, News Corporation's DirecTV and the Dish Network reaching 25 per cent of US homes between them. The cable networks, which grew rapidly in the 1980s before satellite became a significant force, were built on analogue technology, and now as many as 80 per cent of US homes have a cable connection (Gomery 2006a: 24). The 1996 Telecommunications Act included legislation requiring that cable television boxes no longer use mutually incompatible decoding, or conditional access (CA) systems. The intention was to open up a market in cable receivers so that competition would result in falling prices and allow viewers to replace analogue boxes with digital. Progress was relatively slow: by the end of 2005, just under 40 per cent of cable boxes in use were digital (Ofcom 2006b: 130).

For terrestrial television, the challenge was greater. With just a small number, fewer than one in ten households, relying exclusively on terrestrial signals for their television reception, the task of switching over to digital might seem straightforward. However, the terrestrial networks remain very popular, capturing the biggest slice of the viewing audience at peak times; in fact, such was the importance of the terrestrial networks that they were able to increase the rates charged to advertisers by record amounts in 2004 (Gomery 2006b: 27). In most cases of course the terrestrial channels are watched via the cable relay services, but on secondary sets around the home they are received through an aerial. Thus the transition of terrestrial television from analogue to digital operation was a process of significance similar to that in other countries. Galperin (2004) describes the process of transition as a series of battles between vested industry interests, regulators and the government. Frequencies originally allocated in principle for television as long ago as in the 1950s remained unused for many decades by broadcasters until, in the mid-1980s, an expanding telecommunications industry sought their use for 'personal mobile communications', or pagers and phones. In order to keep control of these frequencies, the existing terrestrial broadcasters persuaded the regulator that they should be reserved for the imminent arrival of high-definition television (HDTV). A Japanese system, Hi Vision, was being developed by broadcaster NHK, based on analogue technologies. Suddenly US broadcasters became enthusiasts, having shown little interest up to that point. Having persuaded the regulator to retain existing frequency allocations for television, the broadcasters, who were keen on the idea of an internationally agreed HDTV standard as it opened up a global market for programmes, found themselves up against the American Electronics Industry, which favoured investment in a US-developed HDTV system as a counter to the growing dominance of the Far Eastern electronics companies. In the end, it was European opposition to the Japanese system that prevented it being adopted at the international standards meeting in 1986 (at about the same time as the Eureka digital radio project was being launched as a counter to Far Eastern dominance of the consumer electronics sector). With the US broadcasters and electronics companies momentarily satisfied, in their different ways, little further progress was made on HDTV until General Instrument announced in 1990 that it had developed a means of compressing HDTV signals using digital techniques so that it would fit into a 6 MHz frequency channel, as already used in US analogue television, and three further competing systems emerged in the following months (Orlik et al. 2007: 61). For the regulator, the FCC, this confirmed that the way forward for terrestrial HDTV would be through the introduction of digital broadcasting: by requiring US broadcasters to use one of their digital channels for HDTV, they could continue also to transmit standard definition (SD) pictures to the public via other digital channels (and simulcast in analogue), and so the transition to digital could be an orderly, if slow one. The implication was that existing terrestrial broadcasters would have to be automatically allocated additional capacity for this purpose, and not surprisingly this was met with approval by the broadcasters who saw this as both an important way of excluding new entrants from terrestrial television (who might otherwise be allocated parts of the new digital capacity) and also recognised that digitisation allowed the prospect for them to transmit more SD channels than hitherto. Thus terrestrial broadcasters, local and networked, could become multichannel operators and begin to compete with the powerful cable companies and growing satellite services. Once again, they felt it necessary to talk up HDTV in order to acquire the rights to the new frequencies but in fact were more interested in securing the transition to DTT based on SDTV in order to offer more channels. In 1992, the Bill Clinton/Al Gore administration was elected to the White House, and the 'digital future' was now much more focused on the information society agenda, with digital television's role being as a provider of digital communications services as much as television, so broadcasters were able once again to quietly ignore HDTV in favour of the potential for DTT to offer additional SD television channels and interactive digital services of an as yet unspecified nature.

At the end of 1996, after much wrangling between broadcasters and the computer industry over the best way to code and transmit pictures, the FCC decided on a standard for DTT and broadcasters, by now freed from obligations to carry HDTV, were nevertheless required to begin the roll out of DTT from November 1998. The FCC's targets were that all terrestrial broadcasters would have begun DTT transmissions by 1 May 2002, and that the switchover to all-DTT transmissions would be complete by the end of 2006. However, given that more than two-thirds of households used cable as their principal means of receiving television, the beginning of the process of conversion of *terrestrial* services to digital was just one part of the complex jigsaw puzzle. A television cable can equally well carry analogue and digital signals, and the terrestrial broadcasters were due to simulcast both signals as well as begin new, digital-only channels. Cable operators were already required by the FCC to carry terrestrial broadcasters' analogue channels, but what would be the requirement now that digital broadcasting had begun? Should cable companies be required to carry all of the new digital channels? Once more, battles ensued between broadcasters, cable operators and the FCC, and the regulations eventually required that cable companies would be required to carry only one of the terrestrial broadcasters' signals, analogue or digital, though the broadcaster could also negotiate with the cable company for further stations to be carried. Crucially, if the cable company did carry a digital signal, or an analogue simulcast of a digital channel, it would count towards the broadcasters' targets for rolling out the digital service. As noted earlier, however, the slow take up of digital cable boxes made the growth of digital television slower than anticipated, matched by the equally slow take up of digital receivers for terrestrial television. In 2000, 33 million receivers were sold, but only 40,000 of these were suitable for DTT reception and, in Galperin's words, 'With every new analog TV set sold, the switch-off of analog stations inched a step beyond December 31, 2006' (2004: 118). When it became clear that most terrestrial broadcasters would miss the deadline for launching DTT services (in the event, only one-third of all broadcasters met the 2002 deadline) the date for switching off analogue transmissions was quietly deferred until 2009. By the end of 2005, of the 9 per cent of US households solely dependent on terrestrial reception of television, less than half received it via digital signals.

Radio

Digital terrestrial radio, like television, operates on a number of different standards, with the Eureka DAB standard being most widely adopted. The US, initially in favour of Eureka DAB, eventually settled on a different standard, In Band On Channel or IBOC, after intense lobbying by the commercial radio companies, represented by the National Association of Broadcasters. (Confusingly, 'DAB' is occasionally used in the US to refer to digital radio generally; in this book, as in most countries where the standard has been adopted, 'DAB' refers to the specific system developed in Europe under the Eureka programme.) Japan, meanwhile, has adopted a system known as Integrated Services Digital Broadcasting (ISDB), and all three are incompatible with each other, that is, a receiver designed to work with DAB will not work with IBOC or ISDB and vice versa, while further standards have also emerged in recent years. While multiple and incompatible standards also exist in digital television, this was also true of analogue television (NTSC, SECAM and PAL all being widespread), whereas analogue radio's FM and AM techniques are universal. Given the portability of radio receivers (in comparison with television at least) this new incompatibility might be regarded as a problem, but digital radio is yet to become as widely adopted anywhere as digital television, and so standards continue to evolve.

Within Europe, as noted earlier, there are wide variations in the take up of digital terrestrial radio. The DAB system has been adopted across Europe, in principle at least, although in a number of countries transmissions are only beginning. Following the UK, governments in Germany and the Netherlands were initial DAB enthusiasts and, together with Norway and Sweden, began an early roll out of transmitters. But while Germany has a similar geographical coverage to the UK, it has almost no DAB listeners, sales of receivers numbering thousands rather than millions. The licensing and roll out of transmitters in Sweden and the Netherlands was suspended in 2006, and so listener figures remain static, while in Finland, DAB transmissions were switched off altogether in 2005. Neighbouring Scandinavian country Denmark, however, began to catch up with the UK levels of receiver sales by 2006. Elsewhere in Europe, coverage has grown only slowly, and the numbers of DAB stations on air and the number of receivers sold are correspondingly relatively small. This variability is in contrast with developments in digital television. While levels of digital television in some countries are low, there is near-universal acknowledgement that progress *will* need to be made towards an all-digital television, even if sometimes the rates of progress are slow. With radio, in contrast, some countries' hesitations are based on uncertainty about which format will be successful for digital radio, or indeed if there is public demand for digital radio at all. Marketing strategies in countries where digital radio has been relatively successful have had to change focus from one based on the supposed superior sound quality to one emphasising the number of new radio stations, and where markets are already served with a large number and variety of analogue radio stations, as they are in many countries, the attraction of digital radio is likely to remain limited. Thus, again in contrast with television, few countries have discussed the eventual switch off of analogue radio, with even fewer giving dates.

The IBOC system in the US, renamed HD Radio for marketing purposes (as in 'high definition' radio to mirror HDTV developments), began to be adopted by broadcasters during 2006, with receivers beginning to appear in stores as a marketing campaign was launched. The adoption by the industry of the HD Radio standard rather than DAB was widely regarded as based not upon technological criteria but instead on the fact that it allowed existing radio broadcasters to retain their frequency allocations and exclude newcomers to the market (Ala-Fossi and Stavitsky 2003). In this respect, the introduction of HD Radio followed a similar pattern to HDTV, driven by the desire of the incumbent broadcasters to maintain their dominant position, and thus migration to digital radio is anticipated to be similarly slow, dependent more on factors such as any inadequacy of existing analogue radio reception rather than the superiority of digital radio. Where there has been some success in US digital radio is in the launch of two satellite services, XM in 2001 and Sirius the following year. These subscription services offer radio free of advertising (and with some terrestrial stations carrying 15 minutes of advertising per hour, 'ad-free' radio can prove attractive) and operate without regulation on content, prompting 'shock jock' Howard Stern for example to move from terrestrial radio, where his outpourings had resulted in huge fines, to the less-regulated satellite platform, although the $500 million contract offered to Stern by Sirius may also have been persuasive (Orlik et al. 2007: 237). While these services had 15 million subscribers between them in 2007, these figures were lower than either company had anticipated and neither had become profitable by that time, resulting in a bid to the FCC to permit the two companies to merge.

The uncertainty over the future of digital radio is underlined and compounded by the emergence of new formats or standards. When the Eureka DAB programme was first planned, as we have seen, it was acknowledged that the market for radio receivers was 'virtually saturated', and thus there was no guarantee that the new technology would produce the new market for electronic goods that was hoped for. The slow progress of DAB allowed further technological developments to take place that, in the absence of high levels of adoption of DAB, might stand an equally good chance of being adopted as the standard for digital radio. HD Radio was one of these, but other formats also emerged to challenge DAB. Digital Radio Mondiale (DRM) was developed in the late 1990s, principally by broadcasters and electronics companies which were involved in high frequency or short wave international broadcasting. Drawing on some of the techniques as DAB, but with more advanced coding methods, it was also clear that the DRM system would work in the FM or VHF part of the spectrum that broadcasters originally had envisaged being replaced by DAB. An alternative being pursued in Finland and studied elsewhere is a portable version of the digital television standard, known as Digital Video Broadcasting Handheld (DVBH) to carry both television and radio to portable devices (DAB can also carry television alongside its radio content). A rather more incremental change was the incorporation of similar advanced coding techniques being incorporated into DAB, a system adopted by the WorldDMB industry body in 2007 and known as DAB+. DAB+ allows radio stations to be carried on a DAB multiplex at less than half the bit rate as DAB, meaning still more stations can be carried, or alternatively offers superior sound quality for similar bit rates. However, incrementally different or not, all three, DRM, DVBH and DAB+ are incompatible with DAB; the millions of DAB receivers already sold in the 'successful' markets of the UK, Denmark and Norway, for example, will not work on any of these new systems. As new formats are agreed, newer receivers will incorporate multi-format decoding circuits; some radios launched during 2008 are indeed backwards compatible and thus able to receive DAB, DAB+, DRM, as well as all analogue wavebands. Backwards compatibility is relatively straightforward; full forwards compatibility is, clearly, an impossibility (although some measure of software upgradeability can be incorporated). The plethora of digital terrestrial radio formats either in use or in development is summarised in Table 5.2.

Those countries which have not yet begun digital radio broadcasting on a significant scale are, therefore, faced with a number of options as to which

Abbreviation	Name	
DAB	Digital Audio Broadcasting	Operating since 1995, to varying levels in numerous countries
DMB	Digital Multimedia Broadcasting	Development of DAB, able to deliver mobile TV
HD Radio	'High Definition' Radio	Developed as 'In band on channel' (IBOC) in US as an alternative to DAB
DRM	Digital Radio Mondiale	'Digital short wave', intended for HF, MF and LF frequencies.
DRM+	'DRM plus'	Extension of DRM to operate in VHF (FM) frequency band
DAB+	'DAB plus'	Based on DAB but with more efficient coding
DVBH	Digital Video Broadcasting Handheld	Development of digital television standard suitable for mobile TV and radio

Table 5.2 The main digital radio formats in use (or being trialled) by 2008

format to adopt. They are unlikely to adopt the 'old' DAB system, as all other systems offer improved coding and thus greater efficiency in use of spectrum. For example, in 2006 Australia announced that it was to adopt DAB+ as its chosen system for digital radio and passed legislation the following year in anticipation of broadcasting beginning in 2009. Countries like the UK, however, face the irony of its relatively successful adoption of DAB making the introduction of DAB+ or any other more recent system problematic. With Ofcom beginning its second phase of licensing in 2007, some suggested that all new licences should use DAB+ coding; however, others within an industry which has marketed so strongly (and relatively successfully) the benefits of digital radio fear this would seriously damage the confidence of both those listeners who have already bought DAB receivers and, perhaps more importantly, those on the brink of so doing. Thus, countries joining the digital radio circus later on may well find themselves at a technical advantage over the first movers for many years to come. Even in the post-analogue world then, the issue of how to introduce new technological developments into an established or, more accurately, establishing market will need to be confronted again and again.

In a speech to the NAB's 2003 conference, BBC Director of Radio Jenny Abramsky repeated the claim echoed by many within the radio industry: 'radio must go digital if it is not to go into long term decline. If radio were the only medium not to go digital it would soon become obsolete' (Abramsky 2003). Yet this bald statement is not supported by evidence; as we have seen, new media technologies do not tend to render old ones obsolete, and digital radio always faced an uncertain future. Brian Winston describes three categories of social necessity for the successful development of new technologies. The first is a need created by the development of another technological system – the growth of the railways created an opportunity for the development of the telegraph, for example, as we saw in Chapter 1. The second type occurs where a group of social changes directly stimulates demand for new products to serve those changes – such as the rise of the modern business corporation stimulating demand for office technologies. His third category is the 'strictly commercial' need, as opposed to any wider social need, for example, when a new product such as the compact disc or MiniDisc is launched into an uncertain market. According to Winston, of the three this third category is 'less certain in guaranteeing diffusion and producing less significant innovation than either the consequences of social change or the effects of other technological advances' (1998: 9). While the development of analogue radio in the first quarter of the 20th century chimed with social changes that helped secure its prominent place in society and thus fulfilled the social necessities of Winston's second category, digital radio was conceived both in Europe and in the US as little more than an economic challenge to the Far East and an opportunity for commercial consolidation of European electronics and broadcasting industries. If Winston is correct, with a set of 'social necessities' based purely on commercial needs, we should not be surprised if digital radio struggles to become completely successful in replacing its analogue forerunner in the near future (Lax 2003).

Digital Quality and Channel Quantity

As noted in passing in the discussion above, the traditional trade off in communications technologies between a system's capacity and its ability to deliver high quality, faithful communication is one that persists in the digital realm. Analogue FM radio gives better audio quality than AM, but requires more bandwidth to do so; the superior 625-line television pictures use more bandwidth than the 405-line system they eventually replaced. Once converted to digital signals, capacities are measured as the bit rate rather than as bandwidth, but the principles are comparable, and broadcasters have faced a choice as to what bit rates to use to carry their various radio and television channels. We have seen that the quality of digital delivery also depends on the detection and correction of transmission errors, and this protection depends on adding redundancy, that is, data which carries no picture or sound information. In general, greater levels of protection are afforded at the expense of more and more redundancy. Yet, the higher the number of bits allocated to transmit a single radio station or television channel, of course, the lower the number of stations or channels that can be carried on the multiplex.

An issue of rather minor public debate (far too minor in the opinions of some) is the choices that broadcasters have made in most cases. It is generally acknowledged, for example, that the low bit rates adopted by most DAB broadcasters, in order to maximise the capacity of their multiplexes, offer sound quality that is worse than a quality analogue FM receiver (for example, Lax 2003; Holm 2007). Similarly, the effort to incorporate the maximum number of television channels into its three multiplexes resulted in ITV Digital reducing its levels of protection, with the consequent unreliability of its service. Even now, at times of high 'data demand' within a multiplex (for example, when a radio station is temporarily added to a multiplex, or when sports television programmes leave little opportunity for data reduction) the listener or viewer can experience poor sound quality or pictures that break up (or, simply, the transmission in mono on digital of a radio service transmitted in stereo on analogue). Such degradation is the direct result of the compromise between achieving reliably high quality reception and carrying the maximum number of stations or channels.

While the existence of such problems is rarely disputed, it raises a series of questions (which certainly will not be answered here). Firstly, at a purely technological level, it demonstrates that the widely accepted assertion that digital technology is 'better' than the analogue it replaces requires some qualification. For whom is it better? Most radio listening is not to high-end equipment but to small receivers with low specification sound systems in poor acoustic environments – but not all listening, and digital listening is unquestionably a worse experience for some. Secondly, though it is not the first time that a superior technology has been rejected in favour of an inferior competitor (most obviously, VHS's supremacy over Betamax), it is probably the first time that governments have enacted legislation or introduced policy to ensure that this is what will take place. A third question relates to the question of the subjective nature of quality: how should a technical judgement about sound or visual fidelity be judged against the increase in content provision that digitisation presents? Yet the perception of quality is one which has never been consistent, either across media (should we expect radio to sound as good as a CD?) or throughout history (Nyre 2008).

Switchover Strategies

From the many examples of digital radio and television transition, we can identify a number of strategies to bring about conversion from analogue to digital.

Content strategies

The history of analogue subscription television shows that making certain content such as key sports events only available on particular platforms helps speed up the adoption of that platform. However, this is not without its difficulties. As recently as 2005, there was a public and political outcry that (following an unusually successful season) the rights to show cricket test matches in England had been bought by BSkyB and live cricket could only be seen on payment of a subscription. Moving some of the most popular programming to exclusively digital platforms could easily create political problems for governments. Alternatively, promoting *new* programming that is only available on digital is more acceptable, as this is seen as additional to the existing offering but runs the risk that those who are content with the options as they are will not be likely to change. For example, satellite subscription radio is moderately successful in the US partly because it does not carry the 'painful number of commercials – 13 to 17 minutes an hour on average and more during peak "drive times" at rush hour' that, for many, plagues analogue radio

(Bary 2003: 17). However, many commentators believe that this model would not be persuasive in those European countries which are already served with advertisement-free, public service radio on their analogue service.

Carrot and stick

The US has announced a date (17 February 2009 at the time of writing) on which analogue television will be switched off. This is seen as an incentive for the public to purchase set top boxes or digital receivers, but to soften the blow all households can claim two $40 vouchers redeemable against new equipment. In the UK, the first designated television switchover area, Whitehaven in Cumbria, was heavily marketed with leaflets and advertising ahead of the October 2007 switch. Low income households were similarly eligible for a free set top box or discount on receiving equipment. Six months before the switchover, the number of households equipped for digital reception matched the national figure at 70 per cent, although 75 per cent still had at least one analogue receiver. The industry body overseeing the transition anticipated the remaining 30 per cent would leave it until the last minute before obtaining equipment, producing a rush of some 18,500 homes trying to buy a set top box over a two-week period (Ofcom and Digital UK 2007).

Conclusion: Technology, Policy, Economy

Digital technologies (if we take a liberal definition) go back as long as electronic communication itself, while the theoretical principles that underpin its operation today were established 80 years ago. Their practical realisation in the development of computer technology during and after the Second World War was incorporated into broadcasting systems only after a further half century or so, delayed largely because of the complexity and quantity of the digitised data produced. However, the accounts given above of digital television and radio around the world show that this is not the whole explanation. Digital television in particular has been welcomed as a technology of the information society, but not simply because its digital nature means it could fulfil that role. The cable networks of the 1980s were expected also to be catalysts to new wired nations, but manifestly failed to become such things. Television though, unlike cable, was already in almost everyone's home and thus could bring the information age to all.

In fact, digital television and certainly digital radio have not proved as popular as anticipated, and this is not because the technology fails to work: its technical success may be qualified but it does deliver greater capacity at least. That capacity though has generally been used to offer enhanced quantity rather than quality – digital television and radio tend to mean more television and more radio, but not very different television or radio. It is in the realms of policy and economy that we can find the most convincing explanations for this turn of events. The roll out of digital broadcasting has largely left broadcasters to their own devices, with little regulation for fear of compromising their competitiveness in an unfettered global economy.

Computing, Communication and Convergence

6

The personal computer is now, justifiably, regarded as the central technology in communications systems. When connected to the internet, we might use it for anything from sending email to watching television. The one thing that most people do not directly use a computer for is performing mathematical calculations, the original purpose behind the computer. However, as with all digital technologies, whether we are in fact writing an email message or viewing images on the screen, the computer's role is to interpret such forms of communication as sequences of numbers, and to perform computations, that is, to process those numbers using mathematical rules. During its 60-year history then, the computer could be described as having undergone a transition from calculator to communicator, a transition that reflects principally the changing economic demands within our society.

Origins of Computing: The Calculator

The often repeated history is that computers came into being after the Second World War. Most have heard of the machines devised to break the secret Enigma codes used by German forces, not least because the story has been told in a successful film. However, this development follows a far longer pattern of the use of technology for speeding up mathematical processes, driven by the needs of an advancing industrial society. As Shurkin notes, 'For most of human history counting was scarcely necessary' (1984: 19). The development of mathematics and science in the great civilisations of the Middle East and Asia took place largely without the use of mechanical aids to calculation, and much scientific enquiry was based on Aristotelian science that had little need for numbers (Brose 1998: 18). However, over the 200 years from the 16th century, the escalation of warfare in Europe, the growth in trade and the rapid expansion of industrialisation all required increased application of science and mathematics and so introduced new demands and accelerated the development of knowledge and understanding in these fields. As mathematics became more sophisticated, methods were developed to allow complex calculations to be performed more quickly, such as the drawing up of log tables and trigonometry tables. Mechanical devices, such as 'Napier's bones', devised by John Napier in 1617, made the application of these methods quicker still or, equally, permitted the solution of ever more complex mathematical problems. While simple in design (tools like Napier's bones consisted of an assembly of marked sticks) these instruments nevertheless embodied sophisticated mathematical techniques, based on logarithms, which remained in use well into the 20th century in the form of the slide rule, used by students and mathematicians prior to the arrival of the electronic calculator in the 1970s. During the 19th century, Boolean mathematics was developed, based on the use of logical operators such as AND, OR and NOT, a method which could also be expressed using the binary numbers 0 and 1, the basis eventually of course for digital technologies, but which was also used by Charles Babbage (sometimes known as 'the father of computing') to develop his 'difference engine' and, later, the concept of the 'analytical engine'.

It was not just mathematical and scientific knowledge that developed rapidly during this period. Technology advanced dramatically too, both benefiting from advances in science and also contributing to its development in the form of tools and instrumentation for further exploration. As industrialisation progressed, based on the cotton industry in England from the 18th century and elsewhere in the coming decades, the same social forces that eventually gave rise to the telegraph played a part in the development of calculating machines. The expansion of industry and trade, and the massive population movements upon which this expansion depended, demanded more mathematics: in order to make industry work, calculations were required for financial purposes, to build and improve machinery, to plan for raw materials to be sourced and moved and so on; the migration of thousands from the countryside to towns and cities would also require a detailed knowledge of local populations which had never been needed before. In *The Condition of the Working Class in England* (1999 [1845]) Frederick Engels famously documented the miserable conditions in which many members of this new working class were forced to live, with cramped dwellings and poor sanitation shared by large numbers of families, and campaigners and sporadic social unrest forced governments to respond to the consequences of this mass migration. As they began to organise data gathering through a ten-yearly census, amongst other methods, the sheer size and constant movement of populations made such things a complex exercise, and they too turned to technological assistance. By the end of the 19th century, desk calculating machines had changed from being mere 'hand-made curiosities for the wealthy' to becoming standard, indispensable items of office equipment, as would typewriters and telephones in the ensuing decades (Campbell-Kelly and Aspray 1996: 2). In the 1890s, the US government bought a series of machines to process its own ten-yearly census results. The 1880 census had taken seven years to process, its final report numbering more than 21,000 pages, six times as many as the 1870 census. At that rate of increase, it would not have been possible to count the coming 1890 census before the next one was due in 1900, and it had become clear that a mechanised means of processing the census data would be needed. The tabulating machines, devised by Herman Hollerith specifically to process the census, used a system of holes punched in cards and paper tape to record the data, which could then be read by metal pins passing through the holes and conducting electricity as the cards passed through the machine. Their use in the 1890 census not only cut the processing time to two and a half years but also allowed more sophisticated calculations and tabulations to be made from the raw data. The system of punched cards, dating back to the cards used in the Jacquard cotton weaving looms at the beginning of that century and intended also to be employed in Babbage's difference engine, lived on well into the computer era, and the success of the Hollerith machines in such a high profile exercise helped to open up the idea of the benefits of mechanised technology for information processing. The legacy of the punched card system can even be identified in the disputed US presidential elections of 2000, where arguments raged over whether voting cards in Florida could be counted if they had not clearly been punched right through; a whole new taxonomy including 'hanging chads', 'dimpled chads' and even 'pregnant chads' emerged in the law courts of that state over the following months (Borger 2000).

From calculator to computer

Over the decades from the end of the 19th century to the 1930s, ever more advanced office machinery was sold to businesses, including calculating machines, with and without punched card inputs, for use in financial processes and stock control. The beginning of the Second World War in 1939 prompted further research into calculating machines, just as warfare had accelerated developments in mining and metallurgy four centuries earlier (Brose 1998: 10–14). This time the pressing need was for ballistics calculations: the path taken by a shell depended on a host of variables that could not readily be calculated in the field, such as wind speed and direction, elevation, speed of target and so on. Instead, ballistics tables were produced and printed in a booklet, to which the weapon operator referred. Each booklet contained around 3000 possible trajectories, and such was the complexity of the calculations that the time needed to produce the 3000 table entries could keep a hundred-strong team occupied for up to a month. With new weapons being produced more and more frequently during the course of the war, the length of time taken in the calculation of trajectories became the determining factor in the rate of their deployment. In efforts to speed up wartime calculations, work began on projects using electronic rather than electromechanical technologies. These included the Electronic Numerical Integrator and Calculator project (ENIAC) at the Moore School of Electrical Engineering at the University of Pennsylvania, while the Colossus project at Bletchley Park in England was the culmination of the development of similar electronic calculating machines designed to break the German Enigma naval codes. Colossus began operation at the end of 1943 and was used successfully to decode encrypted messages, while ENIAC did not actually become operational until after the end of the war, six weeks after the dropping of the first atomic bomb over Hiroshima in August 1945, an event to which it was initially anticipated to contribute its calculating power.

While these machines were important developments in the history of computing, they were not actually computers but advanced calculators. However, the term 'computer' *was* in use at the time: it was used to refer to the people who carry out computations or calculations. Thus the ballistics tables at the time were indeed calculated 'by computer', that is, by mathematicians, including an increasing number of women, who were allocated the considerable if routinised and sometimes tedious task. The distinction between calculator and computer is subtle but significant and for Winston reflects a cultural or ideological difficulty with the idea of a 'thinking machine' (1998: 147–8). He suggests that the idea of constructing a machine that could replicate the human process of thought offended the prevalent Cartesian notion that held that all things in nature were mere assemblies of particles, and humans were uniquely distinguished in being capable of thought. During the 1920s and 1930s, however, just as mechanical understandings of the physical nature of the world were being challenged by Einstein's relativistic theories, mathematics was also recognising that its axiomatic explanations of the world might not be the whole story. Working at Cambridge University, Alan Turing wrote *On Computable Numbers* in 1936, in which he suggested it might be possible in principle to build a machine that could do all the calculations, that is, could compute everything, that a human 'computer' was able to do. This challenge went beyond mathematics – the machine would be 'universal' in that it might be extended to any area of human activity and thought that could be expressed mathematically, however complex (Hodges 1997). While this was all highly theoretical, Turing did indeed experiment with real mechanical devices used for code breaking and was recruited at the outbreak of the Second World War by the British government to lead a number of the projects at Bletchley Park. By 1945, the mechanical calculators which had been used for the complex calculations needed for warfare were well advanced, but only with the logical structure suggested by John von Neumann did the notion of the electronic computer begin to become established, going some way towards a practical realisation of the machine that Turing had conjectured.

Von Neumann had collaborated with John Mauchly and John Presper Eckert on the development of ENIAC. While working with them at the Moore School, he considered how a planned successor to ENIAC might improve upon one of its major defects. ENIAC was of course a massive machine, with its 40 units weighing 30 tonnes and taking up a room some 10 m wide and 15 m long. It contained 18,000 vacuum tubes (like the glass valves used in pre-War radios) and generated 150 kW of waste heat. It had taken over two years to design and build, but by the time it was finished it could process 5000 calculations every second. However, its programming was hard wired, as it would be described today: to set up the circuits to perform a particular calculation meant connecting them together with hundreds of patch leads, similar to an old, manual telephone exchange. Once so wired, it could perform the calculations as required, but to re-programme it to perform a different set of calculations would require a complete rewire, and this could take two or three days to perform. Von Neumann suggested using the memory circuits, which in ENIAC were being used only to hold the data being used in the calculations, to also hold the instructions, or the programme. When this was incorporated into ENIAC's successor, this had the immediate advantage of speeding up the time needed to programme (or re-programme) the machine; the instructions could now be read into the memory from a punched card, taking just a few seconds and, once there, would remain until changed. Processing speeds were also increased, but holding the instructions in the machine's electronic memory also enabled the crucial possibility of the programme being dynamic rather than static, treating its own instructions as data and changing its operation in response to the results of its calculations. Here, we have a machine that is not just performing a fixed set of calculations, but which also responds to the results of its calculations in different ways, and this forms the essence of the computer. While some way off Turing's 'thinking machine', the stored programme computer, as von Neumann's architecture became known, laid the foundations for the ideas of artificial intelligence many years later (Campbell-Kelly and Aspray 1996: 93).

This distinction notwithstanding, the fact that ENIAC clearly belonged to the 'calculator' rather than 'computer' category did not prevent the media responding to its public launch in February 1946 by heralding this new 'electronic brain' (Martin 1995). The use of this term in a report in *The Times* in November 1946 precipitated a flurry of correspondence decrying the description, including one from Charles Darwin, director of the National Physical Laboratory, who referred to plans to develop the laboratory's own 'advanced computing engine' based on Turing's ideas. Darwin argued (1946):

> The new machines will in no way replace thought, but rather they will increase the need for it, both because the machines themselves will call for high qualities of intellect in their use, and also because as a tool they will open up new fields for study.

Meanwhile, the successful demonstration of ENIAC could not heal the growing rift between its original developers, Mauchly and Eckert, and the newly successful von Neumann and his collaborators. Things came to a head over intellectual property rights at the Moore School and, one month after showing ENIAC to the world's press, Mauchly and Eckert both resigned in order to start a business making computers.

The Electronic Business Machine

The idea that a computer could do more than perform sophisticated calculations was implicit in Turing's original 1936 paper. The computer, as a 'symbol manipulator', could process data representing all manner of quantities and so had obvious applications in business, which had now become used to employing technology to speed up office functions. While developing ENIAC, Mauchly and Eckert had paid a number of visits to the US Census Bureau to promote the use of their machines in processing census data, and by the time they left the Moore School in Spring 1946, like Hollerith half a century earlier, they had secured a contract to build a number of stored programme machines known as the Universal Automatic Computer (UNIVAC). Struggling to gain financial backing for their business, it was not until 1951 that the first UNIVAC was completed, and even then they did not deliver it to the Census Bureau until December 1952 as, being the only completed and working machine, they wanted to keep it to demonstrate to other prospective customers. The first machine built and delivered was to the US Air Force at the Pentagon in June 1952, and by the end of 1954 about 20 had been built and sold, at a price of about £1 million for a complete system (Ceruzzi 2003: 27).

The only other country where developments in computing were taking place on any significant scale was the UK; as Campbell-Kelly and Aspray explain, 'Britain was the only country other than the US not so devastated by the war that it could establish a serious computer research program' (1996: 99). In fact, it was in the UK that the first two stored programme computers were actually completed, at the Universities of Cambridge and Manchester in 1949.

Here, businesses had been rather slower than in the US in adopting office technology, and interest in computing for business purposes was correspondingly less enthusiastic. Nevertheless, a number of pioneering companies sought to engage with the emerging technology, one of which was the catering company J E Lyons, which also ran a chain of tea and coffee shops across the UK. Having worked with (and helped fund) Maurice Wilkes's team at Cambridge, Lyons began construction of a machine for use in stock control and payroll processing, derived from Wilkes's Electronic Delay Storage Automatic Calculator (EDSAC). The project leader at Lyons, Raymond Thompson, kept a log of events in the development of the Lyons Electronic Office (LEO), and some of its entries suggest just how pioneering its efforts were: for example, '16 November 1951: Brigadier Hinds writes to offer us £300 for carrying out some ballistic computations for the Ministry of Supply' (Lavington 1980: 72). The log reveals that the contract for these calculations was received in January 1952, meaning that a catering company was engaged by the British military for calculating missile trajectories! Even so, the computer remained at the testing stage until it was finally considered completed in December 1953 and was put into routine service. On 5 November 1954, Thompson was able to write in his log: 'Teashops General Report for Wembley teashops has entry: "The head staff at this shop would like to give thanks for LEO. This is a wonderful time saver, and work saver, and we are grateful for it"' (ibid.: 73). Thompson went on to head a spin-off company manufacturing and supplying updated versions of LEO to business customers, but only 13 of its successor, the LEO II, were ever sold, a low level of sales that continued in Britain over the next decade. In contrast, sales of computers to industry in the US were much more successful.

In 1949, in the early days of computing, Thomas J. Watson Sr, the president of US office machinery company International Business Machines (IBM), reportedly stated that the world market for computers might be around twelve in total. Eckert and Mauchly, with their contract secured for the Census Bureau, clearly believed differently. Their financial difficulties however meant that when business machinery company Remington Rand offered, in effect, to take over Eckert and Mauchly's business, they were ready to accept and thereafter operated as a subsidiary of the corporate giant. Keen to save the business, Remington Rand arranged a publicity stunt with broadcaster CBS – to run a television programme in which a UNIVAC would be used to predict the outcome of the 1952 US presidential election. Basing the calculations on early returns from states that had proved decisive in previous elections, as election night wore on UNIVAC was predicting a landslide for Dwight Eisenhower, a result that was at odds with conventional opinion polls, which had predicted a close race with his rival Adlai Stevenson. The UNIVAC prediction was so out of line that before broadcasting these predictions its operators adjusted the machine to produce a rather more credible prediction, a narrower Eisenhower victory. Of course, the eventual outcome was that Eisenhower won by 442 electoral votes to 89, remarkably close to the earlier, suppressed UNIVAC prediction (438 to 93), and a spokesman quickly admitted on air the earlier tinkering that had taken place. Had the programmers not buckled but instead stuck to UNIVAC's original prediction, the impact would no doubt have been even more spectacular, but nevertheless the surprise result proved a dramatic demonstration of the prowess and even superiority of the computer in comparison with human endeavours (Campbell-Kelly and Aspray 1996: 121–3). The event helped to establish an already growing interest in the business applications of computers, and numerous US companies began to build and sell computers, but the already massive IBM competed strongly with Remington Rand's UNIVAC and during the 1950s came to dominate the industry. As industry leader, it was responsible for a considerable number of innovations such as the use of magnetic disks for data storage and the gradual replacement of valve tubes with transistors, and computers became bigger and more powerful, with more and more data being stored. The 'mainframe' computer became the norm, particularly for large organisations, with the various elements such as processing circuits, card readers, memory in the form of tape spools (as some of the only moving parts in the system, the tape cabinets were often the focus of early film and television portrayals of the computer) and so on housed in separate cabinets linked by cables, all housed in climate-controlled rooms. To 'access' the computer meant a trek to the computer room with a sheaf of punched cards which would be handed to the operator, followed by a repeat journey some hours (or days) later to retrieve a printout of the resulting data on pages of fanfold paper.

Further developments during the 1960s began to change the way in which computing was viewed. Rather than a mainframe being separated from its users, in the sense that customers passed their jobs onto operators and programmers who would then set up the computer to process that series of jobs in turn, real-time access and time sharing made more efficient use of the mainframe. A number of programmers could access the computer simultaneously, each running and modifying their respective programmes without exceeding the capacity of the machine, since in practice at any one time only a few would actually be drawing on its processing power. The speed at which the computer ran exceeded that at which the programmers would be sending or requesting data. This permitted remote working via 'dumb terminals' or workstations, essentially keyboards and screens connected to the mainframe but possessing no processing or memory of their own. The idea of a centralised computer resource and remote access to that resource (via cables for example) was similar to the way in which utilities such as water or electricity were supplied to consumers, and the notion of a computer utility began to excite interest. Just as it made economic sense to centralise power generation in a small number of highly industrialised complexes, and deliver the power down lines to its users, so the same could apply in computing: ever more advanced mainframe computers could share their processing power among any number of users. In 1970, Paul Baran of the RAND corporation imagined a 'home computer console' connected to the central mainframes for sending and receiving messages, or for paying utility bills, or sending questions to 'information banks' (Campbell-Kelly and Aspray 1996: 217). This is similar to how Bell (and others) had noted that one of the telephone's key advantages over the telegraph was the lack of a 'gatekeeper', the telegraph operator, and so the telephone might become a utility routinely used by the general public, in a way the telegraph never could. These ideas of course did not go away, even when the particular technology suggested by Baran did not succeed in the domestic sphere, but have remained as objectives for those who saw the computer as more than a machine that would serve the needs of big businesses, such as those who later looked to the cable television system and more recently those envisaging the internet as offering similar capabilities.

What prevented the success of the computer utility, apart from its lack of an obvious application, was a combination of economic difficulties for the large computer companies (part of a general, global economic recession in the early 1970s) and the emergence of the integrated circuit (IC) or, colloquially, the 'silicon chip'. Developed, as so often, as a response to military demands (this time the Cold War rather than the actual war which had earlier spawned the transistor), the IC used photolithographic techniques for 'writing' electronic circuits into slivers of semiconductor material such as silicon or germanium, by diffusing other elements into the surface through a mask. These elements changed the electrical properties of the semiconductor, and the photographic reduction technique allowed these properties to be changed on a tiny scale. It was possible to incorporate hundreds, later thousands, of transistor circuits into a piece of silicon just a few square millimetres in size, whereas a single component transistor (also made out of silicon) would itself have dimensions of a few millimetres. Just as the transistor had reduced both size and power requirements of electronic equipment in comparison with valve or tube devices in the 1950s, two decades later the IC reduced them one stage further and so made it possible to incorporate computer-processing circuits into a much smaller space. The mainframe systems still had a role, but for more modest computing requirements an organisation might be able to satisfy its needs with a much smaller, and much more affordable, dedicated installation of its own. The minicomputer, as it became known, could operate as a stand-alone device or, more commonly, operate as a small time-sharing system with a number of minicomputers connected together, perhaps sharing a common printer or large capacity memory disk. The deployment of minicomputers, particularly into colleges and universities, exposed far more people to computing and programming and, rather than it remaining the preserve of the specialist, researchers, educators and hobbyists began to learn programming skills simply as a tool to allow them to incorporate computers into their work. It is certainly debatable whether, as Ceruzzi suggests (2003: 135), the arrival of the miniskirt in the fashion world (and the popularity of the Mini car) at the same time as the term 'minicomputer' was coined helped to make computing more glamorous, but, sitting on desks in individual offices and laboratories, alongside telephones, books, pens and paperclips, minicomputers began to become more familiar pieces of equipment, and their users would come to regard them as their personal machines.

The Personal Computer

The story of the emergence of the personal computer is steeped in mythology, and it is a story too recent for its history to have become properly established. As Campbell-Kelly and Aspray point out (1996: 233):

> Scores of books and hundreds of articles, written mostly by journalists, have appeared in response to a demand from the general public for an understanding of the personal computer. Much of this reportage is bad history, though some of it is good reading. Perhaps its most serious distortion is to focus on a handful of individuals, portrayed as visionaries who clearly saw the future and made it happen: Apple Computer's Steve Jobs and Microsoft's Bill Gates figure prominently in this genre. By contrast, IBM and the established computer firms are usually portrayed as dinosaurs: slow-moving, dim-witted, deservedly extinct. When it comes to be written, the history of the personal computer will be much more complex than this. It will be seen to be the result of a rich interplay of cultural forces and commercial interests.

This interplay does indeed include these individuals and others and also includes a vibrant, anti-establishment, 'counter culture' movement from the 1960s and 1970s. As Ceruzzi says, the myth that these players were solely responsible for the birth of the personal computer is 'about half right' (2003: 215). The wrong half is that which firstly ignores the role of the established corporations, which, were it possible, would happily have ignored any counter cultural tendencies; and, secondly, where it fails to acknowledge the importance of the early visionaries' shrewd commercial moves. All authors quoted here note the similarities between the emergence of the personal computer and the history of radio in the first half of the last century, as described in

Chapter 2. That history began with the development of some technological capability for radio transmission, but with uncertainty over its application, before its ready adoption by amateur enthusiasts and its eventual incorporation by a few dominant organisations. In the case of the personal computer, the crucial technology initially found application in a separate sector.

The electronics industry continued to advance its development of the integrated circuit, packing ever more components into each chip (so called 'large scale integration' and later very large scale integration or VLSI). ICs were used in a range of electronic devices, as well as in the components of the minicomputers and mainframes, but their capacity for miniaturisation was deployed to greatest advantage in items like calculators, where electronics began to replace the electromechanical operation of the desk machine. The potential market for calculators was enormous, and as they became cheaper they also became more sophisticated. IC manufacturer Intel, asked by one calculator company to come up with a still more demanding design, built a versatile logic device that could be programmed for particular applications so that it could be produced in larger numbers and tailored to different products, not just calculators. The 4004 chip, as it was known, was announced in 1971 and was the basis for the microprocessor, containing all the programmable processing components within a single IC. Electronic calculators became portable and shifted from the desk to the pocket (at least, to large pockets). The more expensive were programmable, that is, the user could use the keys to enter codes which made the calculator do particular calculations beyond those already available on its keys. The typical user was a professional who had a need for calculations in his daily life but who might tinker at home at the end of the day. From this growing number of programmable calculator owners, as with any group of enthusiasts (such as the radio enthusiasts before the 1920s), clubs formed, newsletters were published, and tips, stories and favourite programmes were shared. Meanwhile, computers remained bulky devices intended for use in larger, corporate environments and provided little incentive for development of the microprocessor: 'If it was generally known that enough transistors could be placed on a chip to make a computer, it was also generally believed that the market for such a chip was so low that its sales would never recoup the large development costs required' (Ceruzzi 2003: 217). Indeed, for much of the 1970s the electronics industry and the computing industry remained separate sectors of activity.

In addition to calculators, microprocessors were also used extensively in electronic games, such as Atari's 'Pong' which was developed for amusement arcades before being sold as a console to be plugged into a television set. Electronics enthusiasts' magazines such as *Popular Electronics* and *Radio Electronics* had long described home construction projects for hobbyists and also began including ICs and microprocessors as prices fell. Enthusiasts clubs met regularly across the US but particularly in California, where the electronics industry was concentrated (in Silicon Valley). One such hobbyist was Ed Roberts, who supplied kits to readers of electronics magazines. In 1974, he designed and built a prototype computer based on microprocessors. Known as the Altair 8800, it was splashed across the front cover of the January 1975 issue of *Popular Electronics* which described it as 'the most powerful minicomputer project ever'; it was available as a sub-$400 kit and created a storm of interest amongst electronics enthusiasts and calculator enthusiasts alike.

It was not only the electronics hobbyists who seized upon the Altair. There also developed in the US, particularly in California at the end of the 1960s, a 'computer liberation' movement (Streeter 2004; Mosco 2005). This was one strand within what became known as the counter culture, which was in large part a reaction to the US wars in Cambodia and Vietnam. It expressed itself culturally through alternative, 'hippie' lifestyles and college dropouts, and politically through student riots and campaigns for civil rights. There was certainly a strong anti-science, anti-technology current, partly a response to the high technology nature of the warfare waged particularly in Vietnam but also expressed earlier in publications such as Rachel Carson's *Silent Spring*, credited by many as starting the environmental protection movement. However, there was also a vocal 'alternative technology' lobby which sought to 'reclaim' technology from the big corporations and harness it for public good. For example, E F Schumacher published his famous *Small is Beautiful* in 1974, which argued amongst other things for a harmonious embrace of technology on a 'human scale', while radical scientists set up campaigning groups such as Science for the People and, in the UK, the less-catchily named British Society for Social Responsibility in Science (for an account of these groups see Werskey 2007). In a similar vision to Paul Baran's computer utility, the computer liberators of this tendency argued that computing power could bring information and communication to all, and to achieve this computing should be cheap. In the early 1970s, some, such as the Computer Memory Project, succeeded in putting remote terminals (connected to a mainframe) into public libraries. The arrival of the Altair, however, brought the possibility of a personal computer within reach.

The Altair excited the interests of both groups: the computer liberationists were enthused by the potential affordability of personal computing power, while the calculator and electronics enthusiasts embraced the arrival of a 'proper' computer. However, we would not recognise the Altair as a computer today. It was a simple box (once assembled from its kit components) with a line of toggle switches, which could be set to input binary code one line at a time, and eight LED indicators showing the execution of the programme. Nevertheless, the excitement spawned new computer clubs, including the influential

Homebrew Computer Club in Menlo Park, Silicon Valley (where, incidentally, Thomas Edison had set up a laboratory a hundred years earlier, developing the phonograph amongst other things). Soon, in July 1975, the first computer shop opened in Los Angeles, and the first home computing magazine, *Byte*, was launched. A 'world wide' Altair conference was planned for March 1976. Ideas, successes and failures were shared in the computer clubs and before long, further kits were being sold which allowed peripherals to be connected to the Altair to enhance its usability, such as teletypes (a kind of combined keyboard and screen), television sets and audio cassette tape recorders which meant data could be stored and shared. Again, this kind of collective endeavour was reminiscent of the early radio enthusiasts' clubs and lives on now perhaps in the open source software movement.

In what was a precursor of things to come, two college friends, Bill Gates and Paul Allen, who had messed around with computer programming on a time-sharing mainframe to which their school had access, saw the magazine cover announcing the Altair's launch and approached Ed Roberts, offering to write a software compiler for it which would allow owners to programme it using the popular BASIC programming language. They set up a company, 'Micro-Soft' (later removing the hyphen) and developed the compiler by the middle of 1975, which Roberts then sold as part of the kit. Gates, however, argued that he had never been directly employed by Roberts, and so it was he, Gates, who owned the rights to the software. He went on to argue in public, including at the Altair conference, that for Altair enthusiasts to copy the software was illegal and that programmers should have an incentive to produce good software. Rather than the software simply being one contributory component of the total kit, alongside the case, the switches, boards and wires, Gates (who was the son of a lawyer, and was himself studying law at Harvard at the time) saw very early that the software would become every bit as significant in the development of computing as the hardware itself and sought to secure his place in that future.

Another computer enthusiast at the time was Steve Wozniak, who had messed around with electronics since childhood, dropped out of college (a common occurrence in the 1970s) and put together a rudimentary microprocessor-based computer in his spare time while employed in a junior role at the Digital Equipment Corporation (DEC). Without knowing much about the Altair, he showed his prototype, which he called the Apple, to the Homebrew Computer Club, prompting his friend Steve Jobs to urge him to market it through the local computer shop. Jobs helped Wozniak develop the Apple into its successor, Apple II, and decided to market it as a finished package rather than as a kit, so it came as a complete box with screen and keyboard. It was to be marketed as a 'home computer', and its first advertisement described how it could be used for managing bank accounts, keeping recipes, or keeping track of biorhythms (this *was* the 1970s, and Jobs had spent the requisite period of his youth travelling in India). Again, much like Baran's suggestions for the computer utility, this was a completely misjudged market; only a particularly 'enthusiastic' computer user would keep the machine in the kitchen and use it for looking up recipes, and there remained little compelling domestic application for the personal computer at that time (Campbell-Kelly and Aspray 1996: 249). Hobbyists continued to develop the computer, however, and software started to become available which allowed the personal computer to be used by those without specialised knowledge of the hardware. For example, VisiCalc was a spreadsheet for personal computers that became widely used in small offices and in the homes of those who used computers at work. By the end of the 1970s, a number of computers were now available, many through high street shops, and the market was beginning to be taken seriously by the large computer companies. IBM, as a supplier of mainframe and minicomputers to big business, saw little role for itself in a small personal computer market, but by 1980 this had grown sufficiently important for it to plan its own personal computer. Having been able to watch the development of the market, IBM adopted a number of new practices such as outsourcing, both of hardware and software. It considered a number of suppliers of its operating system software before settling on Microsoft.

The IBM brand gave significant credibility to the personal computer, in both the small office and the developing home market, and sales were huge. In contrast with Apple, IBM's decision to outsource suppliers meant they did not control the design of the microprocessor circuitry, and a number of other computer manufacturers began to copy the basic structure; the IBM system slowly became a standard adopted for the personal computer. The competition amongst manufacturers of these IBM clones helped reduce prices and sales expanded further. With each clone requiring Microsoft's disk-operating software (MS-DOS, which *was* legally protected) to run it, this growth generated huge revenues for Microsoft. Before long, manufacturers offering computers which were not based on the IBM system had stopped production; only Apple remained as a competitor to the IBM clones, and its sales were becoming tiny in comparison. Apple's response was to challenge the clones in the area of software rather than hardware.

GUI, WIMP and WYSIWYG

Computing generates more than its fair share of abbreviations and acronyms, many contrived, and no fewer than three describe the next transformation in the personal computer's fortunes. The computers sold to homes and offices until the 1980s, whether based on MS-DOS or the Apple II's operating system (also written by Microsoft), were based on the command line interface, that is, on instructions typed in word by word. It was tedious, clumsy and required the learning of a new language. For example, to transfer a document from the computer's hard drive onto a removable disk could involve the user in typing lines of text, appearing on the screen thus:

```
C:> COPY C:\DATABASE\FILE.DOC
=A:\RECORDS\FILE.DOC
C:> CD A:\RECORDS
A:\RECORDS> DIR
FILE.DOC
A:\RECORDS>CD C:
C:>
```

A simple typing mistake in entering the commands would stop the system in its tracks; yet, as the only system on offer, computer users put up with it. Given the ease with which a file is copied with today's graphical interfaces, it is hard to imagine that so many did so, and though sales of personal computers were growing, it did not establish itself as a 'standard' piece of domestic equipment for some decades. The introduction of the graphical user interface (GUI), sometimes denoted by its essential elements of windows, icons, mouse and pointer/pull-down menu (WIMP), helped in this development. Though it is often assumed it began with the Apple Macintosh's launch in January 1984, the origins of the GUI go back much further to developments on making the computer more 'human friendly' undertaken at the US Defense Department's Advanced Research Projects Agency (ARPA, from which the internet also originated). When ARPA changed its research strategy at the end of the 1960s, a number of its computer scientists moved to the newly established Palo Alto Research Center (PARC) set up by Xerox, the office photocopier company. Xerox was feeling the pressure of competition from Japanese copier manufacturers and was seeking to expand its market by developing an 'electronic office'. With its influx of specialist computer scientists, it was responsible for a number of innovations but failed to capitalise on any of them. As work began on the Alto office computer system during the 1970s, a graphical interface was designed, and text display and editing systems in which the text appeared on the screen as it would be printed out: the so-called 'what you see is what you get' (WYSIWYG) format. As this was intended for an office system, based on a minicomputer, it was never adapted for the personal computer as it emerged during those years, and when the Xerox office machine was launched, it was too expensive in comparison with the plethora of alternatives that were by then on the market. Other companies, more used to selling into commercial markets, began to adopt the techniques, while Steve Jobs from Apple, in which Xerox by now had a stake, visited PARC and saw the GUI system in 1979. A failed attempt to launch a GUI-based Apple computer in the business sector was followed by the development of the Macintosh by Jobs and Jef Raskin, to be aimed once again at the domestic market. Despite a huge advertising budget and spectacular launch commercial directed by Ridley Scott in 1984, sales were low. The domestic market, small as it was, was still not a place for a $2000 device whose application was unclear. It was rebranded as a business computer, with an even higher price tag but failed to shift the stranglehold that the IBM compatible had established, and the Macintosh made inroads only into a specialised sector, notably the print and graphics industry, where its GUI gave it a distinct advantage. Equally, the dominance of the IBM/MS-DOS combination also made the specialist software required for the limited Macintosh market very expensive, and it could neither match the range nor price of software applications already developed for the IBM/MS-DOS machines. Nevertheless, the Macintosh made the command line interface of MS-DOS seem dated, and Microsoft paid Apple under a licensing arrangement to use its graphical look to develop its own GUI, launched in 1985 as Microsoft Windows.

In planning the development of Microsoft Windows, two options were available: to design the new GUI from scratch, as a direct replacement for the text-driven MS-DOS, or alternatively to leave MS-DOS as the command structure for the IBM system with an additional overlay on top, presenting the user with the easier-to-use graphical interface. The former approach would be more efficient in using the machine's processing power, but would have the disadvantage that all existing software, which had been written for MS-DOS, would be rendered unusable on new machines. The second approach was adopted: MS-DOS was the basic interface, hidden most of the time from the user by the GUI, but accessible should the user be running MS-DOS software. Windows applications would in time come to be written, but meanwhile the computers could continue to work. This follows a familiar pattern, such as seen in television, where once a particular technology becomes well established, it becomes difficult to introduce innovative developments as the technology improves, and for economic reasons a technically inferior system is adopted. This proved the case with Windows: because the first machines were effectively running two sets of software, MS-DOS with the Windows overlay, they ran much more slowly than similar machines running MS-DOS alone. This in turn accelerated and steered developments in chip technology, and only with the emergence of the Intel 386 processor at the end of the 1980s did Windows run at speeds comparable with earlier MS-DOS machines.

The history of the personal computer, when it comes to be written, is likely to avoid the characterisation of it as a simple battle between Macintosh/Steve

Jobs and IBM/Bill Gates. Instead, it is likely to demonstrate a cycle of development similar to many other technologies considered here. The role of hobbyists in adopting and adapting the technology early in its development, and the desire by some to appropriate it for purposes which reflected the political climate of the time are not unique. Key decisions which played a large part in deciding which of the many technological options would be adopted were made on economic rather than technological grounds, and those companies and individuals which were often the most innovative were rarely the most economically successful. Furthermore, despite the undoubted dramatic technical progress that has been made in computing, at the domestic level at least it remained rather unremarkable, far less significant than broadcasting technologies or consumer durables like video recorders. Repeated attempts to identify a domestic application for the computer threw up the most banal examples of its potential, a trend which Nicholas Negroponte, amongst many others, continued with the emergence of the internet, as we shall see. As Winston says, 'It rapidly became clear that the appetite to replace one's cookbooks, balance one's cheque-book, keep track of one's stocks or spend happy evenings recalculating one's mortgage over different terms and interest rates was limited' (1998: 236). Even with the growing adoption of the internet, the penetration of home computers is typically only one in two households in the most advanced technological societies. Winston contrasts the first three decades of the computer's time with that of the automobile: after a similar time there were some 23 million cars in the US, and 'with the automobile came a complete remaking of the entire environment: paved streets, petrol/gas stations, car-parks, the decline of urban centres' (ibid.: 239). Though such a comparison is readily challenged, it offers a reminder that the role of technology in epoch making is not novel, but one that is bound up with the economic and political climate that both steers its development and in turn is also changed by it.

From Computation to Communication: Networks and the Internet

The time sharing of mainframe computers demonstrated the benefits of connecting computer terminals together and, once the personal computer became widespread, it was natural to explore ways of connecting them together. Connecting a set of personal computers together in a local area network (LAN) in order to share a common printer was, and remains, a common practice. The difference was that the computer-processing power, and much of the storage memory, was dispersed amongst each computer on the network rather than being held centrally with the mainframe architecture. This meant that for most of the time, programme execution was taking place on the local machine, the network being exploited only occasionally for access to the shared devices. Not having data travelling back and forth through the network simply for the purpose of processing allowed computers to work faster, and mainframe architecture was rapidly outdated by the network architecture of linked personal computers. The client-server architecture is a variation where one machine in the network, the server, stores data which is then 'served' to any of a number of linked client machines, which then process information locally; the client might also, if permitted, update the data held on the server by sending the data in the reverse direction.

Such networks require common sets of rules by which to operate. Known as protocols, these rules determine how traffic is delivered on the networks and how computers attached to the network are identified, or addressed, so that data can be sent to or retrieved from each. Two well-known protocols, for example, are those used for internet traffic: the transmission control protocol (TCP) and the internet protocol (IP).

Xerox's PARC was innovative in the development of networking architecture in the early 1970s, as in other areas such as laser printing, and the resulting Ethernet became a standard for linking computers and sharing data (though again Xerox failed to profit from its development as much as other companies). These early developments, inherited from its ARPA origins, were later adopted within academic and other networks, for linking separate mainframes and minicomputers. However, it was a number of years after its emergence that personal computers began to be networked – after all, most of these were bought initially for personal use rather than to be shared with anyone else. Each ran its own software, installed by the owner or user for her own purposes, and there was no reason why the data on one such computer should be compatible with that on any other. Networking here was not an obvious thing to do until they became commonplace in office environments, when the connection of LANs began to make economic sense for resource sharing and for backing up valuable corporate data. However, these remained *local* area networks, serving immediate and localised needs rather than creating the geographically dispersed networks seen in large organisations such as universities. Different LANs could be, and often were, using different protocols, which made perfect sense while they were intended to operate as discrete networks. Should it become desirable to connect these separate networks together for any reason, the different protocols could prove problematic. This was not yet the era of the internet.

Meanwhile, the infrastructure that was forming the backbone of the big, wide area research networks in the US, mainly comprising ARPANET owned by the military, was transferred to the National Science Foundation (NSF) in the 1980s, in order to allow its expansion to include academic and other public institutions. With what were seen as prohibitive costs, the NSF agreed to allow commercial use of its planned network. Online commercial services were already in existence by this time, offering business information to corporate clients using personal computer networks. We have seen (in Chapter 4) how videotex systems such as Prestel, and the French Minitel in particular, were also making headway into this market, particularly in Europe where sales of personal computers had been slower. In the US, services were aimed at computer users and CompuServe and America Online (AOL) were the biggest providers. By the early 1980s, videotex services were available via an interface to users of personal computers, removing the need for separate videotex terminals (Aumente 1987: 13). In the academic sector, no fewer than 2800 databases were available online, many of these being commercial enterprises (Williams 1985). Electronic messaging was also part of the networking experience and had been developed from the outset with ARPANET in the 1970s. So CompuServe's customers would each have an email address, as would AOL's, but because they did not use consistent protocols, they were not connected to each other and a CompuServe customer could not email an AOL customer; the multitude of services available in different countries across the world were also not able to connect to each other, and often an individual or a business would have multiple email addresses, one on each of a number of different services, in order to be contactable by other users, just as in the early days of the telephone, businesses would have different telephone numbers on a number of services. Still, then, this was not the internet.

The emergence of what is now known as the internet was a process which resulted from the gradual adoption of the common pair of protocols, TCP and IP (referred to together simply as TCP/IP). TCP establishes the rules for how computer data is broken up into sections known as 'packets' for transfer over a packet switched data network (PSDN, see Box 6.1) while IP controls the addressing of computers and data. IP addressing consists of a series of numbers in an internationally agreed, hierarchical addressing format. This is no different in principle from the telephone system, in which a unique telephone number identifies (in the case of the landline network) any handset's geographical location by country, region and area within that region. Before this standardisation of protocols, different countries, and different local networks within countries, worked to their own rules . The US and the UK, for example, used different formats for email addresses: bill@cityname.edu in the US for example and jill@uk.ac.cityname in the UK. With eventual agreement on what would become the international standard format for packet switching and addressing, and thus email and server addresses, progress could be made on linking up any computer network with any other network, anywhere in the world – the interconnection of networks.

With growing adoption of TCP/IP, finally, the internet could be said to have arrived.

Box 6.1 Packet Switched Networks

Packet switching makes more efficient use of network infrastructure than previous architectures. It is readily contrasted with the circuit switching technique used in telephone networks and differs because, essentially, data moves in networks as a one-way transfer (although if the transfer back and forth is quick enough it can appear to be two-way), while the telephone network genuinely consists of two-way connections.

In a circuit switched network, communication between network nodes (such as telephone calls) requires a circuit to be opened all the way from one node to the other, to allow live conversations to take place. As demand grows the network's capacity can quickly be used up and more infrastructure must be added. In Figure 6.1 A wishes to contact G, and so a circuit is established between the two nodes and remains open until one or other disconnects the circuit. If D wishes to contact E at the same time, in this simplified illustration a separate circuit must be established to avoid interference with A to G's communication.

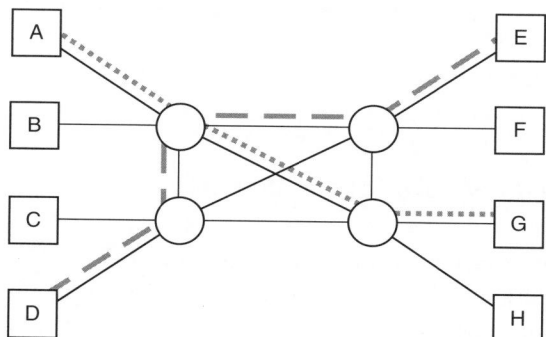

Figure 6.1 Circuit switched network

In contrast, a packet switched network is based on two techniques. The data comprising a message is broken up into small sections, packets, each addressed to identify its source and destination (Figure 6.2). This time when A communicates with H, each message packet (numbering ten in total in this example) moves one stage in the network at a time. This 'store and forward' system means it is not necessary to establish a complete route from source to destination, and the same link in the network is available for other messages such as one from D to F. At each switching point on the network, the packets may be held briefly until there is a space free in the network to send it on the next leg of its journey. Eventually all the packets arrive (by various routes) at the destination where they are reassembled into

Box 6.1 (Continued)

the original message. The small size of the data packets and need to send them only over small segments of the network at a time makes message transfer more efficient in its use of the network.

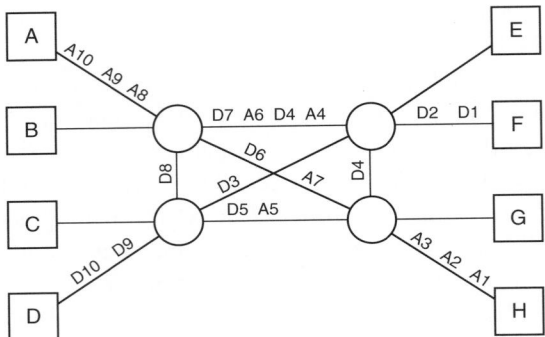

Figure 6.2 Packet switched network

World Wide Web: A GUI for the Internet

In 1993, Tim Berners-Lee, a physicist working at the CERN proton collider project in Switzerland, developed an interface using hyperlinks to navigate through a computer network. While the GUI was now a standard way of using the personal computer, until Berners-Lee's innovation, accessing other computers over the internet was still a text-based process. To get a file from another computer, or to access an online database used protocols known, respectively, as file transfer protocol and telnet, and would require the typing in of laborious ftp and telnet commands including typing in the full server addresses and file names. This represented a throwback to the command line interface of MS-DOS and others, before Macintosh and Windows, and made the internet accessible mainly to (once more) specialist computer users and enthusiasts. Berners-Lee's ideas allowed for the development of a GUI which would execute ftp and telnet (and other) commands by clicking on text or graphical links on the screen, embedded in which would be the various commands needed. The hypertext transfer protocol, http, written to allow this simple execution of commands, meant that all internet access could take place through a common browser, and the World Wide Web (WWW) as it became known, was the platform through which almost all internet access and transfer now took place. No longer was it necessary to have a specialist knowledge of computer language and addresses to access data, and equally it became straightforward to place data in the 'public domain', where it could be searched for and accessed by anyone browsing the Web, rather than those who had prior knowledge of the data's location.

In 1995, the NSF transferred ownership of the internet's 'backbone', the cables and other infrastructure carrying the bulk of the internet's traffic, to the private telecommunications sector. While commercial access to the internet had been available for some time, it was still considered primarily to be a public resource in a similar way to a public utility, and before the WWW interface its use tended to be restricted to those likely to use it in that way (such as public sector workers). Those commercial services that existed tended to be aimed at these users, offering access to electronic databases and so on of use to researchers and professional users. Now, with commercial ownership of the hardware established and access made potentially much easier for the general computer user through the Web, businesses were encouraged to explore the internet as a route to customers. Dozens, or at times hundreds, of commercial internet service providers sprang up within a year or so, and enabled public access through gateways to the internet, and it became fully open for business. Web content began to reflect this much more commercial approach to 'data' communication, with the development of more sophisticated graphical and audiovisual content published alongside conventional, text-based material. With the inclusion of advertising, this new emphasis encouraged technical developments allowing, for example, shopping and other financial transactions to take place. What had begun as a technological system intended to facilitate easy exchange of computer material between researchers, and then evolved into a common interface for searching electronic databases, was now beginning rapidly to be transformed into an electronic marketplace.

Now, the era of the fully commercialised internet had begun.

Convergence

Whatever else the term 'convergence' means in the context of communications technologies, it has spawned a number of unpleasant lexical offspring. In their various attempts to capture the novelty of convergence, commentators have described content as 'edutainment' or 'infotainment' while the beneficiaries of such developments are now 'viewers' or 'prosumers' (Toffler 1980). The intention of course is to suggest that technological developments are changing the way we communicate, blurring boundaries between different media and allowing us to interact more with our media rather than consume in a passive way. The earlier discussion on digital television introduced the notion that the new technology could be seen as more of an information resource than a simple, one-way television service, with access to services and information from a range of sources. This resemblance of digital television to the internet also has its mirror image in the streaming or downloading of television programmes over the internet, to be watched in most cases on a computer screen.

What is Convergence?

In an effort to understand what convergence means, we can consider three overlapping spheres in which it is assumed to be taking place: the technological sphere, that of the corporate and organisational world and the cultural sphere.

Convergent technologies

Digital technology is often held up as being the root cause of convergence. With all forms of technological communication migrating to digital technology, the ease with which its electronic signals can be processed means that there is no fundamental difference between the data produced by images, sounds or text. Indeed the head of the MIT Media Lab, Nicholas Negroponte, suggests hyperbolically that there is almost nothing that cannot now be reduced to bits of digital data (Negroponte 1995). The convergence of telecommunications and computing was seen first in the 1970s with the development of videotex and later in computer-based client-server networks such as those of CompuServe and AOL; and the subsequent adoption of internet protocols in the 1990s means that now any platform is available to be used by any medium. So data can be carried over the wires of the internet, of course, but increasingly that same data is carried wirelessly to computer users on the radio waves, for example, in Wi Fi or 3G mobile networks. While networks previously were confined to transfer of text and simple images, the data reduction techniques deployed in audio and video make it possible to stream good quality sound (radio programming) over the internet, and reasonable quality video (television), particularly as the limited capacity of a standard telephone line (and the failure of the cable industry to connect optical fibre networks to homes) has been overcome with the development of ADSL technology – broadband telephone lines are now the most popular means of internet connection to the home in the UK. Equally, digital storage formats such as disks, tape or solid state systems (for example 'flash' memory cards) simply store data, irrespective of what that data represents. With the increased processing power of computers over the years, even a basic home computer can receive data from a still camera, video camera, downloaded audio and so on and process or manipulate that data as desired. The range of options for output of that data is equally expanded: physical formats such as DVDs and memory sticks can hold video or data files, or the output can be uploaded to a web server for 'publishing' over the internet; advanced portable devices such as mobile phones and 'personal media' like mp3 players, containing their own computer processing abilities, can store and play this data in all its forms. Automated filtering software such as that used in personal video recorders (for example TiVo) and RSS computer feeds make it easier to select material for downloading over networks to computer stores. Here then, convergence centres around the embedded computer as processor and store for all manner of media and communications content, with inputs from a whole range of sources and outputs to a similar variety of devices and outlets.

Organisations

These technological changes are reflected in the practices of businesses and other organisations. Certain business models are clearly challenged by new technological developments. Video and DVD rental shops, for example, face an uncertain future if films can be readily downloaded over networks (although many remain in business even though their demise has long been forecast). Other businesses are moving out of their traditional areas. For example, in the UK, BT, for many years the dominant force in telecommunications, now offers a subscription television service in competition with cable and satellite operators. The blurring between telecommunications and broadcasting has encouraged such companies to look for strategic alliances or mergers, exemplified in 2000 by the biggest merger in corporate history: print media, film and broadcast giant Time Warner merged with internet service provider AOL in a $190 billion venture in an attempt to secure part of the coming converged world. As Williams wrote at the time (Williams 2001: 197; see also Golding 1998):

> Clearly, the commercial logic of the deal is impeccable: AOL has access to the massive content resources of the Time publishing empire and the film, music and television of CNN, Warner Bros., Time Warner Cable, and much more, whilst Time Warner gets access to the world's largest online and e-commerce platform.

Similar cross sector alliances have taken place throughout the industry, with Microsoft for example investing heavily in the shares of cable companies Telewest and NTL. On a rather smaller scale, mobile phone retailer Carphone Warehouse has partnered with radio companies in operating a number of the UK's digital radio multiplexes, as the use of digital radio signals for data delivery to handheld devices begins to emerge as a potential market (Lax 2007a: 118).

Convergent cultural forms

In previous times, in the analogue world perhaps, we have associated telephones with wires, broadcasting with radio waves and text with print media. Although such an association was never absolute, with digital technology we find point-to-point telephone communication carried by radio waves, 'broadcasting' down wires to computers, while 'print' media publish text, audio and video on their websites. These developments in our use of media and information represent an acceleration of the pace of change in comparison with, say, the introduction of video recording or colour television. Television broadcasters are now having to consider how programming might be configured so that it can be watched both on huge HDTV screens and on tiny handheld screens a few millimetres across. Radio stations, whose programmes were often premised on the understanding that they were ephemeral and often live, now must consider that these same programmes may well be stored and played back at a much later date. Where once we would turn to broadcast news for breaking stories but to newspapers for deeper analysis and commentary, now newspapers break news on their websites, while at the end of their bulletins broadcasters suggest we visit *their* websites for more coverage and analysis. Broadcasting, long regarded as a one-way medium, now incorporates a degree of interactivity through offering web forums and other means of responding to programmes, replicating the letters pages found in newspapers. While the transition between different media (here including the internet) is not seamless, most people continuing to *watch* television and *use* a computer as separate activities, the rebranding by manufacturers of high specification computers as 'media centres' reveals an expectation that the eventual incorporation of television, computer, video recorder, audio player and so on into a single box, though long anticipated, remains a continuing objective.

Early talk of convergence focused primarily on the first of these three categories. The expansion in the 1980s and 1990s of computer networks beyond corporate intranets and into the public arena led to fevered speculation about the emerging 'wired' lifestyle. Where the cable television systems had proved to be mere extensions of existing broadcast television rather than enabling a new, data enriched world, computer networks and the enhanced functionality offered by a computer in comparison with a television set meant that anything was possible. With a fixation purely on the technology, and an apparent dislocation from the rest of the world, commentators suggested exciting futures. As noted, Nicholas Negroponte generated much media interest around the time of the publication of *Being Digital* (1995). Its very title suggested that new technologies would become completely embedded in our lives. In newspaper interviews, he suggested that networked sensors woven into clothing would identify us and unlock the doors to our homes as we approach (and switch on the lights, kettle and run the bath if we so desired). 'The home could become a very different kind of place. Your refrigerator, for instance, could tell your toaster that it's almost out of bread' (cited in Hunt 1994). In a similar vein, in 1994, Bowen described the future home of 2008, in which operating an electric toothbrush would, helpfully, switch on the electric kettle in the kitchen (Bowen 1994: 1). On a rather grander scale, the first UK issue of *Wired* magazine invoked the spirit of Tom Paine (declaring him a 'digital revolutionary') and his pamphlet *Common Sense* written in 1776 in the prelude to the American Declaration of Independence. *Wired* celebrated those 'in the vanguard of the digital revolution' and, slotted between full page advertisements for Porsche cars and Macintosh computers, reprinted Paine's 200-year-old declaration, 'We have it in our power to begin the world over again'.

The emphasis in much of the commentary around this time was that convergence between computing and communication technologies was bound up with individual expression and freedom. From the libertarian stance of *Wired* to the self-help 'virtual communities' espoused by Howard Rheingold (1994), new technologies were seen as an opportunity for individuals to free themselves from the constraints of legislation or bureaucracy. Others celebrated the anonymity of participation in online communication, with the proliferation of immersive environments or role-playing games into which one could escape from 'real life' (Turkle 1996). This was a period when postmodern thinking was in the ascendant in some academic and intellectual circles, and political ideas tended to coalesce around the triumph of free-market capitalism following the collapse of the Eastern bloc (which presented a world view seen by some as at least an alternative to Western market capitalism). The emphasis on the individual and the freedom to reinvent oneself chimed with these ideas of self-help and individual expression; at the same time, the rampant political triumphalism might have given increasingly pessimistic liberals a greater incentive to find another world into which to escape, or at least consider the possibilities of new technologies as offering a novel, alternative way to a different kind of society. The opening up of the internet to those looking solely to the commercial benefits offered by convergence was not welcomed by those who had regarded it principally as a resource for the public good. However, when US Vice president Al Gore made his 'Buenos Aires' speech during the 1994 mid-term election campaigns, he had signalled clearly that this expansion of networks was to be at least in part a commercial undertaking (Gore 1994):

> ...we now have at hand the technological breakthroughs and economic means to bring all the communities of the world together...To accomplish this purpose, legislators, regulators, and business people must do this: build and operate a Global Information Infrastructure. This GII will circle the globe with information superhighways on which all people can travel. These highways – or more accurately networks of distributed intelligence – will allow us to share information, to connect, and to communicate as a global community. From these connections we will derive...a greater sense of shared stewardship of our small planet.

In 1995, Richard Barbrook and Andy Cameron published *The Californian Ideology*, a critique of the libertarian, free market tendencies of many of the emerging ideas about the convergent, online world and contrasting these with the radical, left-leaning countercultural and computer liberation ideas of the 1970s (Barbrook and Cameron 1995). This provoked a furious response from Louis Rossetto, the editor of *Wired*, who appeared to confirm Barbrook and Cameron's points by attacking their 'attachment to failed 19th century social and economic analysis' and listing the 'failures' of European policy: 'High European taxes which have restricted spending on technology and hence retarded its development; state telco monopolies which have kept prices high and service bad...; social welfare policies which reward parasitical living rather than risk-taking', before concluding, 'it's time to encourage competition, risk taking, democracy and meritocracy' (Rossetto 1995). A similar neoliberal political association with the new networking technologies was proclaimed with the publication in 1994 of *Cyberspace and the American Dream*, calling itself 'a Magna Carta for the knowledge age'. Following Toffler's earlier suggestion of three 'waves' of economic development, the authors suggested that the new, 'Third Wave' economy meant nothing less than overthrowing old ideas of regulation of markets, taxation and limitations on freedom. Described by Winner as a 'right wing manifesto', providing a 'new injection of seltzer' into 'Toffler's simplistic wave theory of history, barely fizzing a couple of years ago', the 'Magna Carta' concluded by declaring: 'It is time to embrace these challenges, to grasp the future and pull ourselves forward. If we do so, we will indeed renew the American Dream and enhance the promise of American life'

(Winner 1996: 64–5; Dyson et al. 1996: 308). The identification of this convergent trend was clearly as much for its political and economic possibilities as technological.

In more recent years, the convergence debate has focused on the growing use of digital tools for personal expression and 'social networking'. Described by some as an alternative media, increasing numbers are writing blogs, recording podcasts and posting video clips to the web, using computers certainly but also mobile phone cameras, personal media players and so-called smartphones among the plethora of small, portable capture and storage devices now available. These tools are augmented by sophisticated editing and authoring software that allows images to be manipulated, video footage and music or other audio material to be edited and Web pages to be created relatively easily. Social networking websites such as Facebook and MySpace allow all these individual postings to be linked up, shared between groups of people or automatically 'pulled' from the Web onto one's own computer (or similar device). The convergence here is certainly technological in that telecommunications and computing are brought together as with earlier notions of convergence; there is also a convergence with broadcasting technologies, to the extent that posting video and audio onto the Web could constitute broadcasting. The same tendencies for existing media and communications companies to move into new areas is also evident: for example, News Corporation bought MySpace in 2006, while in 2007 music streaming site last.fm was acquired in a £140 million takeover by CBS.

The extent to which we might be witnessing new cultural forms is less clear. Claims that these new communications tools and practices are replacing existing forms have to be rejected as premature on the simple grounds that 'traditional' media continue to survive and show little sign of diminishing in popular support. While newspaper sales continue a downward trend begun long before the internet could have had an impact, television viewing remains more-or-less unchanged from previous decades, while 'old fashioned' radio listening, if anything, is increasing, for example in the UK up from an annual average of 985 hours in 1999 to 1066 in 2003 (Ofcom 2004: 35). Each medium of course has changed in order to adapt to or incorporate the new interactive technologies, typically by linking programmes or newspaper articles to associated websites with forums and other interactive opportunities. Only in one aspect can we discern possible significant change: traditional media usage amongst young people in particular does appear to be affected by the use of the internet. Ofcom research (based on survey responses, in other words perceptions rather than actual observation) suggested that internet users aged between 15 and 24 were the group which experienced the greatest reduction in consumption of traditional media (other than television) thanks to their online activities (Ofcom 2006c: 43). It is too early to say whether this is a real or perceived trend and whether, as these younger internet users age, they will return to more traditional patterns of media consumption. Overall then, rather than replacing existing media, new media is as much about the augmentation of existing media. With blogs easily linked to existing media, for example online news articles, the commentary and further linking to additional stories create a means by which, amongst the inevitable trivia and narcissism, a nascent form of 'citizen journalism' might emerge (for example Tumber (2001) contrasts the rise of internet journalism with the decline of political reporting in the mainstream media). While the 1990s ideas of convergence might have been a response to or, in some cases, an embracing of the emerging neoliberal politics, in the early 2000s a more radicalised politics shifted focus from a critique of globalisation (seen first in the 1999 'Battle of Seattle') to an anti-war activism following the post-9/11 invasions of Afghanistan in 2002 and Iraq in 2003, seen most publicly in the mass demonstrations of 15 February 2003. The World Wide Web became a focus for campaigners, politicians and observers alike (Couldry and Curran 2003; de Jong et al. 2005). Political blogging is increasingly considered an important part of campaigning, an importance reinforced by the growing reliance on blogs by the existing print media. Newspapers regularly augment the traditional letters pages with extracts culled from blogs, and politicians, always keen to 'connect' with their electors, are equally ready to publish blogs (Coleman 2005).

The themes of this new debate about the consequences of convergence are control and flexibility. The technological focus of the convergence debate is no longer the joining of communications and computer technologies but on technologies for acquisition and origination, and technologies for consumption. New digitised technologies allow far more people than before to capture moments of everyday life or to construct their own stories, to manipulate and to publish those stories. In the context of a more widespread radicalised politics, with a critique of neoliberalism and increasingly globalised media corporations, though of course not always articulated as such, some novel forms of organising and linking ideas and stories are beginning to emerge. Yet novel means of cultural expression do not render old ones obsolete or unimportant. The mainstream media in its various forms, although embracing and adapting to emerging possibilities, remain as popular and significant as ever for the majority of people, and for political campaigning, such widely used sources remain a target for publicity; as Jordan says, 'Protest without media coverage is like a mime performance in the dark: possible but fairly pointless' (1998: 327). Neither do new cultural forms or new technologies automatically connote a new power upon their users. Downing suggests that there is no reason to imagine that the South African Apartheid system, for example, would have fallen any quicker had the internet been available at the time. Even so, he says, 'like free speech, it is better to have the internet's potential than not to have it' (Downing 2005: 160).

Convergence is Not New

The commonly accepted explanation of convergence, indeed one that has been reflected above, is that it begins with the emergence of computer communications, or networks, in combination with telecommunications (in the 1970s) and continued in the 1990s to incorporate existing mass media (print and broadcast) with the development of digitised content transferable over the internet. Certainly these phenomena are real but, it would be wrong to imagine that similar phenomena had not occurred previously. Though ostensibly describing those who talk of the 'information society' (see Chapter 8), Kumar could equally well be considering commentators on convergence when he says that they 'attribute to the present developments which are the culmination of trends deep in the past. What seem to them novel and current can be shown to have been in the making for the past hundred years' (Kumar 2005: 44). Already, at the beginning of this book, and therefore from the earliest days of electrical communication, we saw that the telephone was being developed simultaneously as a point-to-point communication device and as a proto-broadcasting service. The videophone, a logical extension of the voice telephone to incorporate moving images, has been imagined almost as long as the telephone has existed, and portrayed in science fiction film repeatedly over the decades: *Metropolis* (1926), *2001 A Space Odyssey* (1968) and *Blade Runner* (1982) are just some examples. While the numerous attempts to market the videophone (for instance, Bell in 1971, BT in 1993) failed, it could be regarded as an early example of one sector (telecommunications) borrowing techniques from another (television). Radio offers a further example: in its early days, radio stations were not operated simply by 'radio broadcasters' but run by a variety of organisations such as department stores and newspaper companies. A number of these newspapers explored novel uses of radio technology. In March 1939, *Radio Craft* magazine described the launch of a facsimile newspaper delivered by radio. An afternoon edition of the St Louis *Post-Dispatch* would be transmitted over the airwaves to a radio receiver, which would also contain a printing device, and the newspaper, complete with pictures, would be printed out on a roll of paper like a modern day fax machine. The receiving devices, manufactured by RCA, were expensive at $260, but this did not stop a number of newspapers exploring similar systems before the lack of subscribers ended interest in providing the service (Anon 1939). Indeed, though radio is rarely considered to be at the forefront of technological or cultural change, it could be argued that radio has embraced the convergent potential of technological change more wholeheartedly than most media. In recent years, for example, radio has changed from a simple one-way transmission delivered over the airwaves to a radio receiver to a multi-platform service available on mobile phones, the internet and digital television. Its form has also adapted to changing technology: just as newspapers have long held archives of their publications, now often available on the internet, radio too has begun to archive its programme output, either for 'catch-up' time shifted listening over the internet or for download as podcasts to be listened to later. Such services are proving popular with internet users but, again, while a convincing instance of technological convergence, few would suggest that it constitutes a cultural transformation.

As a final example, digital imaging is commonly assumed to be a recent practice dependent upon the emergence of the 'multimedia' computer, yet it also has a longer history. McFarlane describes the use of telegraph lines for the transatlantic transmission of pictures using digital techniques in the 1920s, while Prendergast traces the uses of computers for manipulation (or enhancement) of photographs back to the early 1960s (McFarlane 1972; Prendergast 2003). The whole issue of the journal in which McFarlane's article appeared almost four decades ago was introduced with the explanation: 'This special issue has been motivated by the realization that more and more frequently the computer is taking a major role in the processing, transmission, reception, enhancement, and restoration of natural quality images or pictures' (Andrews and Enloe 1972: 766).

Conclusion

A brief history of the computer illustrates its changing primary function from one of calculation to one of communication. Comparisons with the history of radio, as noted by those authors upon whose work much of this chapter is based, are apposite, in particular in recording the engagement with and shaping of the technology's development by its users. While this occurred early on in radio's history, at a time when few had a clear vision of what radio might eventually become, the computer's first decades were shaped by some very precise intentions of its designers, though less clear appreciation of potential customers. The promotion by libertarians and progressives of the personal computer for its radical social potential recalls the efforts of the earliest proponents of radio broadcasting and the later rise of pirate radio stations. It is this degree of engagement with computing technology which perhaps explains the willingness to see the more recent adoption of myriad digital communications devices as heralding some new convergent age in which all can share. However, rather than being a novel phenomenon driven by recent changes in technology, the longer history of convergence suggests that while change is certainly taking place in all three areas considered above – the technological, the organisational and the cultural spheres – there does not exist a simple, causal relationship between the three. Despite the recent, undeniably rapid advances in the technologies of communication, the most important of our three categories has been the changes in organisational structures. Convergence of corporations from previously disparate sectors has not been technologically driven so much as economically and politically enabled. The recent years during which convergence has been most celebrated are precisely those when regulations keeping the sectors separate have been dismantled. Legislation limiting the number of radio stations a company may own, or restricting television channel ownership by a newspaper owning company have been relaxed, as have restrictions on overseas companies buying media and communications organisations. Formerly state-owned telecommunications operators have been privatised and allowed to invest freely in other sectors, while public service obligations on commercial broadcasters have been relaxed or eliminated altogether. For governments, media policy has become aligned with industrial policy, as the media has been regarded as key to enhanced economic competitiveness (Freedman 2003, 2008). The UK government's media department, for example, explained this clearly (DCMS 1998):

> A major objective of the review [of regulation] is to ensure that we have a regulatory structure which will allow the UK to gain maximum economic and social benefit from the process of convergence while securing the required quality and variety of programming and adequate consumer protection. Where appropriate, lighter-touch regulation applied consistently across the converged market will give the communications industry the confidence to invest in the development of new digital services.

In this context, 'convergence' in the technological or cultural spheres should not surprise us. As competitive entities, companies will seek every possible avenue for generating revenue from consumers, and the breaking down of regulatory barriers between platforms focuses energies on removing any technological barriers. This is a task in progress rather than one completed. Television broadcasting and internet streaming are still not equivalent. At times of surges in demand (for example the 9/11 terrorist attacks or publication of controversial inquiry reports), internet networks jam, and to find the latest news we turn once again to broadcast television or radio. Consequently, while cultural forms and user practices are changing (as ever they do), they have not yet done so on a scale that constitutes a social transformation and appear far from doing so; most news is still consumed through television, newspaper circulations continue a longstanding, steady rather than accelerated decline, and blogs and internet journalism have yet to have the impact that stories on either of these two older media create on a regular basis. If we seek evidence for transformations and apparent convergence, it is to be found most clearly within the economic arena.

Mobile Communications 7

In Chapter 2, we saw that the advantages of communication without the physical constraint of wires was anticipated during the second half of the 19th century, and turning this into a practical possibility made Guglielmo Marconi both famous and wealthy over the following years. Marconi saw that the Admiralty would gain a clear benefit from being able to communicate beyond the horizon, as the limits of existing methods were breached by the increasing speed of warships and other vessels. The crude spark transmitters made Morse code communication possible over great distances, not just between places where connecting a physical cable would have been impossible (such as shore and ship) but also where it would have proved much more expensive to do so. His transatlantic demonstration showed that Morse signals could cross oceans and suggested that the benefits of the huge efforts 40 years earlier to lay a transatlantic telegraph cable might have been more cheaply realised using radio wave techniques.

The advantage Marconi's signals had was the potential range of wireless transmissions; the disadvantage was their poor selectivity. The burst of radio signals meant it was difficult to send more than one message at a time without interference. Later, techniques in tuning of radio transmissions were improved, but most attention during this period had focused on the beginnings of broadcasting. However, better tuning also aided radio's one-to-one capability and maritime radio communication benefited, while law enforcement and the armed forces became the first to deploy land-based mobile radio services. In 1921, the Detroit Police Department began using one-way radio transmissions to officers out in patrol cars. This would consist of a simple Morse or other coded message, and the officers would then need to call back to their headquarters from a standard, wired telephone in a 'police box' (mostly familiar these days as *Dr Who*'s Tardis in the BBC television series) or from a public telephone. Later, Motorola developed two-way devices for service in World War II that allowed voice communications, the 'Handie-Talkie' and the 'Walkie-Talkie' (Dutton et al. 2001: 12). However, these were private systems, intended to work over a limited geographical area and between those who had been granted access by being provided with the transmitter-receiver devices. Today's mobile or cellular phone owes little technologically to those days, though conceptually the advantages of being wireless are similar. (Note: although the term 'cell phone' or 'cellular phone' is strictly more accurate than 'mobile phone', as a satellite phone for example is also mobile but uses quite a different technology, 'mobile phone' will be used here interchangeably with cell phone, as both terms are in common usage.)

An additional historical footnote in this conceptual history is provided by Jon Agar's lively account of the mobile phone. He describes how Swedish electrical engineer Lars Magnus Ericsson, whose company made telegraph and telephone equipment, installed a telephone in his wife's car in 1910 (by this time he was retired, and this episode was more in the spirit of a hobby than a commercial endeavour). The telephone was powered by cranking a handle, and connected to the public telephone network by, apparently, using poles to connect wires to the overhead telephone lines alongside the road (Agar 2003: 8–9). This was not truly mobile of course – the car had to be parked each time the telephone was to be used – but it demonstrated an early connection between communication and mobility, the private automobile being the emblematic mobile technology of the 20th century, and of course Ericsson's company went on to be one of the major agents in the mobile phone's development.

Frequency Re-use and the Cellular Structure

The automobile is the obvious host for a mobile radio telephone. The power requirements can be supplied by the vehicle's own battery, or supplementary batteries carried, and the significant weight of the device is easily transported. For the emergency services, private mobile radio (PMR) became as essential in the post-War period as it had earlier proved in the armed forces. Domestic versions were later used by taxi operators and companies running vehicle fleets. In order to run such services, the use of the electromagnetic spectrum must be managed, just as in other areas of radio communication such as broadcasting. From the earliest days of radio broadcasting, frequency management had sought to ensure that listeners could choose from a number of different stations without interference, some of these being local and others national. With the scarcity of radio frequencies in comparison with the demand for them, a particular frequency channel could be allocated to a number of different stations provided they were sufficiently geographically separated that their respective transmission areas would not overlap (see Box 2.2). This re-use of frequencies could equally be used in PMR – a taxi company in one city might be allocated the use of the same radio channels as one in some other, distant city. After all, in most cases, PMR users such as taxi companies are only interested in communication over a limited area. By confining the transmission area, by careful choice of transmitter sites and power, the re-use of frequencies thus makes efficient use of scarce spectrum, allowing larger numbers of users to access the airwaves than if the transmissions radiated over large regions or even national distances; the mobile phone system built upon the route taken by PMR by breaking an area down into small transmission cells, far smaller than coverage areas used in PMR (Figure 7.1).

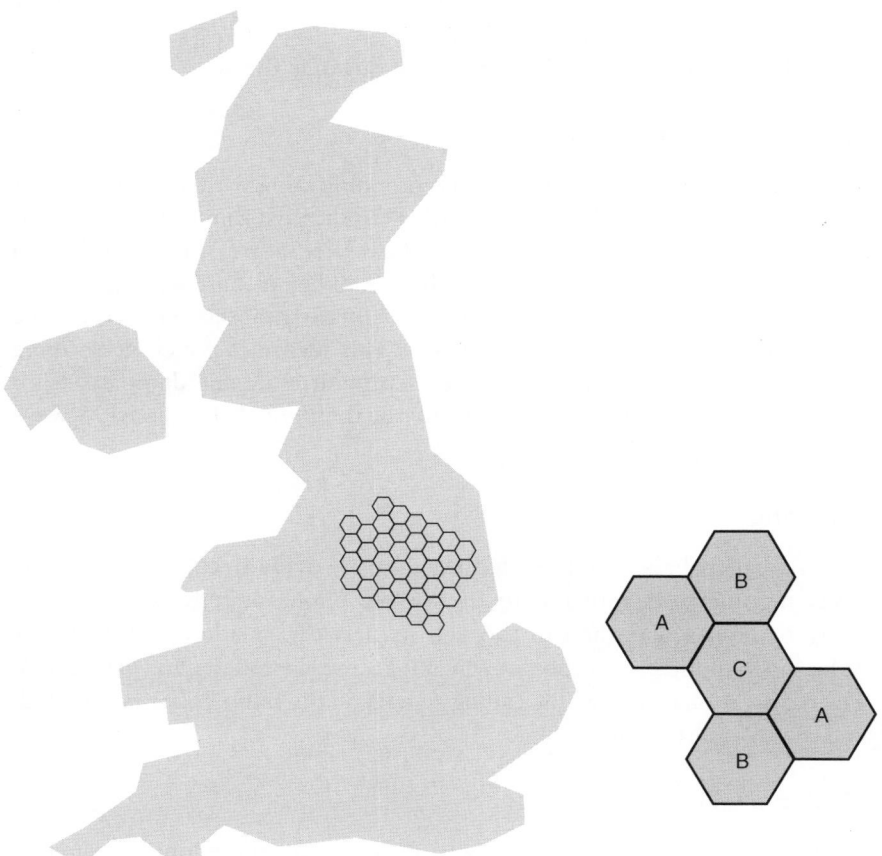

Figure 7.1 Mobile phone cells. The country is divided into a network of cells. Each is assigned a frequency band for the transmission and reception of mobile phone calls, with different frequencies in adjacent cells and frequency re-use employed in a similar manner to radio (see Figure 2.2). Although cell transmission areas overlap, like radio transmitters, a mobile phone is allocated by the operator's control system to a single transmission cell at any time, changing cell as it moves around the country (see Box 7.1)

Box 7.1   Making and Taking Calls: how the mobile works

The operation of the mobile phone depends crucially on a number of technological features:

- Each cell has at its centre a base station, with a mast that transmits and receives radio signals;
- the phone itself is also both a radio transmitter and receiver;
- a phone operating company's entire network of base stations are linked and also provide access to the PSTN;
- at all times the location of any phone is lodged in the network's database.

Identifying Location

Even when the phone is not in use it is communicating with nearby base stations (unless it is actually switched off). Periodically (about once a second) the phone sends out a paging pulse, which carries information including its number. This signal will be received by a number of base stations within range, but the one to which the phone is currently closest will receive the strongest signal. To the mobile network, this identifies which geographic cell the phone is in, and this is stored temporarily on the database. With a pulse being repeated every second or so, the phone's location is always known to the network.

Receiving a Call

When a caller dials a mobile number, they are actually calling the mobile operating company rather than the mobile phone directly. The network operator then routes the call through its network (made up of cables or radio links) to the base station in which it knows the called phone is located. The base station transmits the calling signal and the radio link is established, and the call goes ahead.

Making a Call

When a mobile phone user begins to make a call, the phone transmits a calling signal. The base station nearest the caller picks up the strongest signal and the call is then routed via that base station through the network and connected with its destination, whether this be another mobile or a PSTN phone.

Crossing Cell Boundaries

If while on a call the mobile phone is in motion and approaches the edge of a cell, the phone's transmissions will become within range of adjacent base station, as well as the one in its current location. By means of a comparison between the relative signal strengths of these two (or three) signals it is clear when the cell boundary has been crossed, and the call is then re-routed, or 'handed over' to the base station in the next cell. Although in the early days handover might have been noticed by a short gap in the call, nowadays the caller will not notice the transition.

Some cells, such as those in areas of high population (and therefore user) density, or difficult geographical terrain, may be very small, perhaps 100 m or so across, while others in more rural areas can be measured in kilometres. In urban areas, where at busy times the capacity of one cell might be exhausted, a phone might be routed through an adjacent cell if it is within range. In this way, loads can be balanced and services made as accessible as possible.

A further distinction between a PMR service and the mobile or cell phone service is that a PMR user would usually operate only within a restricted area served by a single transmitter, as indicated above, whereas the mobile phone is intended to be a device which can work anywhere in the country, or indeed anywhere the world, that is, in any cell. Further, it is important to the user that any call transfers seamlessly as cell boundaries are crossed, for, given that some cells may be less than a kilometre across, a conversation on a high speed train, for example, can easily traverse a number of cells, and the call must be handed over from one to the next. It is this cellular structure, and the consequent efficient use of spectrum, that allowed the mobile phone to become the mass item it is today. 'Public' use of radio telephones between the 1950s and 1980s was restricted to a small number of business users, and these worked on a similar basis to PMR with typically city-wide coverage areas but unlike PMR could connect to the 'normal' landline network, the public switched telephone network (PSTN) to use its full title. This geographic arrangement restricted the number of users: in 1976, there were only 545 customers able to use the service in the whole of New York City, with another 3700 on a five-to-ten year waiting list, despite the high costs of the service (Farley, cited in Gow and Smith 2006: 25). By this time, then, demand from business users was clearly outstripping supply, and the development of the cellular network, where now many tens of separate cells would cover an area like New York City, helped to enable the expansion of the service. However, the idea of the cellular network had been first proposed in 1947 by a Bell Labs engineer, the appropriately named

D H Ring. While the technology was not then ready to implement the idea, given that the transistor only emerged from the same research laboratories in that same year, it is nevertheless surprising that the cellular network should not have been implemented for another four decades. The barriers were more than technological, they were also social. Post-War institutions were in general hierarchical and paternalistic, and businesses had little obvious need for any additional telephony that could not already be provided by public pay phones and hotel phones. The telephone system in many countries was a publicly owned utility like power and water supplies; for example, until the 1980s, telephones in UK households remained the property of the General Post Office, BT's forerunner. The notion of a personal telephone, let alone a mobile device not fixed to the network, was one that neither arose nor would have found favour in that context (Agar 2003: 24–6). Thus Ring's ideas were unpublished for two decades and only put into limited, specialist service along the New York City to Washington DC train corridor in the late 1960s (Gow and Smith 2006: 26).

A further barrier to the widespread availability of mobile telephone services was a delay in agreeing standards for interoperability. While the FCC licensed a number of services to different companies in various parts of the US from the 1970s, these concentrated on serving particular cities rather than aiming to provide a linked, nationwide service. Licensing requirements did not stipulate the particular standard to which phones should operate and 'roaming', the idea of using the same equipment in many different parts of the country, was virtually impossible or at least difficult until the 1990s. The particular charging model adopted in the US, where a mobile phone owner would pay a charge to *receive* a call, meant owners were wary of giving out their numbers, further constraining the mobile phone as an everyday item. Instead pagers became popular, with their wider and more universal coverage and relative affordability. In Europe meanwhile, the Scandinavian countries, Denmark, Norway, Sweden and Finland, sowed the seeds of an interoperable, universal standard that could be expanded across the rest of the continent and, eventually, on a global scale. With strong and shared traditions of natural resources (like the radio spectrum) being used for common public services, these countries collaborated within the Nordic Mobile Telephone (NMT) group on the development of a cellular system. These countries also had relatively small populations dispersed over wide geographical areas, and the mobile phone proved popular – by 1981, in Sweden alone with a population of just over eight million, there were 20,000 users. By the end of that decade the Swedes were using half a million mobile phones (Eurostat 2001).

While the NMT system was adopted by a number of European countries, others began development of their own systems. In all cases, however, these were based on analogue technologies. It was clear that future systems should be digital, and in 1982 the *Groupe Speciale Mobile* (GSM) was formed to further this goal. What NMT had shown was that it was possible for countries to work together to develop a system that would allow roaming, and GSM began testing a new digital standard. During the mid-1980s, a number of new nations joined the European Union and the idea of GSM as a pan-European standard was appealing as a way of building a stronger union. Inevitably taking longer than anticipated to realise, nevertheless an EU focus on a single standard helped countries within Europe and beyond to decide on its adoption, and by 1995 most of Europe was operating GSM (by this time GSM had been adapted to stand for *Global System for Mobile communications*). It also began to be adopted in Australia, Russia, Africa and in parts of the US where digital services were emerging to replace analogue, and by the end of 2004 GSM had become by far the dominant mobile standard with 1.3 billion of the world's 1.7 billion subscribers (Gow and Smith 2006: 50).

Mobile Numbers

The transition of the mobile phone from a vehicle centred device to a portable, personal item has been accompanied by phenomenal growth, with 3.3 billion users at the end of 2007, twice the number of three years earlier. Once it was clear there was a demand from the general public rather than just business users, rapid developments in the technology inside the phone handset made them smaller and less dependent on an external power source. The electronic components were miniaturised further, while batteries became smaller, yet at the same time could hold far more charge, and the mobile phone was no longer the conspicuous, brick sized and weighted appliance that identified the self-conscious 'yuppie' of the 1980s. Two of the key drivers for the accelerated take up was the marketing of 'pay-as-you-go' charging models and one completely unanticipated use of the mobile phone: a non-voice add-on feature known as SMS, for short message service, also known as texting. Seen originally as a kind of one-way paging facility for networks to send information to customers, perhaps prompting a simple reply, it was not conceived as a two-way text-based communication facility, to the extent that when GSM was being rolled out in the 1990s not all telephones had the SMS facility enabled. However, texting has of course taken off: in April 1999, for example, one billion SMS messages per month were circulating in Europe, doubling over the previous six months, but by 2005 that same number was sent per month in the UK alone. Even this number is dwarfed by the 'text capital of the world': in the Philippines, that number of texts is sent every five days (Goggin 2006: 75). There are some very obvious reasons why this might be: it is a cheap form of communication, particularly valued perhaps by those on pay-as-you go tariffs, and it is asynchronous communication. One novel aspect of the mobile phone in comparison with its landline counterpart is the possibility of being interrupted at any time, often not the most convenient, and sending a text message rather than a call can be a more effective way of communicating.

Whatever the causes, the growth of the mobile phone is not just a phenomenon of the industrialised nations. It is an important means of communication in countries which do not have a significant landline infrastructure. The poorest countries of the world have never had access to telecommunications on anything like the same scale as the industrialised nations and, particularly in rural areas, limited access to electricity compounds this absence. In such regions, a wireless, or mobile phone system can be a quicker means of installing telecommunications: the cost of installing a mobile 'line' can be less than one tenth the cost of a wired connection. Public access to the telephone can be provided through mobile phones located in bars or other public spaces or even in informal 'kiosks' in street stalls. Power to public kiosks is sometimes provided by solar panels, or more often from a car battery, and access to telecommunications can be provided more easily than other utilities. Winsbury reports that in South Africa, following the fall of the apartheid system, efforts were made to support rural access to communications (Winsbury 1994: 38):

> In the last few weeks, the informal township, Chris Hani, received five cellular payphones as part of [operator, Mobile Telephone Networks'] project. To get some idea of the significance of this for the community, it is worth noting that Chris Hani currently has no electricity, water or roads. But now it does have telecommunications, operated by a 12 volt car battery.

While this may be a significant technological achievement, it is less clear how valuable it might prove in comparison with provision of access to water and power. A number of global development agencies such as the World Bank have emphasised telecommunications above other services in seeking to aid development but have been criticised as demonstrating a distorted sense of priorities.

The growth of the mobile phone has nevertheless outstripped that of fixed line services most dramatically in the poorer regions of the world. ITU figures show that in 1999 Africa as a whole had a tiny number of mobile phones in comparison with, for example, Europe. As a percentage of fixed connections, however, the mobile in Africa fared similarly to Europe. By 2006, however, there were far more mobile than fixed phones in use in Africa, a much higher ratio in comparison with Europe, and indeed anywhere else in

	1999			2006		
	Fixed lines per 100 population	Mobile phones per 100 population	Ratio, mobile: fixed	Fixed lines per 100 population	Mobile phones per 100 population	Ratio, mobile: fixed
Africa	2.4	1.0	0.41	3.1	21.7	6.99
Europe	38.4	22.4	0.58	39.7	99.3	2.50
World	15.1	8.2	0.54	19.3	29.6	1.88

Table 7.1 Access to fixed and mobile phones by region, 1999 and 2006
Source: ITU.

	Fixed lines per 100 population	Mobile phones per 100 population	Ratio, mobile: fixed
Canada	64.5	57.6	0.89
China	27.8	34.8	1.25
US	57.2	77.4	1.35
UK	56.2	116.4	2.07
Uganda	0.4	6.7	18.58
Mozambique	0.3	11.6	34.92

Table 7.2 Access to fixed and mobile phones, selected countries, 2006
Source: ITU.

the world (Table 7.1). In the poorest countries, the ratio can be as high as 35:1 (Table 7.2). While most of these mobiles are certainly concentrated in urban centres, and the costs of provision still make mobile ownership unaffordable for most rural dwellers, the shared use through the mobile kiosks does mean that it can be argued that the mobile phone has proved as significant, if not more so, for the rural poor in the underdeveloped world than for the relatively advantaged users in industrialised nations (UNCTAD 2008: 243–7).

Certainly, in comparison with the penetration of the personal computer and the internet, about which so much commentary has been written, the mobile phone is a vastly more commonplace communications device just about everywhere in the world. In the UK, in 1997, 20 per cent of the population had mobile phones while just five per cent of households had internet access; by 2004, 60 per cent of the population were internet users, but there were more mobile phones in the country than people. In the same year, across Africa, there were almost four times as many mobile phones than there were internet users. Despite this imbalance, the role of the mobile telephone receives much less consideration than that of the internet, being seen perhaps as simply an augmentation of the telephone. While it is certainly that, it is also potentially a much more elaborate means of communication.

Mobile Computing

Just as a landline telephone enables a number of additional, non-telephone communications activities, so it requires no leap of imagination to realise that similar functionality was part of the mobile telephone from the earliest days. It was possible to receive a fax on a mobile phone (using the phone to print it out from a public fax machine) and a number of phones began to incorporate modems that allowed computers to connect via the mobile network in exactly the same way as those computers could connect via a land-based modem. Though data speeds were often much slower than landline modems (which reached speeds of 56 kbps before being outpaced by broadband connections), they nevertheless made up for their lack of speed in the convenience of not being tied to a desk. Once connected via the mobile phone modem, the computer could access the internet as with any other connection, though usually at a high price given that mobile phone call charges are invariably a number of times higher than landline charges.

Before long, however, the use of the mobile phone as simply a link between the computer (typically a laptop, or a smaller palmtop or 'personal digital assistant' computer) was superseded by the promise of a new generation of mobile phones which would themselves store and process data, in effect operate like small computers. From mid-1999 it was announced that the mobile phone of the future would be more like a handheld computer, streaming data back and forth for display on an enlarged screen, downloading emails and web-like pages complete with tiny images, streaming audio and video content – and still be available for phone calls. The Wireless Application Protocol (WAP) described the way in which data could be delivered to suitably enabled mobile phones. Early offerings included dedicated WAP content and reconfigured Web pages. For these purposes, WAP phones came with larger screens than previous devices and the tendency towards ever smaller phones came briefly to an end. The promise was that data speeds would be much higher than a conventional, landline modem but, nevertheless, when the first devices went on the market the following year, many early adopters were disappointed to find that the devices used a clumsy circuit switching method that meant speeds were more like 9.6 kbps, about the same as Prestel and other videotex services achieved in the 1970s. The circuit switching meant users were charged on a per-minute basis, like any other call, and WAP became known not only as a slow service but one that was also expensive. The visions for a mobile multimedia future portrayed in the media still seemed a long time away. Already, however, data transfer systems for mobile phones were in development that were based on the same packet switching technology that had made internet traffic possible, and the first of these, the General

Packet Radio Service or GPRS, emerged slowly during 2000, effectively stalling the further development of circuit-switched WAP. When it finally appeared in 2001, data speeds were significantly faster than the earlier WAP service, though at around 56 kbps, the same as a landline modem, they were again rather lower than had been predicted. The big advantage of GPRS though was its packet switched mode which meant that it was 'always on', that is, it did not tie up the voice channel, and customers were charged by the quantity of data delivered rather than by the minute, so if the service was running slowly it might be a frustrating experience but it was not costing any more.

GPRS was always seen as a stop-gap measure. A still faster service, the Universal Mobile Telephone Service (UMTS), was seen as the third generation of mobile devices and became known more succinctly as 3G. As digital mobile telephony was the second generation after analogue, GPRS thus became regarded awkwardly as 2.5G, and the speculation shifted to what would really, finally come about with 3G. We have already noted that by this time, even before the technology had been proven to work, UK mobile operators had already paid more than five times the amount anticipated by the government in the auction of the 3G licences and clearly expected to be able to launch a host of revenue-generating services. With the auction coinciding precisely with the bursting of the so-called dot com bubble in 2000, press speculation began to suggest that telecoms companies had over-bid for the licences, a view reinforced when the first 3G services finally began in 2002, once again at speeds far lower than the heady 2 Mbps that had been described. In 2001, French mobile operator SFR defaulted on its €619 m 3G licence payment, while in the UK Vodafone announced that its 3G launch would be at speeds of just 64 kbps, prompting one market research director to declare: 'This is just one more piece of news that reaffirms our view that 3G was never going to be about things like video. Speeds are coming down and down and down and it's getting less and less exciting from a consumer point of view' (cited in Milner 2001). Once again, the mobile networks became known for delivering slower data speeds than had been predicted at high costs, and the market for 3G phones has remained largely limited to business users. Meanwhile, some commentators had noted another struggling sector, the DAB digital radio industry, and suggested that here was 'a match made in heaven' (Rigby 2001).

Non-telephone Mobile Technologies

The difficulty with the idea of using the mobile telephone network as a channel for delivering high bitrate content, such as audio and especially video, is that the more who seek to access such content, the slower the resulting delivery. The capacity of the channel is limited, in much the same way as the wires of the internet, and so when demand grows, the maximum supply of data has to be shared between all those requesting it.

This is in complete contrast with the broadcasting model. As the word denotes, a broadcast transmission is intended to reach the maximum number of people, and if a transmission network has been installed and serves an area with a population of, for instance, 100,000, it makes absolutely no difference whether 10,000, 50,000 or the whole population choose to 'download' the information simultaneously. In other words, viewers and listeners of a popular television or radio programme, with audiences in millions, do not receive worse pictures and sound than those watching a programme carried on the same network pulling in an audience of just a few thousand – 'sharing' the programme between more people makes no more demands on the infrastructure. The DAB digital radio system was conceived with the idea of delivering data alongside its audio information and, in the UK, since the 1996 Broadcasting Act set the original limits, the proportion of the frequency capacity that is permitted to be used for data has been increased over the years from 10 per cent to 30 per cent. By using this data capacity for 'broadcasting' data to mobile phones (or 'datacasting' as some would have it), the limited capacity of the 3G networks could be overcome, and the DAB operators have sought to develop this potential (Lax 2003: 343–4). Broadcasting data is similar to the way in which teletext works: the user cannot request an item to be sent directly to her phone but instead it can be transmitted on a carousel basis and stored or 'cached' in the device. The user selects the information from the cached data for display on her screen. In this arrangement, the 3G telephone network can be employed to offer a unique return path but, given the asymmetric nature of the transactions, with downloaded data invariably much greater in quantity than that uploaded, the telephone network can cope with this. Trials during 2006 showed the potential of using the spare radio spectrum to deliver live television to mobile phones, one operator launching its 'tellyphone' service with its collection of television channels and radio stations at the end of that year (the mobile television service proved short-lived, closing in 2007 due to the low number of subscribers).

A more recent and growing means of accessing data on the move is the wireless local area network facility, often known as Wi Fi, based on the IEEE 802.11 group of standards. Commonly used to supply broadband internet access around the home, public Wi Fi services are increasingly available in places such as libraries, cafes and hotels. The service consists of a small, low power radio transceiver which transmits and receives internet data (that is, in packet form and appropriately addressed) over a limited range. Such access points, or 'hotspots', allow anyone with a Wi Fi enabled device, which might be a laptop computer or a handheld device such as a personal digital assistant (PDA) or sophisticated telephone (the distinction between the latter two is increasingly meaningless) to access data via the internet at broadband network speeds. Once again, theoretically, the more people accessing the service at any one time, the slower it becomes, but given the limited geographical range of such services (within a café or hotel lobby for example) often only a few are likely to be accessing the service simultaneously. Extending this idea, a number of towns and cities are developing wider networks, with access points spread across city centres allowing public access from almost anywhere. Sometimes these services must be paid for, but occasionally they are free.

In comparison with 3G, for many regular users, Wi Fi access is becoming a much more convenient and significantly cheaper way of accessing data while away from a landline, with the advantage that data speeds are often considerably higher. As the number of hotspots increases, coverage can be as good as the 3G networks, particularly in urban centres, though otherwise it can be rather sporadic and unpredictable: with the 3G networks owned by a small number of large telecoms companies, coverage can be expected to increase steadily as the 3G networks are rolled out (that is, transmission masts built or converted), whereas enhancing Wi Fi coverage depends more on the whim of particular individuals such as shop and café owners deciding to install access points. However, as more people come to expect Wi Fi access to be available, and carry suitable devices around, it will make obvious commercial sense for such establishments to offer access, and coverage is likely to increase further. On the other hand, with responsibility for supplying Wi Fi coverage dispersed among many individuals, many of whom may simply be offering it as a service alongside coffee and cakes and may well have no specialist wireless networking knowledge, the reliability of Wi Fi networks is likely to be variable. In comparison, as established national telecommunications operators, the 3G companies are more likely to maintain a consistent, reliable service which may be valuable to those willing to pay the higher costs of the service.

A further distinction between 3G and Wi Fi is now being eroded. The 3G phone service sitting alongside data transfer is also becoming mirrored in the Wi Fi service, as internet telephony (voice over internet protocol, or VoIP) is being accepted as a normal way of making phone calls. A simple headset plugged into a laptop in a Wi Fi hotspot turns it effectively into an admittedly rather cumbersome mobile phone, usually with cost advantages over the traditional mobile phone networks. Increasing numbers of devices (PDAs or phones) are incorporating Wi Fi functionality, and the day when a single communications device (we will call it a phone for now) can switch seamlessly between Wi Fi, GSM, 3G and also the cordless landline facility at home is surely imminent.

Domestic Wireless

As the then radio critic in the *Guardian* newspaper observed, 'There's something curiously satisfying about wireless becoming a current word again' (Karpf 2000). In particular, given the domestic origins of the wireless, or radio, it seems appropriate to consider how wireless communications are pervading the home environment. The most commonplace, and largely taken for granted, is probably the cordless phone, which, were it not for the ubiquitous experience of mobility with the cell phone, might be considered a little more remarkable than it is. However, as testament to the familiarity of the mobile phone, cordless landline phones now emulate their functionality with address books, SIM card slots to allow numbers to be copied, and text facilities. Instead, of more note is the slow but growing take up of wireless data transfer within the home.

For many years, mobile phones, computers and their peripherals have incorporated wireless connectivity. Using infrared waves, much like a television remote control, it has been possible to align a computer and a printer and set it printing without any wired connection. This was never straightforward: sometimes the alignment or proximity of the devices became critical, and sometimes the infrared devices worked to slightly different standards. Bluetooth technology has now largely displaced infrared for connecting communications devices and is found almost as standard in mobile phones, headsets and audio players, where the absence of wires can make life easier by not getting in the way. In other applications, such as connecting computers or cameras and printers, it simply helps by eliminating the need to physically connect devices with wires.

In conjunction with home Wi Fi networks, with a range which covers the whole house rather than simply between devices, wireless communication can be used to stream content from one room to another (for example satellite television can be transmitted to a remote receiver eliminating the need for multiple decoding boxes; or music downloaded to a computer can be streamed to be played through a hi fi system). The same wireless connectivity brings a little closer the idea of the 'smart home', about which there has been speculation for many years (as we noted in the previous chapter) and in which some anticipate eagerly the day when the kettle may be used to close the curtains, or some similar arrangement. However, it would be safe to say that in general, the consequences of applying wireless technologies in the home are largely about convenience rather than being associated with changes in the way we live.

Localisation

At the same time that mobile phones and wireless internet access reflect a more dispersed and transient society, mobile communications operators have not missed the opportunities that arise from the unfamiliarity that this mobility can bring with it. We may find ourselves in a strange city, but our mobile phone will help us out with maps and lists of local services. The cellular structure of the mobile transmission networks means our location (or at least, that of our phones) is always known (and such information is regularly shared on demand with police and other authorities). Some cells, as we have seen, are a mere few tens of metres across, which means our position is known down to the level of which street we might be on. More sophisticated determination of location is enabled by 'triangulation', comparing the relative strengths of the mobile signal picked up by a number of adjacent base stations. Clearly the station we are closest to receives the strongest signal, but by comparing this with that received by two or more others, our location can be pinpointed to within a few metres. While the global positioning system (GPS) used in satellite tracking systems can also do this, for the mobile operators, using their own technology for this purpose enables them to offer a number of location-based services. However, for some people the idea of our mobile phone network operator knowing where we are at all times (and maintaining a record of that information) is more alarming than it is convenient.

So the mobile phone presents a number of paradoxes. While it offers connection and convenience as we travel far and wide, it also serves our need for information about our immediate locality. As well as calling across the world from an unfamiliar place, we can also access the local information we need: maps, obviously, but lists of hotels, restaurants, cinemas and so on too, like a local Yellow Pages. More sophisticated versions of these services, able to pinpoint a phone's location to within a few metres, could direct its owner to his chosen facility in much the same way as vehicle satellite navigation systems do using GPS. If it is to function in this way, the mobile operator needs to know at all times where we are, and if we are to be served with useful information, it also needs to know some of our habits and preferences. Concerns for privacy have to be weighed against convenience, but the rapidity with which the mobile phone has been adopted suggests that for many this potential conflict is readily resolved.

Conclusion: The Mobile, Social World

The near ubiquity of the mobile phone has undoubtedly made life different for individuals and for society at large. Yet it is also possible to see these changes as part of a continuum rather than a dramatic freeing from the ties of wires and cables. As a recent social phenomenon, nevertheless, it is tempting to highlight some of the novel social practices contingent on mobile phone use. For those who have not grown up with mobile phone, the notion of always being contactable irrespective of location represents a significant change from being tied to a particular space. The once familiar idea of calling someone at a known location, their place of work or residence, only to find them 'not in', is now replaced with the equally familiar but opposite demand to state their location: 'Where are you?'; 'I'm on the train'.

New rules of social etiquette arise. Should we phone someone on their mobile if we do not know exactly where they are? After all, they might be in an important meeting. Or, if your phone rings while you have company, should you answer it? When is it acceptable to have one's phone switched off? Such concerns echo the equally heartfelt but, in retrospect, quaint and misplaced worries when the wired telephone originally entered the public realm a century ago. As with most other technologies, once patterns of usage have become established, they exhibit a rich variation and it makes little sense to generalise. Some welcome the mobile phone, others tolerate it for its convenience, while others continue to resent the intrusion of the once private world into public space. The way in which people use the mobile phone varies from the apologetic and discrete to the loud and almost exhibitionist. Special train carriages are set aside in order to keep the exhibitionists and the resenters apart. Yet we might argue that such mixed reactions to novel telephone technologies are not new. The rapid adoption of the telephone answering machine from the 1970s, though largely unremarked upon, caused difficulty for some. Many callers resented being asked to leave a message on a machine: this was somehow rude of the recipient, who clearly could not be bothered to wait at home in case of a call. Later, call-screening facilities added to the suspicion on the part of the caller that their intended recipient might be deliberately not answering. However, for the new *owner* of the answering machine, like the mobile phone, in its early years this technology brought with it a certain social status, implying a particular, busy lifestyle: it instigated a telephone 'mobility' that the actual mobile phone, when it came into being, merely completed. For the first time (unless one had servants or paid for a professional, human-based answering service) it was no longer necessary to stay near the telephone to receive an expected (or unexpected) call or, alternatively, to worry about missing a message while out; and with remote playback of messages via any telephone there was no need to return home to pick up the message and return the call. Like the mobile phone, the answering machine also allowed its owners to customise or personalise their telephone in a public way: the choice of greeting betrayed something of the owner's personality, and it was possible to buy customised greetings in the form of tunes or celebrity voices, perhaps a precursor of the downloadable ringtone.

So rather than considering how the mobile phone has introduced or at least enhanced mobility in our lives, we should instead explore the world into which the mobile phone emerged. This world has become more mobile as the decades pass. Images and information travel across the world as newspapers and later television bring news and pictures into our homes from distant countries; goods are carried over land, sea and by air; the growth of international capitalism means those goods may be assembled in many parts of the world and then marketed worldwide under global brands. Personal mobility too has been enhanced by the automobile and more affordable air travel so that our sense of the world we live in is derived from experiences, some of them personal, taken from a wide array of physical spaces. We can no longer pretend to know only what is happening within our immediate neighbourhood; but, equally, we can expect to keep in touch with our home neighbourhood when we are far away (during flooding in the UK, one man, hundreds of miles from home, found that his house was inundated when, watching satellite television news, he saw pictures of water half way up his front door (Brignall 2007)). Just as Raymond Williams understood that radio meshed with the social changes that he referred to as privatised mobility, equally the development of the mobile phone represents the ways in which broad social changes can shape technological developments.

An Information Society?

The preceding chapters have explored the ways in which electrical and electronic technologies have been used to aid communication for almost two centuries. During that time, the focus of that communication has gradually changed from the needs of business and government as the principal drivers of communications technologies to one in which its use for personal communication is also important. Advanced communication can now be regarded as ubiquitous in any industrialised society, given that almost all businesses and other organisations are connected to the internet, and there is near-universal access to broadcast reception and mobile phones. Such high levels of adoption have prompted repeated speculation and theorisation about the changes in society that may result, and in recent years this has coalesced around the concept of an 'information society'. While loosely defined, the idea of the information society is that not only is the quantity of information available dramatically increased by communications technology, but qualitative changes are taking place in which an individual's role in society is bound up with his relationship to information, that is, access to it and the ability to manipulate it.

With its origins in Daniel Bell's articulation of a post-industrial society (Bell 1973), the information society is often described in terms of its contrast with previous epochs, the industrial society (considered to be over or, at least, in decline) and, before that, the agrarian society. Just as the shift from an agrarian society to the industrial society brought about overwhelming social change and upheaval for individuals, so too it is argued that the information society is bringing about similar social transformations. For example, in agrarian societies, relations between people were based on the feudal system. The aristocracy derived its wealth from its ownership of vast tracts of land on which peasants kept animals and grew crops in order to sustain themselves, paying dues to the aristocratic landlord in the form of money or produce. A close relationship between monarchs, aristocrats and the church helped to maintain the social order, reinforced with violent subjugation when required. This relationship changed with the development of industry and the need for a more organised form of industrial production, with capitalism emerging as a new form of social order based on ownership of factories and material goods (raw materials) and access to a ready supply of manual labour; wealth was no longer derived purely from inherited right (as in the feudal system) but from the profits produced by the new industries. For the new class of factory workers, migrating often unwillingly from the villages to the expanding towns and cities, their manual labour was now a source of 'wealth' in the form of the wages paid by their factory-owning employer. The employee was no longer, in theory, bound to the employer as the peasant had been to the landlord and could take their labour power from employer to employer, but nevertheless such freedom was largely an abstract one as, without employment, there was no source of income. Wider social changes came as industrialists grew wealthier than the old aristocracy, and the power of the monarchy and church similarly weakened in the face of the enhanced role of parliament. Workers' organisations, first craft guilds and later trades unions, fought for improvements in political and economic conditions and, while armies have certainly been used to quell workers' insurrections, unlike the feudal system most battles were fought at the political level.

This explanation is needed in order to distinguish the use of the term 'information society' in a casual sense, meaning merely that there is a lot more information around, to its more significant meaning of a new form of society with novel and quite distinct social relations. It is not uncommon for the emergence of new technological systems to inspire speculation about the future of society. We have seen, for example, how the press, poets and other writers celebrated the arrival of the telegraph, or radio, for its potential to bring enlightenment to every corner of the world, and the same rhetoric can be read today in relation to the internet or social networking websites. Much of this is (and was) rather superficial commentary, but for some the adoption of new technologies does suggest rather more profound change. For Daniel Bell, the post-War change in the focus of production from goods to services in the US (his particular focus) and other advanced societies did indeed represent the emergence of a new phase of social development, post-industrial society, with consequent shifts in status and power (Bell 1970: 394):

> To speak rashly: if the dominant figures of the past hundred years have been the entrepreneur, the businessman, and the industrial executive, the 'new men' are the scientists, the mathematicians, the economists, and the engineers of the new society – in the sense that they will provide the most creative challenges and enlist the richest talents – will be the intellectual institutions. The leadership of the new society will rest, not with businessmen or corporations as we know them (for a good deal of production will have been routinized), but with the research corporation, the industrial laboratories, the experimental stations, and the universities.

Hence intellectual work, based on knowledge and information, become key to one's place in this new society, and the notion of the information society meshes easily with Bell's conception. Indeed Bell used the terms interchangeably: 'The post-industrial society is an information society, as industrial society is a goods-producing society' (Bell 1973: 467). Bell's ideas proved highly influential and during the following years numerous authors welcomed the new era. Alvin Toffler's *The Third Wave* (1980) claimed that the rise of information work promised 'to change all the existing terms of debate, making obsolete most of the issues over which men and women today argue, struggle and sometimes die' (1980: 217); Tom Stonier believed that the new information society meant 'that not only are we more affluent, more resourceful and less likely to go to war, but also more likely to democratise' (1983: 202). Naturally, much of this anticipation was based on the power of computers, which were beginning to become more widely adopted in homes, as well as businesses and the relative affordability of this information machine distinguished the new era. For the enthusiasts, information was the new source of power and, unlike land in agrarian times or money in the industrial age, information could be widely distributed.

Naturally, then, the ideas about the information age of the 1970s and 1980s were reinvigorated in the mid-1990s, as the distributive potential of the internet became widely discussed in the public arena, and the debates were beginning to influence public policy. We have noted earlier the establishment of 'information society' policy groups such as the Task Force in the US and the Bangemann Commission in the EU, and, writing in 1996 the future UK prime minister Gordon Brown stated, 'the defining characteristic of economy is less an individual's ability to gain access to capital and far more his or her ability to gain access to knowledge and to use it creatively' (Brown 1996: 13). The terms 'knowledge economy', 'knowledge society' and 'information society' became used interchangeably, and in this new economy one's position was no longer determined by whether one was the owner of a large corporation or a lowly employee within it but instead by one's access to information. This implied a reordering of society at least as significant as Bell had imagined, with old hierarchies of privilege to be swept away. Such a view was expressed succinctly in Charles Leadbeater's popular account *Living on Thin Air* (2000). He writes:

> Most of us earn our livings providing service, judgement, information and analysis, whether in a telephone call centre, a lawyer's office, a government department or a scientific laboratory. We are all in the thin-air business. That should allow our economies, in principle at least, to become more humane; they should be organized around people and the knowledge capital they produce. Our children will not have to toil in dark factories, descend into pits

or suffocate in mills, to hew raw materials and turn them into manufactured products. They will make their livings through their creativity, ingenuity, and imagination. (p. ix)

Later, he elaborates on these changes:

An economy which becomes more knowledge-intensive has the potential to become more inclusive and meritocratic. Everyone with an education can have a go.... In an economy which trades know-how and ideas, everyone seems to have a chance to make it, working from a garage, their kitchen or their bedroom. Twenty-five year-old drop-outs can create best-selling computer games; a nerd fresh out of college can create the Internet's best browser; a boy with no formal education can become Europe's most precocious fashion designer. (p. 33)

Such views clearly reflect the thinking within a number of governments elected in the late 1990s. The front cover of *Living on Thin Air* carried an endorsement by the then UK prime minister, Tony Blair – 'Leadbeater is an extraordinarily interesting thinker. His book raises critical questions for Britain's future' – and Leadbeater spent some years as a government adviser and member of an influential think tank with close ties to the ruling Labour government. Just as he recalls some of the mythology of the earlier histories of computing entrepreneurs, he also echoes Louis Rossetto's view of public services and welfare provision: while 'the public sector is home to some great brand names: the BBC and the NHS', it also 'suffers not just from poor productivity compared with much of the private sector, but from an innovation deficit as well ... entrepreneurship and risk-taking are discouraged in the public sector' (Leadbeater 2000: 51). This supposed correlation between the power of information and knowledge, and an overturning of traditional public institutions in favour of newer brands and private provision, lends further weight to a sense of the 'end of history', and the emergence of a new epoch.

While Leadbeater's account might reflect the personal experiences of a relatively well-paid, freelance journalist, it draws upon (and elaborates) ideas that have been subject to considerable academic attention. Before the emergence of the internet gave credence to the information society thesis, the world of work was characterised as 'post-Fordist', a reference to the end of an approach to manufacturing based on large runs of similar items. (The Ford Model-T car, built from 1908, is celebrated as the first mass produced item, in which a scientific approach to the work process, known as Taylorism after its progenitor Frederick Taylor, was taken to devise the most cost effective way of organising the manufacture of a vehicle. The process was broken down into its constituent parts, with consequent clear divisions of specialised labour, each employee working only on one particular part of the process.) Fordism was very successful in producing large numbers of standardised products – Henry Ford famously announced that the Model T was available in any colour as long as it was black – but by the 1980s or so markets were perceived to be less interested in standardised products and more in favour of diversity. By introducing information technologies into the manufacturing process, machinery became more flexible: computer numerical control systems allowed stored data to fine tune the machine's output and to use the same machine to manufacture a different product simply by altering the data, rather than changing the machine, making it economic to manufacture short runs of items. The mass production of Fordism was giving way to an era of 'flexible specialisation', with implications for the organisation of industry. The tendency towards larger and larger corporations would be reversed, and industry would emphasise small teams working on specialised projects rather than massed ranks of employees on a production line; this would have consequences for trades unions, typically concentrated in larger workplaces, and social cohesion more generally, and the imminence of post-Fordism was anticipated with trepidation amongst those on the political left (Kumar 2005).

A comprehensive account of the ways in which the world seems to have changed over the last two to three decades was given by Manuel Castells. His trilogy, *The Information Age*, published from 1996 with numerous revised editions, sought to describe the changes in the social, economic and political world by studying cultural and working lives in countries across the globe. He noted the decline of traditional political parties and processes at the same time as the emergence of campaigning, social movement groups. For Castells, this world could not be explained as simply a slightly different version of the industrial society that had gone before, although he did not find the idea of the information society a helpful concept. Instead, he conceived the idea of the 'network society', in which the world is made up of large numbers of interwoven connections which are constantly being formed, broken and re-formed. He traces the origins of network society to the 1970s, when the capitalist world was plunged into crisis with rising oil prices and unemployment ending what had been a long post-War period of rising living standards. Wholesale restructuring took place as companies went bust, some merged with or swallowed up others, and many looked for new areas of economic activity. At the same time, developments in ICTs were growing apace and, as these newly reforming companies sought to incorporate them increasingly into their business, information became more significant in their operations, whether in organising working patterns in machine programming, as described above, or in accessing and sharing market data on a global scale. This growing importance of information to the creation of wealth (Castells describes it as the 'informational mode of development' to distinguish it from agrarian and industrial modes) leads quite naturally to companies operating as networks, and the ongoing, historical process of globalisation meant those networks were international. Like Daniel Bell, Castells emphasises the importance of information work, and the ease with which ICTs allow information to be exchanged means being on the networks is critical. These internationally networked organisations are not the same as the transnational corporations that grew in the 20th century, since, being established before the rapid developments in ICTs, the transnationals had become hierarchical, centralised organisations. New networked organisations instead are flexible and fluid: self-programmed and self-directed teams of information workers come together to work on projects and then disband after that work is done. Hierarchies flatten, and power is devolved from company executives to those information workers on the networks who are at the heart of things. In echoes of the pessimistic view of post-Fordism, the rise of information work's importance leads to a fragmentation of the traditional working class of the industrial age, with those who are either too inflexible or lacking sufficient education left unable to play a full part on the networks. Castells calls this group 'generic labour', numerically much smaller and economically impotent in comparison with the working class in industrial society and increasingly subject to the more flexible class of information labour directing the way in which it must work. This division, however, is different from the capitalist-worker divide of the industrial society; the information networkers are not where they are because of property but because of expertise, and they are not bound to particular roles or organisations as that expertise is readily transferable from employer to employer. The constant flow over the networks creates its own momentum so that the economy is no longer directed by a small number of large corporations but, in short, capitalism (or informational capitalism) is more democratic.

The networked society extends beyond work and into the cultural sphere. For Castells, the multiplicity of television channels available over cable and satellite platforms is the antithesis of networked society, instead contributing to ever greater fragmentation. He suggests that as networks allow increasing interaction between individuals and groups, the mass media will become less significant; while a little more cautious than Howard Rheingold, he also embraces the idea of the virtual community as a new phenomenon of the network society (Castells 2000: 365–89). Politics too demonstrates networking in operation; while the old, hierarchical political parties are largely in decline across the world, with decreasing memberships, the rise of social movements (groups organised around particular issues such as feminism or environmentalism as opposed to whole political orthodoxies) incorporate the fluid and non-hierarchical nature of the networks and increasingly deploy network technologies on an international scale. The generally higher levels of education and networking skills together with the affordability of ICTs mean these new social movements are able rapidly to mobilise support and media attention, and, just as the networks come and go in workplace organisation, so too do the fortunes of social movements.

So Castells shares with the post-industrialists and post-Fordists a view of a new epoch, some version of an information society, in which work, leisure, culture and politics are to be transformed with the application of a whole range of communications technologies. Whether this transformation is for the better, leading to a more egalitarian society, or worse, with greater social fragmentation and disintegration, is debated. As May says, 'Utopians have been confronted by dystopians, but both accept that we are self-evidently entering a new age' (2002: 17).

Exploring the Information Society

It is instructive to investigate some of the aspects of life which are impacted upon by the notion of the information society. For many critics, the promoters of the information society idea are keen to point to changes in society (many of which are undoubtedly taking place) but less willing to acknowledge continuities (Webster 2006: 6–7). Here we will consider the tension between continuity and change in the areas of politics, work and equality.

Politics

Many commentators contrast the declining fortunes of traditional political parties and traditional politics (such as falling voter turnouts in elections) even with the potential offered by growth in the diffusion of new ICTs. Countless articles herald the new Athenian age, where full democratic participation is extended to the many rather than the few. Rather than electing representatives to govern in our names for several years before we have the chance once again to endorse or remove them, technology allows more and more to take part in the political process.

There are different ways in which ICTs can be said to enhance the democratic process. They can make the process more efficient: governments can publish more information, and voters can access that information more easily than before. The same applies more generally, in that the range of sources of information easily available to citizens is increased with access to ICTs. Any campaigning organisation that hopes to gain support has a presence on the Web, at the very least offering an electronic equivalent of a paper leaflet but more often giving some means of contacting the organisation, joining or otherwise supporting it. Of course, the two-way nature of the internet allows both governments and campaigning groups to use the internet to allow deliberation and discussion on political issues, and for many commentators this holds the key to re-engaging voters (and non-voters) in the political process (for example Axford and Huggins 2000; Blumler and Gurevitch 2001). Since the earliest days of computer networking, activist groups have helped establish a number of projects intended to foster 'citizens' networks' in cities around the world (for example Downing 1989; Raab et al. 1996; Tsagarousianou et al. 1998). In more recent years governments have held electronic forums, usually to invite responses to and deliberation about specific policies; for example between 1998 and 2002 the UK government held ten such online consultations (Coleman 2004: 4). Some have argued that the ultimate goal of such networks should be a form of direct democracy, where online discussion goes further than merely allowing the exchange of opinion but culminates in real decision making via online referendums, the outcomes of which would be binding on governments (Budge 1996).

While these forms of political engagement might be regarded as enhancements of the traditional political process, based largely on parliament and political parties, alternative forms of political expression have also made use of ICTs. The so-called alternative media have long made use of new technologies such as offset litho printing, cable television and video recorders, each of which reduced entry or production costs in comparison with previous technologies. The internet goes further in reducing, in many cases, the costs of distribution. For example, Undercurrents is a video-making organisation which began by producing programmes about 'the news you don't see on the news', released on videocassette tape and sent via mail order to purchasers. In 1999, it produced its last edition as the costs of distribution had become a much greater hurdle than the costs of production, and now Undercurrents concentrates on providing training in video making (Forbes 1999). When Indymedia began in 1999, however, it chose the Web as its sole distribution platform. A loosely tied collection of organisations, Indymedia emerged at the time of the protests against corporate capitalism at the World Trade Organisation meeting in Seattle. It encourages activists to post images, audio and video reports to its website from protests around the world, which can then be commented upon and added to by fellow activists (Coyer 2005). With the internet as the distribution platform, Indymedia avoids the costs incurred by Undercurrents, although of course the video clips are of the limited quality and short length associated with internet video, and many activist groups continue to issue longer video material on DVD. Alongside political blogs and other internet-based mechanisms (such as email groups or Web forums) these media forms undoubtedly represent a novel widening of access to political expression.

However, we can recognise novelty, and welcome it, but we must be cautious before concluding that this represents a significant change in politics. It is difficult to contend that technological developments are reinvigorating the democratic process. Measured in conventional terms, certainly the evidence does not support this. Despite the growing levels of internet access and its adoption by governments and politicians in most industrialised nations (for example, political parties and candidates maintaining blogs and podcasts as part of their campaigning armoury), election turnouts and party membership levels continue to fall. Equally, there is little evidence of a sustained political consequence of the new 'alternative media' outlets such as Indymedia and bloggers, and these should rather be seen as a continuation of a longer term trend in seeking alternatives to mainstream media, including print and audio-visual media (Atton 2002). For example, Arterton (1987) identifies a trend from experiments in deliberative democracy in cable television networks. The Ohio-based Qube experiment allowed cable television subscribers to vote via a handset on issues of the day, political or otherwise. Audiences began to fall after the initial novelty had worn off, and participation was low unless the issues were about sport or in the form of game shows, while the phrasing of the issues did not lend itself to deliberation and considered responses (Elshtain 1982). A second attempt in 1993 to repeat the experiment similarly failed to arouse interest amongst cable viewers, and the assumption that a two-way communications medium would encourage participation and deliberation was unsupported (Gomery 2006a: 25).

Instead, early empirical studies have tended to cast doubt on the suitability of internet discussion, such as Web forums, for deliberation and contemplation, with much debate characterised by position-taking and reinforcement of existing, opposing views rather than an approach to opinion formation and consensus (Jankowski and van Selm 2000; Dahlberg 2001; Wright and Street 2007). Given that access to the internet remains differentiated, with a clear correlation, for example, between household connectivity and income, most research concludes that those who are most likely to use new ICTs for political purposes are precisely those who are in any case already politically mobilised in some way or other, and there is little evidence that politically demotivated internet users are becoming newly engaged with the political process. We can conclude instead that the main ways in which new ICTs are used in the political process are for instrumental purposes: they enable campaigning groups and political parties to organise more effectively and mobilise support through rapid communication with their membership. Email and mobile phone communication allow, in principle, more flexible mobilisation and the possibility of more spontaneous activity such as protests, but, despite some journalists' explanations, there are very few examples of this happening (Lax 2004: 222). Instead, political protest in fact continues to require lengthy organisation and to employ many of the traditional campaigning techniques and objectives. The goal is mainstream media coverage, as it has long been, and, to help ensure success, theatre and spectacle are becoming standard features of political protest as social movements become as skilled in their approach to the media as any political 'spin doctor' (Jordan 1998; Scott and Street 2000; Monbiot 2001).

The role of new ICTs in the political process is essentially one of enhancing efficiency. Information access is speeded up so that campaigning literature can be more easily written; the communicative role of the technology also speeds up the dissemination of new information from organisations to supporters and provides a means of communication within groups of supporters, helping members to gain a sense of community perhaps (Wu 2007). This though does not necessarily enhance political efficacy. In this respect, the use of these technologies follows in a long line of others which have been deployed as both campaigning tools and support networks (the 'telephone trees' operated by CND and environmental groups in the 1980s for example), tools which have been adopted equally effectively by political parties and the public relations departments of large corporations, and so it cannot easily be argued that the use of ICTs uniquely confers new political advantage on one or other section of the political process.

Working life

Here, we return briefly to Castells's assertion that profoundly new ways of working are emerging as a consequence of the deployment of new technologies and his anticipation of a large group of highly educated, self-activated and self-directed workers, people rather like Charles Leadbeater in fact. There is little doubt that the workplace is becoming more 'information rich' as ICTs are deployed into all areas of work, including areas of skilled manual work such as engineering and, famously (owing to the bitter industrial disputes at the time), newspaper printing. Ian Angell is even more pessimistic than Castells in his concern at the potential gap between information networkers and 'generic labour' and foresees a society where the main concern will be survival in a new barbarian age (Angell 2000). However, although the introduction of new technology may well impact significantly on some individual work roles, some of the anticipated wider consequences have yet to become apparent. For example, similar concerns about the dramatic impact of ICTs on the workforce were aired in the 1970s and 1980s, as information technology began to be introduced into the workplace. One manifestation was the prediction of widespread unemployment, in particular in manufacturing as machines replaced people. In fact the rise in unemployment that occurred in numerous countries in the

1980s was more attributable to governments' economic policies and proved to be temporary, with the size of the labour force in virtually all countries now higher than at any time previously.

Such paradoxes do not mean that the nature of work is unchanging, and many who argue that a new era is emerging point to the growth of service work, invariably seen as tending to be based on information. Daniel Bell and others since have cited the work of economists Fritz Machlup and Marc Porat as providing evidence for the growing importance of information work to the economy, yet the definition of 'information work' is by no means straightforward, and neither is any attempt to separate different categories of industry (Webster 2006: 12–17). Manufacturing, particularly of the 'high tech' kind, clearly involves information work: are those working within it contributing to the information economy or the manufacturing sector? The transition from agriculture to manufacturing to service work is not linear: certain service jobs, such as laundry services, have been eliminated by the development of technologies like the domestic washing machine, which of course need to be manufactured, a pattern repeated by growing levels of consumption of goods such as televisions and, of course, computers. Furthermore, even in the most advanced industrialised countries, manufacturing has never accounted for more than half of the workforce (Callinicos 1989: 122). Finally, even without the difficulty of definition, it is unhelpful to put all 'information workers' in the same category and assume their experiences of work are broadly the same. For example, in his earlier extract Leadbeater suggests that the call centre worker and lawyer 'are all in the thin air business', but it would be hard to conclude that each will experience the same conditions and rewards from their daily work.

Indeed, the call centre offers a compelling argument against the equation of 'information work' and 'information society'. As the paradigmatic instance of information work, the call centre is undoubtedly a new technology phenomenon of the 1990s and early 21st century. By utilising some of the most sophisticated technologies available, service sector functions which once would have required teams of specialists placed across the breadth of a country to provide national service delivery can now be concentrated and centralised into a small handful of call centres. Location is largely irrelevant – when we call 'customer services' the same telephone number might connect us to someone in any one of a number of cities in the world, someone able to access our details and respond using a programmed set of rules. Their call logging systems also afford unparalleled levels of scrutiny, supervision and management, in an almost entirely mechanised manner. The way that calls are routed to operators, together with the flowcharts for responding to queries, resemble precisely the Taylorist 'scientific management' of work in the early 20th century and the similarities between call centre work and 'old fashioned' assembly line production have not escaped a number of commentators. For example, as Poynter and de Miranda conclude (multiclausally) in their call centre study (2000: 194):

> ...the telecentre [call centre] provides little evidence to support the optimistic scenario that the new forms of work organisation in the financial services sector founded on the extensive use of ICTs facilitate the emergence of new kinds of institutions and enterprises and new patterns of employment that achieve a decisive break with the often alienating and repetitive forms of work that were associated with the industrial 'past'.

So while we might find examples of new technologies being associated with some change in patterns of work, the degree of transformation is partial and not nearly as decisive as Castells, Leadbeater and others would suggest. Rather than implying the novelty of the information economy or knowledge society, actual working practices and relationships show more resemblance to than difference from what went before in the 'old' industrial society.

Equality and meritocracy

One of the more appealing claims for the information society is that it is likely to be a fairer, more equal society. The logic is compelling: if the source of wealth is access to knowledge and information, as opposed to access to capital, as Gordon Brown put it (above) then that access can be provided relatively cheaply given the falling costs of computer power and communication technologies. The riches of society (and not just material riches) can be made more widely available – in Leadbeater's words, 'everyone with an education can have a go', and this need not just apply to the wealthier nations of the world, as these low costs mean developing nations can also expect to leapfrog the industrial phase of development and become part of the information economy. As more and more government services migrate to the Web, and government consultations take place online, policy is directed at preventing the emergence of a 'digital divide', in which those without access to the technology or the skills in its use would become increasingly marginalised or excluded. This reflects very clearly Castells's anticipation of a split between networked and generic labour and for Castells, as for Leadbeater, education is the key to success in the information society. Of course, it is suggested that education itself can be provided more equitably with new technologies, as Bill Gates has articulated (1995: 294):

> ...virtual equity can be achieved much more easily than real-world equity. It would take a massive amount of money to give every grammar school in every poor area the same library resources as the schools in Beverley Hills. But when you put schools on-line, they all get the same access to information, wherever it might be stored.

Public policy in many countries is now focused on two objectives: ensuring that education is widely accessible and engenders full familiarity with the tools of the information society and seeking to provide free access to ICTs through public provision in places like libraries and community centres. So in the UK, as elsewhere, education policy has included a number of technology-focused initiatives from the mid-1990s such as the establishment of a National Grid for Learning and a commitment to providing internet connection to all schools. To enable universal access to ICT, the 'People's Network' policy resulted in most libraries having free public internet terminals and similar schemes in almost all other industrialised countries. For example 'Networking the Nation' in Australia and the 'Community Networking program' in the US both sought to bring high speed internet connections to dispersed rural populations (Simpson et al. 2004; Strover et al. 2004). Just as the public transport system provides for those who do not have access to a car, so the provision of public terminals enables those who cannot afford a home computer connection to access information via the internet.

Of course, these developments were not entirely new. As we have seen, efforts have been made since the 1970s to provide public information access using videotex or cable television systems, but the much greater investment of public monies has accelerated that process dramatically in the last two decades, as the 40-year-old debate about the post-industrial or information society has emerged from the realm of academic debate to becoming the basis of public policy. While the UK is fairly typical in having around 65 per cent of its homes connected to the internet, the public provision of access means that, in principle, access is much more widely available. Of course, access does not become universal by virtue of terminals placed in libraries and other public locations, and digital divide campaigners have argued for some equivalent 'universal service' entitlement for the internet as has been traditional in many parts of the world for the telephone service (Wilhelm 2001; Hudson 2006). In particular, the gap between wealthy and poor countries has been a focus for development organisations and the World Summit on the Information Society, convened by the ITU in 2003, sought to provide an initiative in widening access.

These policy goals, widespread access to education and to technology, are key to the idea of a fairer and more egalitarian world. For those following the logic of the information society, success or otherwise should be a product simply of one's level of education rather than inherited privilege. Castells suggests that those on the networks are more successful than generic labour by virtue of higher levels of expertise. A meritocracy should thus come into being where success is directly related to merit, that is, a successful person is rewarded not because she was born with the right connections, or inherited wealth, but because she has made the effort to become highly educated and flexible (Lax 2007b). Logically, where education is available to all (as it is in many advanced industrialised societies) and access to the network's technologies is universally available, everyone can indeed 'have a go' and thus have an equal chance of success, and ultimately society should become a place where it is easier to climb the rungs of the social ladder.

However, a fundamental difficulty with suggesting that new ICTs mean less inequality in the information society lies in the fact that inequality is continuing to grow. The United Nations Development Programme noted in 2005 that the world's richest 500 individuals had a combined income greater than that of the poorest 416 million; the 2.5 billion people living on less than $2 a day accounted for 5 per cent of global income, while the richest 10 per cent account for 54 per cent, disparities which are increasing year on year. Within individual countries, similar inequalities exist, and these are not simply related to that country's prosperity: inequality in both the US and the UK, for example, indicated by the so-called Gini coefficient, is significantly greater than in Albania or Ethiopia (UNDP 2005: 4, 55). While the bare figures indicate current levels of inequality, studies of 'social mobility' seek to reveal barriers to reducing that inequality. Social mobility measures the extent to which being born into a poor family means you are likely to remain poor later on through life or, conversely, being born into a relatively advantaged social position means that position is more likely to be maintained later in life. The logic of the information society implies that social mobility should be increasing; yet longitudinal studies in the UK show that social mobility is in fact decreasing, with people born into poverty in the 1980s having *less* chance of escaping poverty later on in life than those born in earlier decades (Blanden and Gibbons 2006). Similar patterns of low or decreasing mobility have been studied in the US (Corak 2004; Hertz 2006). So the existing differences in material wealth are compounded with increasing barriers to closing those gaps.

So the different fortunes enjoyed by a call centre worker and a lawyer are not simply a result of differences in educational achievement, reflecting individual effort on what supposedly amounts to a level playing field. Instead, we see that even in the most 'advanced' countries, inequality is increasing while social mobility decreases, and thus to argue for the existence of a new society on the basis of grouping all information labour together as though sharing a common interest in that society is unsustainable, and the continuing divisions between classes of people owe more to the traditional relationships of an industrial society.

The Role of Technology

The arguments for a new 'information society' face the difficulty that so many aspects of life appear familiar. As Kumar puts it, 'the development and diffusion of information technology have introduced no fundamentally new principle or direction' (2005: 57). Yet the belief persists, in large part because of its intuitive credibility given this technological growth. In 2002, Leadbeater reflected on the 'breathtaking possibilities of technology' to deliver and distribute information (2002: 30):

> By 2007, the hard disk in the average television set top box should have enough memory to store all the songs ever recorded. By 2010, it should be able to take every film. Telecommunications bandwidth is doubling every 12 months. The capacity of fibre to transmit information has increased by a factor of 16,000 in less than five years; it will soon carry everything we can say, write, compose, play, record, film, draw, paint or design. The entire contents of the US Library of Congress could be passed through an optical switch in less than three seconds.

While this might well be an accurate record of the changing capabilities of new technologies, it is, so to speak, to view technology with one eye closed (Mosco 2005: 10). The eye that remains open focuses solely on the *material* aspects of technology, and critics of the notion of the information society readily admit that ICTs (along with certain other technologies) have indeed developed and dispersed extremely rapidly in the last few decades. Their capacity, in principle, to enable significant social change to come about is also undeniable, but this is not the same thing as to conclude that it has done so. The tendency amongst those who equate dramatic technological change with consequent social change in effect sees technology as an autonomous object, not in itself subject to social forces. Thus Castells sees it as a fortuitous coincidence that the restructuring of capitalism occurred at the same time as there were dramatic developments in computing and communications technologies. Leadbeater sees technology as progressing along some straightforward linear trajectory as if obeying an internal, natural logic. Of course, on the face of it, this can all seem quite credible, and describing some of these beliefs as fundamental laws, such as 'Moore's Law' (which holds that every 18 months computer technology doubles its processing power) only enhances the sense that this advance is beyond social causation, just like the law of gravity, for example. This view of technological progress as autonomous and asocial is referred to as technological determinism, and it lies behind many historical accounts of social change.

However, many historians and social scientists have questioned whether technology drives history in this linear manner (Smith and Marx 1994). Counterposed to a belief in technological determinism is a range of theoretical approaches to understanding the role of technology in the wider social world. The starting point is to reject the idea of viewing the technology as a fixed entity, a 'black box', in favour of seeing technology as a social process. In addition to its material constitution, technology develops in response to a social context which includes economic and political influences. Thus, we have seen how the initial developments in radio technology, including its transition from wireless telegraphy to broadcasting, involved not only progress in its material elements but also commercial needs (such as Marconi's identification of potential markets) and political intervention (in the form of government regulation in allocating broadcasting spectrum or raising revenues through licences). Without each of these elements (and more) radio would not have developed in the way that it did. In an equally obvious way, it would be rather naïve to attempt to understand the history of the transistor or the computer without recognising the political influences of the Second World War. In his history of radio and television technologies, Raymond Williams notes the importance of 'intention': technology does not simply evolve autonomously, but is 'developed with certain purposes and practices already in mind' (Williams 1990: 14). These 'macro' social forces have been identified particularly in studies of the introduction of new technologies into the workplace, where the particular technologies adopted have been those which reflect most clearly the interests of the employers rather than of the employees (Noble 1986; Huws 2003).

An alternative approach looks more closely at each stage in the social development of technology. This social constructivist approach to the development of technology hinges on the notion of contingency, that is, the idea that at any critical stage in the development of a technology, from initial conception to subsequent adoption (or failure), a number of development paths are possible, but at that moment a number of factors impel development down one particular route. Sometimes those influencing factors might be the same macro forces identified in other studies but often are identified as internal, 'micro' forces such as organisational structures or the whims of individual researchers (Bijker et al. 1987). This introspective examination of the microdevelopment of technology can have the effect of privileging particular groups in their influence over technological innovation (such as the researchers directly involved), while neglecting the consequences of the wider political forces which undoubtedly also influence developments.

Whether the 'macro' or 'micro' approach is taken, both views convincingly undermine any idea that technology is a self-acting force; instead they make it clear that any technological innovation is a social product. This is not to say, however, that we can replace technological determinism with a social determinism in which the technologies we end up with can be predictably mapped from a particular set of social forces. Turning to Williams once again, he says (1990: 130):

> Technological determinism is an untenable notion because it substitutes for real social, political and economic intention, either the random autonomy of invention or an abstract human essence. But the notion of a determined technology has a similar one-sided, one-way version of human process. Determination is a real social process, but never (as in some theological and some Marxist versions) as a wholly controlling, wholly predicting set of causes. On the contrary, the reality of determination is the setting of limits and the exertion of pressures, within which variable social practices are profoundly affected but never necessarily controlled. We have to think of determination not as a single force, or a single abstraction of forces, but as a process in which real determining factors – the distribution of power or of capital, social and physical inheritance, relations of scale and size between groups – set limits and exert pressures, but neither wholly control nor wholly predict the outcome of complex activity within or at these limits, and under or against these pressures.

Just as technologies are themselves social, the consequences of their use are also subject to social forces rather than being simply determined by a preconceived idea of their purpose. Given that technological developments are predominantly initiated and pursued by governments and the larger business corporations, the *tendency* of the introduction of most technologies is to reinforce rather than subvert the existing structures of society. But as Williams says this is not a wholly determining force, and so while the development of information technologies in the 1970s and 1980s could be seen, on its introduction into the workplace, as helping to reinforce employers' control, the same technologies were claimed by the computer activists of the time as a potential source of liberation.

Given this tendency of technological innovations, as the consequences of social processes, to reinforce existing social forms, it becomes understandable, perhaps, why technological determinism comes to be seen as a credible explanation. Bimber (1994) describes a 'normative technological determinism', in which it is assumed that technology orders our world not because of any intrinsic attributes but because the norms upon which progress is judged, condition behaviour and an unwitting acceptance of the importance of technology. Thus, rationality and efficiency are privileged over ethical and political considerations, and so we think nothing of giving personal information to call centre operatives because we know that the technology demands it be given in a certain way; similarly, on a macro level, we understand that society must invest in technology to compete economically and that we must ensure all schools have access to the internet (Cavanagh 2007: 142–3). With technological innovation concentrated in large private and public organisations, these norms become self-reinforcing and overwhelming to the point where technological determinism can provide a convincing explanation. The apparent linear nature of technological development also encourages a belief in some internal logic of technological progress. For example, the emergence of *terrestrial* HDTV broadcasting might seem a natural development of the existing standard definition but, on another reading, makes only limited technical sense given the higher capacities of the alternative satellite and cable platforms. Instead, as is clear particularly in the US, for example, HDTV can only be understood as a consequence of economic considerations with the television networks seeking to maintain their position in the market. MacKenzie and Wajcman explain the paradox (1999: 12):

> ...the *compelling* nature of much technological change is best explained by seeing technology not as outside of society, as some versions of technological determinism would have it, but as inextricably part of society. If technological systems are economic enterprises, and if they are involved directly or indirectly in market competition, then technical change is forced on them. If they are to survive at all, much less to prosper, they cannot forever stand still. Technical change is made inevitable, and its nature and direction profoundly conditioned, by this. And when national economies are linked by a competitive world market, as they have been at least since the mid-nineteenth century, technical change outside a particular country can exert massive pressure for technical change inside it.

Thus 'Moore's Law' on computer processing power may be a reasonably accurate observation, but it is not an explanation, as some natural feature of the technology. Instead even a dubious belief in it allows it to become self-fulfilling for economic reasons: if electronics companies compete to sell their processors on the basis of speed, each will understand, reasonably, that the other competitors are working to build faster processors, not least because the others too have the same understanding. So, while a belief in technological determinism might be plausible, a little reflection and examination reveals that, rather than abstracted from society, technological development is inherently social. Such debates are not entirely new. As long ago as 1926, Russian revolutionary Leon Trotsky addressed an audience with the same question (Trotsky 1973: 229):

> 'Does culture advance technology or does technology advance culture?' asks one of the written questions lying before me. It is wrong to put the question that way. Technology cannot be counterposed to culture for it is the mainspring. Without technology, there is no culture. The growth of technology advances culture. But the science and general culture that have arisen on the basis of technology constitute a powerful aid to further growth of technology. Here we have a dialectical interaction.

Technology and the Information Society

Viewing new ICTs as autonomous agents of change is a recurring tendency amongst those who argue for the idea of the information society as being wholly different from what has gone before. This though is not sustainable, for it is necessary, as argued above, to see technological developments as fundamentally social developments. In this case, we have to ask what are the social forces which act upon the specific technologies of the information society. Here we see how little appears to be different. Just as we have noted the importance of economics and political regulation in the development of all earlier communication technologies, the same forces appear to be as important today. The level of regulation may be different, or at least the objectives differently expressed, but the economic imperative behind regulation is unchanged. As noted earlier, the UK government is typical of most in stating explicitly that the objective of regulation is to gain economic advantage over competitors, indicating that even though more corporations are operating across national borders, the role of national governments remains important. To look solely at technological developments and their implicit possibilities as an explanation for a new information society would be a mistake.

Even judged at the level of technology alone, however, comparisons are not straightforward. It is often claimed that the rates of technological change are now greater than we have ever known, and this is likely to be true in a quantitative sense on more-or-less any measure, given that new technological developments depend heavily for their success on previous technologies. In a qualitative judgement, however, the conclusions might not be so straightforward. Golding distinguishes between those technologies that enable truly new forms of social activity, previously impossible or even unimaginable, and those technologies which merely make processes more efficient or convenient by speeding them up or making them portable. He argues that in comparison with the 'miracle' of 19th and 20th century telephony, for example, the hype about email communication is overblown, while the earlier social consequences of the electric telegraph vastly exceeded those of current ICTs (Golding 2000: 171). We have noted earlier the rapid rise in the number of automobiles and radio sets in the early decades of the 20th century, changes which equally could be considered as momentous, but which are not claimed uniquely to have brought about a new kind of society.

If the information society advocates are overstating the transformative powers of new ICTs, they are continuing a rich tradition. For as long as they have been recorded, politicians, writers and undoubtedly academics have heralded the end of one era and the beginning of another, brought about by some new technology or other, and this is all around us today. The 'death of distance' and the 'end of history' are common proclamations for the 'digital age'. Yet, Mosco reminds us, this is in spite of history (2005: 118):

> History, geography, and politics ended in the 1850s when the telegraph was introduced. They ended again a few decades later when electrification lit up the cities, but the myths were largely forgotten when electricity literally withdrew into the woodwork. The end came once more when the telephone brought about a renewal of these myths. But who now refers to our era as The Age of the Telephone? In the 1920s, the arrival of radio brought along its own cast of mythmakers who saw it marking a radical change in time, space and social relations.

And so on, with television, then satellite and cable communications, and finally information and communication technologies. Why does the cycle of proclamation continue? Politicians, quite naturally, want to be associated with progress and are willingly supported by the media, which are always looking for a good story: announcing the 'end of history' is more interesting than 'more of the same'. Public relations firms and advertisers wish to promote a vision of a better, more enticing world. More generally than these instrumental purposes, there are powerful cultural pressures which lift us out of the everyday and make us seek to believe that our era alone is responsible for transforming the world (ibid.). For all that we would like to believe that technological developments can deliver a better world, and of course in many instances they do, there is nothing automatic in that process. A full understanding of communication technologies thus requires, in part, a technical one (how do they do the things they do) but demands in equal measure a historically informed appreciation of their role in the wider, social world.

Bibliography

Abramsky, J. (2003) 'The future of radio is digital. Speech by Jenny Abramsky to the NAB Conference.' BBC Press Release, 20 October.

Agar, J. (2003) *Constant Touch: A Global History of the Mobile Phone* (Cambridge: Icon).

Ala-Fossi, M. and Stavitsky, A. (2003) 'Understanding IBOC: Digital technology for analog economics.' *Journal of Radio Studies* 10(1) 63–79.

Anderson, J. and Anderson, B. (1993) 'The myth of persistence-of-vision revisited.' *Journal of Film and Video* 45(1) 3–12.

Andrews, J. and Enloe, L. (1972) 'Scanning the issue.' *Proceedings of the IEEE* 60(7) 766–7.

Angell, I. (2000) *The New Barbarian Manifesto: How to Survive the Information Age* (London: Kogan Page).

Anon (1939) 'First daily newspaper by radio facsimile.' *Radio Craft* March. Available at http://www.lightningfield.com/david/radiofax/. Accessed 30 June 2008.

Arterton, F. (1987) *Teledemocracy: Can Technology Protect Democracy?* (Newbury Park, Ca.: Sage).

Atton, C. (2002) *Alternative Media* (London: Sage).

Aumente, J. (1987) *New Electronic Pathways: Videotex, Teletext and Online Databases* (Newbury Park, Ca.: Sage).

Axford, B. and Huggins, R. (eds) (2000) *New Media and Politics* (London: Sage).

Bannister, M. (2001) 'Digital radio: A costly dud.' *The Times* 7 September, p. 23.

Barbrook, R. and Cameron, A. (1995) 'The Californian Ideology: A critique of West Coast cyber-libertarianism.' Available at www.hrc.wmin.ac.uk/theory-californianideology.html. Accessed 21 June 2007.

Barton, R. (1968) *Telex* (London: Pitman).

Bary, A. (2003) 'A sound idea.' *Barron's* 18(7) 17–20.

Bell, D. (1970) 'Notes on the post-industrial society' in M. Olsen (ed.) *Power in Societies* (London: Collier Macmillan).

Bell, D. (1973) *The Coming of Post-Industrial Society* (New York: Basic Books).

Benoit, H. (1997) *Digital Television: MPEG-1, MPEG-2 and Principles of the DVB System* (London: Arnold).

Bijker, W., Hughes, T. and Pinch, T. (eds) (1987) *The Social Construction of Technological Systems: New Directions in the Sociology and History of Technology* (Cambridge, Ma.: MIT press).

Bimber, B. (1994) 'Three faces of technological determinism' in M. Smith and L. Marx (eds) *Does Technology Drive History? The Dilemma of Technological Determinism* (Cambridge, Ma.: MIT press).

Blanden, J. and Gibbons, S. (2006) *The Persistence of Poverty Across Generations: A View from Two British Cohorts* (Bristol: Policy press).

Blumler, J. and Gurevitch, M. (2001) 'The new media and our political communication discontents: Democratizing cyberspace.' *Information, Communication and Society* 4(1) 1–13.

Borger, J. (2000) 'Future hangs on hunt for elusive particle.' *Guardian* 13 November.

Bowen, D. (1994) *Multimedia: Now and Down the Line* (London: Bowerdean).

Brants, K., Huizenga, M. and van Meerten, R. (1996) 'The new canals of Amsterdam: An exercise in local electronic democracy.' *Media, Culture & Society* 18(2) 233–47.

Brecht, B. (2000 [1932]) 'The radio as a communications apparatus' in M. Silberman (ed. and trans.) *Brecht on Film and Radio* (London: Methuen).

Briggs, A. (1961) *The History of Broadcasting in the United Kingdom. Vol. 1: The Birth of Broadcasting* (Oxford: Oxford University press).

Briggs, A. (1965) *The History of Broadcasting in the United Kingdom. Vol. 2: The Golden Age of Wireless* (Oxford: Oxford University press).

Briggs, A. (1970) *The History of Broadcasting in the United Kingdom. Vol. 3: The War of Words* (Oxford: Oxford University press).

Briggs, A. (1977) 'The pleasure telephone: A chapter in the prehistory of the media' in I. de Sola Pool (ed.) *The Social Impact of the Telephone* (Cambridge, Ma.: MIT press).

Briggs, A. and Burke, P. (2002) *A Social History of the Media: From Gutenberg to the Internet* (Cambridge: Polity).

Brignall, M. (2007) 'In the wake of disaster.' *Guardian* (Money section) 28 July, p. 7.

Brose, E. (1998) *Technology and Science in the Industrializing Nations 1500–1914* (Atlantic Highlands, NJ.: Humanities press).

Brown, G. (1996) 'In the real world.' *Guardian* 2 August, p. 13.

Browne, D. (1982) *International Broadcasting: The Limits of the Limitless Medium* (New York: Praeger).

Budge, I. (1996) *The New Challenge of Direct Democracy* (Cambridge: Polity).

Bussey, G. (1990) *Wireless: The Crucial Decade 1924–34* (Stevenage: Peter Peregrinus).

Cairncross, F. (1998) *The Death of Distance: How the Communications Revolution will Change Our Lives* (London: Orion).

Callinicos, A. (1989) *Against Postmodernism* (Cambridge: Polity).

Campbell-Kelly, M. and Aspray, W. (1996) *Computer: A History of the Information Machine* (New York: Basic Books).

Carey, J. (1992) *Communication as Culture: Essays on Media and Society* (New York: Routledge).

Case, D. (1994) 'The social shaping of videotex: How information services for the public have evolved.' *Journal of the American Society for Information Science* 45(7) 483–97.

Castells, M. (2000) *The Rise of the Network Society*, Second edition (Oxford: Blackwell).

Cats-Baril, W. and Jelassi, T. (1994) 'The French videotex system Minitel: A successful implementation of a national information technology infrastructure.' *MIS Quarterly* March, 1–20.

Cavanagh, A. (2007) *Sociology in the Age of the Internet* (Maidenhead: Open University press).

Ceruzzi, P. (2003) *A History of Modern Computing*, Second edition (Cambridge, MA.: MIT press).

Coleman, S. (2004) 'Connecting parliament to the people via the internet.' *Information, Communication and Society* 7(1) 1–22.

Coleman, S. (2005) 'Blogs and the new politics of listening.' *Political Quarterly* 76(2) 273–80.

Corak, M. (ed.) (2004) *Generational Income Mobility in North America and Europe* (Cambridge: Cambridge University press).

Couldry, N. and Curran, J. (eds) (2003) *Contesting Media Power: Alternative Media in a Networked World* (Oxford: Rowman and Littlefield).

Cowan, R. (1997) *A Social History of American Technology* (New York: Oxford University press).

Coyer, K. (2005) 'If it leads it bleeds: The participatory newsmaking of the Independent Media Centre' in W. de Jong, M. Shaw and N. Stammers (eds) *Global Activism, Global Media* (London: Pluto).

Crisell, A. (2002) *An Introductory History of British Broadcasting*, Second edition (London: Routledge).

Curran, J. and Seaton, J. (2003) *Power without Responsibility: The Press, Broadcasting, and New Media in Britain*, Sixth edition (London: Routledge).

Cusumano, M., Mylonadis, Y. and Rosenbloom, R. (1992) 'Strategic maneuvering and mass-market dynamics: The triumph of VHS over Beta.' *Business History Review* 66(1) 51–94.

Czitrom, D. (1982) *Media and the American Mind: From Morse to McLuhan* (Chapel Hill: University of North Carolina press).

Dahlberg, L. (2001) 'The internet and democratic discourse: Exploring the prospect of online deliberative forums extending the public sphere.' *Information, Communication and Society* 4(4) 615–33.

Darwin, C. (1946) 'The "electronic brain".' Letter to *The Times* 13 November, p. 7.

DCMS (1998) *Memorandum to Select Committee Enquiry into Audio-Visual Communications and the Regulation of Broadcasting*, January. (London: Department for Culture, Media and Sport).

de Jong, W., Shaw, M. and Stammers, N. (eds) (2005) *Global Activism, Global Media* (London: Pluto).

DNH (Department of National Heritage) (1995) *Digital Terrestrial Broadcasting: The Government's Proposals* White Paper, Cm.2946. (London: HMSO).

Douglas, S. (1987) *Inventing American Broadcasting, 1899–1912* (Baltimore: Johns Hopkins University press).

Douglas, S. (2004) *Listening In: Radio and the American Imagination* (Minneapolis: University of Minnesota press).

Downing, J. (1989) 'Computers for political change: PeaceNet and Public Data Access.' *Journal of Communication* 39(3) 154–62.

Downing, J. (2001) *Radical Media: Rebellious Communication and Social Movements* with T. Villarreal Ford, G. Gil and L. Stein. (Thousand Oaks: Sage).

Downing, J. (2005) 'Activist media, civil society and social movements' in W. de Jong, M. Shaw and N. Stammers (eds) *Global Activism, Global Media* (London: Pluto).

Dutton, W., Elberse, A., Hong, T. and Matei, S. (2001) ' "Beepless in America": The social impact of the Galaxy IV pager blackout' in S. Lax (ed.) *Access Denied in the Information Age* (Basingstoke: Palgrave).

Dyson, E., Gilder, G., Keyworth, G. and Toffler, A. (1996) 'Cyberspace and the American Dream: A Magna Carta for the knowledge age.' *The Information Society* 12(3) 295–308.

Edison, T. (1878) 'The phonograph and its future.' *The North American Review* 126 (May–June) 527–36.

Elshtain, J. (1982) 'Democracy and the QUBE tube.' *The Nation* 7 August, 108–10.

Engels, F. (1999 [1845]) *The Condition of the Working Class in England* with an introduction and notes by David McLellan (Oxford: Oxford University press).

Enticknap, L. (2005) *Moving Image Technology: From Zoetrope to Digital* (London: Wallflower).

Eureka (1986) *Eureka 147 Project Form*. Available at www.eureka.be/inaction/project-GenInfo.do. Accessed 23 May 2007.

Eurostat (2001) *Telecommunication Indicators in the Eurostat Area* Working group, Statistics on Communication and Information Services, Document ITU/EN. Available at www.itu.int/ITU-D/ict/statistics/at_glance/Eurostat_2001.pdf. Accessed 28 April 2008.

Fischer, C. (1992) *America Calling: A Social History of the Telephone* (Berkeley: University of California press).

Flew, T. (2005) *New Media: An Introduction* (Melbourne: Oxford University press).

Flichy, P. (1995) *Dynamics of Modern Communication: The Shaping and Impact of New Communication Technologies* (London: Sage).

Forbes, D. (1999) 'Sucked down.' *Free Press* 110 (May–June) 2.

Forester, T. (ed.) (1980) *The Microelectronics Revolution: The Complete Guide to the New Technology and its Impact on Society* (Oxford: Blackwell).

Forester, T. (ed.) (1985) *The Information Technology Revolution* (Oxford: Blackwell).

Freedman, D. (2003) *Television Policies of the Labour Party, 1951–2001* (London: Frank Cass).

Freedman, D. (2008) *The Politics of Media Policy* (Cambridge: Polity).

Galperin, H. (2004) *New Television, Old Politics* (Cambridge: Cambridge University press).

Gates, B. (1995) *The Road Ahead* (London: Penguin).

Goggin, G. (2006) *Cell Phone Culture: Mobile Technology in Everyday Life* (London: Routledge).

Golding, P. (1998) 'Global village or cultural pillage: The unequal inheritance of the communications revolution' in R. McChesney, E. Meiksins-Wood and J. Foster (eds) *Capitalism and the Information Age: The Political Economy of the Global Communication Revolution* (New York: Monthly Review press).

Golding, P. (2000) 'Forthcoming features: Information and communications technology and the sociology of the future.' *Sociology* 34(1) 165–84.

Gomery, D. (2006a) 'Cable television – US' in D. Gomery and L. Hockley (eds) *Television Industries* (London: BFI).

Gomery, D. (2006b) 'Satellite television – US' in D. Gomery and L. Hockley (eds) *Television Industries* (London: BFI).

Goodwin, P. (1998) *Television under the Tories: Broadcasting Policy 1979–1997* (London: BFI).

Gore, A. (1994) Remarks prepared for delivery by Vice President Al Gore, ITU conference, Buenos Aires, 21 March. Available at w2.eff.org/Infrastructure/Govt_docs/gii_gore_buenos_aires.speech. Accessed 22 June 2007.

Gow, G. and Smith, R. (2006) *Mobile and Wireless Communications: An Introduction* (Maidenhead: Open University press).

Gregory, R. (1998) *Eye and Brain: The Psychology of Seeing* (Oxford: Oxford University press).

Gross, L. (2003) *Telecommunications: Radio, Television and Movies in the Digital Age*, Eighth edition (Boston: McGraw-Hill).

Hollander, E. (1992) 'The emergence of small scale media' in N. Jankowski, O. Prehn and J. Stappers (eds) *The People's Voice: Local Radio and Television in Europe* (London: John Libbey).

Headrick, D. (1991) *The Invisible Weapon: Telecommunications and International Politics 1851–1945* (New York: Oxford University press).

Hendy, D. (2000) *Radio in the Global Age* (Cambridge: Polity).

Hertz, T. (2006) *Understanding Mobility in America* (Washington: Center for American Progress).

Hilliard, R. and Keith, M. (2005) *The Broadcast Century and Beyond: A Biography of American Broadcasting*, Fourth edition (Burlington, Ma.: Focal).

Hodges, A. (1997) *Turing: A Natural Philosopher* (London: Phoenix).

Hollins, T. (1984) *Beyond Broadcasting: Into the Cable Age* (London: BFI).

Holm, S. (2007) 'Audio quality on the air in DAB digital radio in Norway.' Paper presented at 31st International Conference of the Audio Engineering Society, London, 25–27 June.

Hood, S. and Tabary-Peterssen, T. (1997) *On Television*, Fourth edition (London: Pluto).

Horstmann, I. and MacDonald, G. (2003) 'Is advertising a signal of product quality? Evidence from the compact disc player market 1983–1992.' *International Journal of Industrial Organization* 21(3) 317–45.

Howells, R. (2003) *Visual Culture* (Cambridge: Polity).

Hudson, H. (2006) 'Universal access to the new information infrastructure' in L. Lievrouw and S. Livingstone (eds) *The Handbook of New Media: Student Edition* (London: Sage).

Humphreys, P. and Lang, M. (1998) 'Digital television between the economy and pluralism' in J. Steemers (ed.) *Changing Channels: The Prospects for Television in a Digital World* (Luton: University of Luton press).

Hunt, R. (1994) 'The man machine.' *Guardian* (Weekend magazine) 12 November, p. 36.

Huws, U. (2003) *The Making of a Cybertariat: Virtual Work in a Real World* (New York: Monthly Review press).

ITAP (1982) *Cable Systems: A Report by the Information Technology Advisory Panel* (London: HMSO).

Jankowski, N. and van Selm, M. (2000) 'The promise and practice of public debate in cyberspace' in K. Hacker and J. van Dijk (eds) *Digital Democracy: Issues of Theory and Practice* (London: Sage).

Jeppesen, S. and Poulsen, K. (1994) 'The text communications battlefield: Installed base, externalities and the fall of the teletext system.' *Telecommunications Policy* 18(1) 66–77.

Jordan, G. (1998) 'Politics without parties: a growing trend?' *Parliamentary Affairs* 51(3) 314–28.

Karpf, A. (2000) 'Amazing future of the wireless.' *Guardian* 4 March, p. 4.

Keith, M. (2002) 'Turn on...tune in: The rise and demise of commercial underground radio' in M. Hilmes and J. Loviglio (eds) *Radio Reader: Essays in the Cultural History of Radio* (New York: Routledge).

Kellner, D. (1985) 'Public access television: Alternative views.' *Radical Science* 16, 79–92.

Kellow, C. and Steeves, H. (1998) 'The role of radio in the Rwandan genocide.' *Journal of Communication* 48(3) 107–28.

Kieve, J. (1973) *The Electric Telegraph: A Social and Economic History* (Newton Abbot: David & Charles).

Kogawa, T. (1993) 'Free radio in Japan: The mini FM boom' in N. Strauss and D. Mandl (eds) *Radiotext(e)* (New York: Semiotexte).

Kumar, K. (2005) *From Post-Industrial to Postmodern Society: New Theories of the Contemporary World*, Second edition (Malden, Ma.: Blackwell).

Lavington, S. (1980) *Early British Computers: The Story of Vintage Computers and the People who Built them* (Manchester: Manchester University press).

Lax, S. (2003) 'The prospects for digital radio: Policy and technology for a new broadcasting system.' *Information, Communication and Society* 6(3) 326–49.

Lax, S. (2004) 'The internet and democracy' in D. Gauntlett and R. Horsley (eds) *Web Studies*, Second edition (London: Arnold).

Lax, S. (2007a) 'Digital radio and the diminution of the public sphere' in R. Butsch (ed.) *Media and Public Spheres* (Basingstoke: Palgrave Macmillan).

Lax, S. (2007b) ' "Access denied": Arguments about equality and access to new media in the information society' in V. Nightingale and T. Dwyer (eds) *New Media Worlds: Challenges for Convergence* (Melbourne: Oxford University press).

Lax, S. (2009) 'Broadcasting: Radio' in J. Petley and G. Williams (eds) *The Media in Contemporary Britain* (Basingstoke: Palgrave Macmillan).

Lax, S., Ala-Fossi, M., Jauert, P. and Shaw, H. (2008) 'DAB, the future of radio? The development of digital radio in four European countries.' *Media, Culture & Society* 30(2) 151–66.

Leadbeater, C. (2000) *Living on Thin Air: The New Economy* (London: Penguin).

Leadbeater, C. (2002) 'Globalisation: Now the good news.' *New Statesman* 15 (1 July) 29–31.

Lewis, P. (2002) 'Radio theory and community radio' in N. Jankowski and O. Prehn (eds) *Community Media in the Information Age: Perspectives and Prospects* (Cresskill, NJ.: Hampton).

Lewis, P. and Booth, J. (1989) *The Invisible Medium: Public, Commercial and Community Radio* (Basingstoke: Macmillan).

Li, T. (1978) 'Optical fiber communication: The state of the art.' *IEEE Transactions on Communications* 26(7) 946–55.

Lister, M., Kelly, K., Dovey, J., Giddings, S. and Grant, I. (2003) *New Media: A Critical Introduction* (London: Routledge).

MacKenzie, D. and Wajcman, J. (eds) (1999) *The Social Shaping of Technology*, Second edition (Buckingham: Open University press).

Martin, C. (1995) 'ENIAC: press conference that shook the world.' *IEEE Technology and Society Magazine* 14(4) 3–10.

Marvin, C. (1988) *When Old Technologies were New: Thinking about Electric Communication in the Late Nineteenth Century* (New York: Oxford University press).

Mattelart, A. (2003) *The Information Society: An Introduction* (London: Sage).

May, C. (2002) *The Information Society: A Sceptical View* (Cambridge: Polity).

McChesney, R. (1993) *Telecommunications, Mass Media, and Democracy: The Battle for the Control of US Broadcasting, 1928–1935* (New York: Oxford University press).

McChesney, R. (2000) *Rich Media, Poor Democracy: Communication Politics in Dubious Times* (New York: New Press).

McFarlane, M. (1972) 'Digital pictures fifty years ago.' *Proceedings of the IEEE* 60(7) 768–70.

McLean, D. (2000) *Restoring Baird's Image* (London: Institution of Electrical Engineers).

Milner, M. (2001) 'Orange value outstrips its parent.' *Guardian* 7 September, p. 22.

Monbiot, G. (2001) *An Activist's Guide to Exploiting the Media* (London: Bookmarks).

Moore, J. (1989) 'Communications' in C. Chant (ed.) *Science, Technology and Everyday Life 1870–1950* (London: Routledge).

Moores, S. (1988) ' "The box on the dresser": Memories of early radio and everyday life.' *Media, Culture & Society* 10(1) 23–40.

Morus, I. (2000) ' "The nervous system of Britain": Space, time and the electric telegraph in the Victorian age.' *British Journal for the History of Science* 33(4) 455–75.

Mosco, V. (2005) *The Digital Sublime: Myth, Power and Cyberspace* (Cambridge, Ma.: MIT press).

Murphy, B. (1983) *The World Wired Up: Unscrambling the New Communications Puzzle* (London: Comedia).

National Statistics (2002) *Family Spending: A Report on the 2000–2001 Family Expenditure Survey* (London: The Stationery Office).

Negrine, R. (1994) *Politics and the Mass Media in Britain*, Second edition (London: Routledge).

Negroponte, N. (1995) *Being Digital* (London: Hodder & Stoughton).

Noble, D. (1986) *Forces of Production: A Social History of Industrial Automation* (Oxford: Oxford University press).

Nyre, L. (2008) *Sound Media: From Live Journalism to Music Recording* (London: Routledge).

O'Connor, A. (1990) 'The miners' radio stations in Bolivia: A culture of resistance.' *Journal of Communication* 40(1) 102–10.

O'Connor, A. (ed.) (2004) *Community Radio in Bolivia: The Miners' Radio Stations* (Lampeter: Edwin Mellen press).

Ofcom (2004) *Radio – Preparing for the Future. Phase 1: Developing a New Framework* (London: Ofcom).

Ofcom (2006a) *Digital Dividend Review* (London: Ofcom).

Ofcom (2006b) *The International Communications Market 2006* (London: Ofcom).

Ofcom (2006c) *The Communications Market 2006* (London: Ofcom).

Ofcom (2008) *Digital Progress Report. Digital TV, Q4 2007* (London: Ofcom).

Ofcom and Digital UK (2007) *Switchover Progress Report, Q1 2007* (London: Ofcom).

Opel, A. (2004) *Microradio and the FCC: Media Activism and the Struggle over Broadcast Policy* (Westport, CT.: Praeger).

Orlik, P., Anderson, S., Day, L. and Lawrence, P. (2007) *Exploring Electronic Media: Chronicles and Challenges* (Malden, Ma.: Blackwell).

Parker, E. and Dunn, D. (1972) 'Information technology: Its social potential.' *Science* 176(4042) 1392–9.

Parsons, P. and Frieden, R. (1998) *The Cable and Satellite Television Industries* (Needham Heights, Ma.: Allyn & Bacon).

Pedrick, G. (ed.) (1947) *World Radio and Television Annual. Jubilee Issue* (London: Sampson Low, Marston and Co.).

Pool, I. de Sola, Decker, C., Dizard, S., Israel, K., Rubin, P. and Weinstein, B. (1977) 'Foresight and hindsight: The case of the telephone' in I. de Sola Pool (ed.) *The Social Impact of the Telephone* (Cambridge, Ma.: MIT press).

Pool, I. de Sola (1983) *Forecasting the Telephone: A Retrospective Technology Assessment of the Telephone* (Norwood, NJ.: ABLEX).

Poynter, G. and de Miranda, A. (2000) 'Inequality, work and technology in the services sector' in S. Wyatt, F. Henwood, N. Miller and P. Senker (eds) *Technology and Inequality: Questioning the Information Society* (London: Routledge).

Prendergast, T. (2003) *The Ontology of the Photographic Image in the Digital Age* PhD Thesis, University of Leeds.

Raab, C., Bellamy, C., Taylor, J., Dutton, W. and Peltu, M. (1996) 'The information polity: Electronic democracy, privacy and surveillance' in W. Dutton (ed.) *Information and Communication Technologies: Visions and Realities* (Oxford: Oxford University press).

Rajar (2008) 'RAJAR data release, Q4 2007.' News Release, 30 January.

Rheingold, H. (1994) *The Virtual Community: Finding Connection in a Computerized World* (London: Secker and Warburg).

Rice, J. (1980) 'Fiber optics – a bright information future.' *Library Journal* 105(10) 1135–7.

Rigby, R. (2001) 'Digital radio and mobile phones: A match made in heaven?' *Marketing Week* 25 January, p. 47.

Riismandel, P. (2002) 'Radio by and for the public: The death and resurrection of low-power radio' in M. Hilmes and J. Loviglio (eds) *Radio Reader: Essays in the Cultural History of Radio* (New York: Routledge).

Robinson, E. (1935) *Televiewing* (London: Selwyn & Blount).

Robson, N. (2004) 'Living pictures out of space: The forlorn hopes for television in pre-1939 London.' *Historical Journal of Film, Radio and Television* 24(2) 223–32.

Rossetto, L. (1995) 'Response to "The Californian Ideology".' Available at www.hrc.wmin.ac.uk/theory-californianideology-responses1.html. Accessed 28 April 2008.

Scott, A. and Street, J. (2000) 'From media politics to e-protest: The use of popular culture and new media in parties and social movements.' *Information, Communication and Society* 3(2) 215–40.

Shacklady, N. and Ellen, M. (2003) *On Air: A History of BBC Transmission* (Orpington: Wavechange books).

Shurkin, J. (1984) *Engines of the Mind: A History of the Computer* (New York: W W Norton).

Simpson, L. Daws, L. and Pini, B. (2004) 'Public internet access revisited.' *Telecommunications Policy* 28(3–4) 323–7.

Slotten, H. (1996) ' "Rainbow in the sky": FM radio, technical superiority, and regulatory decision-making.' *Technology and Culture* 37(4) 686–720.

Smith, R. (1972) *The Wired Nation. Cable TV: The Electronic Communications Highway* (New York: Harper & Row).

Smith, M. and Marx, L. (eds) (1994) *Does Technology Drive History? The Dilemma of Technological Determinism* (Cambridge, Ma.: MIT press).

Solnit, R. (2003) *Motion Studies: Eadweard Muybridge and the Technological Wild West* (London: Bloomsbury).

Sparke, P. (1986) *An Introduction to Design and Culture in the Twentieth Century* (London: Unwin Hyman).

Standage, T. (1998) *The Victorian Internet: The Remarkable Story of the Telegraph and the Nineteenth Century's Online Pioneers* (London: Weidenfeld & Nicholson).

Steel, M. (1998) 'Email wail.' *Guardian* 9 September, p. 15.

Stonier, T. (1983) *The Wealth of Information: A Profile of the Post-Industrial Economy* (London: Methuen).

Street, S. (2002) *A Concise History of British Radio, 1922–2002* (Tiverton: Kelly productions).

Street, S. (2004) 'Programme-makers on Parker: Occupational reflections on the radio production legacy of Charles Parker.' *The Radio Journal* 2(3) 187–94.

Street, S. (2006) *Crossing the Ether: British Public Service Radio and Commercial Competition 1922–1945* (Eastleigh: John Libbey).

Streeter, T. (2004) 'The internet, the 1990s, and the origins of irrational exuberance' in A. Calabrese and C. Sparks (eds) *Toward a Political Economy of Culture* (Lanham, MD.: Rowman & Littlefield).

Strover, S., Chapman, G. and Waters, J. (2004) 'Beyond community networking and CTCs: Access, development, and public policy.' *Telecommunications Policy* 28(7–8) 465–85.

Sussman, G. (1997) *Communication, Technology, and Politics in the Information Age* (Thousand Oaks: Sage).

Thurlow, C. (2006) 'From statistical panic to moral panic: The metadiscursive construction and popular exaggeration of new media language in the print media.' *Journal of Computer Mediated Communication* 11(3) 667–701.

Tiltman, R. (1933) *Baird of Television* (London: Seeley Service).

Toffler, A. (1970) *Future Shock* (London: Bodley Head).

Toffler, A. (1980) *The Third Wave* (London: Pan).

Trotsky, L. (1973) *Problems of Everyday Life: Creating the Foundations for a New Society in Revolutionary Russia* (New York: Pathfinder).

Tsagarousianou, R., Tambini, D. and Bryan, C. (1998) *Cyberdemocracy: Technology, Cities and Civic Networks* (London: Routledge).

Tumber, H. (2001) 'Democracy in the information age: The role of the fourth estate in cyberspace' in F. Webster (ed.) *Culture and Politics in the Information Age: A New Politics?* (London: Routledge).

Turkle, S. (1996) *Life on the Screen: Identity in the Age of the Internet* (London: Weidenfeld & Nicholson).

UNCTAD (United Nations Conference on Trade and Development) (2008) *Information Economy Report 2007–2008. Science and Technology for Development: The New Paradigm of ICT* (Geneva: United Nations).

UNDP (2005) *Human Development Report* (New York: United Nations Development Programme).

Webster, F. (2006) *Theories of the Information Society*, Third edition (London: Routledge).

Webster, P. (1997) 'Number's up for the Minitel.' *Guardian* 27 August, p. 13.

Werskey, G. (2007) 'The Marxist critique of capitalist science: A history in three movements?' *Science as Culture* 16(4) 397–461.

Wilhelm, A. (2001) *Democracy in the Digital Age* (New York: Routledge).

Williams, G. (1994) *Britain's Media: How they are Related* (London: Campaign for Press and Broadcasting Freedom).

Williams, G. (2001) 'Selling off cyberspace' in S. Lax (ed.) *Access Denied in the Information Age* (London: Palgrave).

Williams, M. (1985) 'Electronic databases.' *Science* 228(4694) 445–50.

Williams, R. (1990) *Television: Technology and Cultural Form*, Second edition (London: Routledge).

Winner, L. (1996) 'Who will we be in cyberspace?' *The Information Society* 12(1) 63–72.

Winsbury, R. (1994) 'Distributive justice: Will digital community wireless telephone be the smart card to play?' *Intermedia* 22 December/January 38.

Winston, B. (1998) *Media Technology and Society: A History from the Telegraph to the Internet* (London: Routledge).

Wright, S. and Street, J. (2007) 'Democracy, deliberation and design: The case of online discussion forums.' *New Media and Society* 9(5) 849–69.

Wu, Y. (2007) 'Blurring boundaries in a "cyber-Greater China": Are internet bulletin boards constructing the public sphere in China?' in R. Butsch (ed.) *Media and Public Spheres* (Basingstoke: Palgrave Macmillan).

Index